Institutions and Investments

SIE *Studies in International Economics* includes works dealing with the theory, empirical analysis, and evaluation of international policies and institutions, in the area of international macroeconomics and finance, international trade theory and policy, as well as international legal and political economy.

Keith E. Maskus, Peter M. Hooper, Edward E. Leamer, and J. David Richardson, Editors
Quiet Pioneering: Robert M. Stern and His International Economic Legacy

Bjarne S. Jensen and Kar-yiu Wong, Editors
Dynamics, Economic Growth, and International Trade

Jagdish Bhagwati and Mathias Hirsch, Editors
The Uruguay Round and Beyond: Essays in Honor of Arthur Dunkel

Kala Marathe Krishna and Ling Hui Tan
Rags and Riches: Implementing Apparel Quotas under the Multi-Fibre Arrangement

Alan V. Deardorff and Robert M. Stern
Measurement of Nontariff Barriers

Thomas Cottier and Petros C. Mavroidis, Editors
The World Trade Forum, Volume I: State Trading in the Twenty-First Century

Rajesh Chadha, Sanjib Pohit, Alan V. Deardorff, and Robert M. Stern
The Impact of Trade and Domestic Policy Reforms in India: A CGE Modeling Approach

Alan V. Deardorff and Robert M. Stern, Editors
Constituent Interests and U.S. Trade Policies

Gary R. Saxonhouse and T. N. Srinivasan, Editors
Development, Duality, and the International Economic Regime: Essays in Honor of Gustav Ranis

Charles P. Kindleberger
Essays in History: Financial, Economic, Personal

Keith Acheson and Christopher Maule
Much Ado about Culture: North American Trade Disputes

Alan V. Deardorff and Robert M. Stern
Social Dimensions of U.S. Trade Policies

Thomas Cottier and Petros C. Mavroidis, Editors
Regulatory Barriers and the Principle of Non-Discrimination in World Trade Law

Bernard Hoekman and Jamel Zarrouk
Catching Up with the Competition: Trade Opportunities and Challenges for Arab Countries

Jun Fu
Institutions and Investments: Foreign Direct Investment in China during an Era of Reforms

Institutions and Investments

Foreign Direct Investment in China during an Era of Reforms

Jun Fu

Ann Arbor

THE UNIVERSITY OF MICHIGAN PRESS

Published in the United States of America by
The University of Michigan Press
Manufactured in the United States of America
♾ Printed on acid-free paper

2003 2002 2001 2000 4 3 2 1

A CIP catalog record for this book is available from the British Library.

Library of Congress Cataloging-in-Publication Data applied for
ISBN 0-472-11178-7 (alk. paper)

Contents

List of Maps, Tables, and Figures

Figures

Abbreviations

AAA	American Arbitration Association
ADR	American Depository Receipts
AIG	American International Group
BIT	Bilateral investment protection treaty
BOT	Build-operate-transfer
BTA	Basic Telecommunications Agreement
CCOIC	Chinese Chamber of International Commerce
CJV	Contractual joint venture
CIETAC	China International Economic and Trade Arbitration Commission
CCP	Chinese communist party
CMAC	China Maritime Arbitration Commission
CT	Compensation trade
CTOEC	China Tianjin Otis Elevator Company
EC	European Community
EIU	Economist Intelligence Unit
EJV	Equity joint venture
EOE	Export-oriented enterprise
ETDZ	Economic and technology development zone
EU	European Union
FAI	Fixed asset investment
FDI	Foreign direct investment
FIE	Foreign invested enterprise
FETAC	Foreign Economic and Trade Arbitration Commission
FSA	Financial Services Agreement
FTAC	Foreign Trade Arbitration Commission
FX	Foreign exchange
GATT	General Agreement on Trade and Tariffs
GDP	Gross domestic product
HKIAC	Hong Kong International Arbitration Centre
HOS	Hechkscher-Ohlin-Samuelson model
ICC	International Chamber of Commerce

ICP	Internet content provider
ICSID	International Center for Settlement of Investment Dispute
IL	International leasing
IMF	International Monetary Fund
IOV	Industrial output value
IPR	Intellectual property rights
ISP	Internet service provider
IT	Information technology
JDP	Joint development project
JV	Joint venture
KOTRA	Korea Trade Promotion Corp.
LCIA	London Court of International Arbitration
MFN	Most favored nation
MIGA	Multinational Investment Guarantee Agency
MNC	Multinational corporation
MOFERT	Ministry of Foreign Economic Relations and Trade
MOFTEC	Ministry of Foreign Trade and Economic Cooperation
MOU	Memorandum of Understanding
NBER	National Bureau for Economic Research
NHTZ	New and high-tech zone
NPC	National People's Congress
NTB	Non-tariff barrier
NTR	Normal Trade Relations
OECD	Organization for Economic Cooperation and Development
OLS	Ordinary least square
OPIC	Overseas Private Investment Corporation
OUD	Old urban district
PA	Processing and assembly
PBOC	People's Bank of China
PRC	People's Republic of China
REITC	Regulations on Encouraging Investment by Taiwan Compatriots
RMB	Renminbi
SAFE	State Administration of Foreign Exchange
SAIC	State Administration for Industry and Commerce
SBSAM	State Bureau of State Asset Management
SCC	Arbitration Institute of the Stockholm Chamber of Commerce

SETC	State Economic and Trade Commission
SEZ	Special economic zone
SOE	State-owned enterprise
SPC	State Planning Commission
TAE	Technologically advanced enterprise
TEC	Tianjin Elevator Company
TRIMS	Trade-Related Investment Measures
TRIPS	Trade-Related Intellectual Property Rights
UNCTC	United Nations Center on Transnational Corporations
UNCTAD	United Nations Conference on Trade and Development
WFOE	Wholly foreign-owned enterprise
WIPO	World Intellectual Property Organization
WTO	World Trade Organization
WWW	World Wide Web

Acknowledgments

Over the past years, I have been blessed to have come into contact with an extraordinary array of excellent scholars and educators. Some have taught me formally in the classroom; others informally through countless conversations and interactions. While researching and writing this book involved long periods of solitary toil, it was marked by a great deal of intellectual guidance, generosity, and collegiality from the faculty at Harvard University and elsewhere and from my friends and colleagues both in the United States and China.

As this book grew out of my doctoral dissertation, first and foremost my gratitude goes to my academic advisers. Roderick MacFarquhar had patience and generosity to supervise my studies for the better part of my years as a graduate student at Harvard. Dwight Perkins, in his usual laid-back demeanor, taught me not only many of the intricacies of transitional economies but also the importance and limitations of quantitative evidence in modeling institutional questions. Yasheng Huang often provided insights and penetrating criticisms of half-baked ideas – frequently over a drink or a basketball game – that one receives only when the best of friends happen to be excellent scholars. My ambition is to bridge the gap between economics, political science, law, and area studies. Robert Bates set high standards for me by demanding constant attention to detail and at the same time asking big theoretical questions. Without his prodding, this book would have failed to clarify the structure the argument should take.

My admiration and thanks also go to Douglass North, who, through his writings, initiated me into the fascinating world of the institutional dimension of economics. In my foray into law, politics, and economics, his theorizing about the role of institutions in economic performance kept me focused on the questions I wanted to answer instead of on statistics. Professor North, in spite of his busy schedule, took time to read the manuscript, wrote detailed comments, and offered helpful suggestions as I was going through the initial draft of the manuscript. Those who are familiar with his work will see its influence on mine.

My debt of gratitude also goes to Jim Alt, Richard Caves, Jeffry Frieden, and Ray Vernon. They, through their teachings at Harvard, kindled my interest in political economy in general, and in international investment in particular. Professors Caves, Frieden and Vernon gave generously of their time and expertise, read part or all of the manuscript, and offered valuable suggestions. Richard Caves and Jeffry Frieden, in particular, provided absolutely critical feedback on the research designs in the pivotal chapters of this book. I also thank Ting Gao and John Ries for reading the manuscript and providing critical and constructive comments. My debt, of course, goes beyond those who read my manusript.

As I was going through various stages of this research project, William Alford, Lawrence Broz, Marc Busch, Richard Cooper, Grzegorz Ekiert, Fred Hu, Huang Jin, Ellis Joffe, Iain Johnston, Devesh Kapur, David Li, Liu Zhi, Lu Feng, Lu Qiwen, Jean Oi, Kathleen O'Neill, Robert Paarlberg, Elizabeth Perry, Ed Steinfeld, Paul Talcolt, Joshua Tucker, Eric Thun, Michael Tomz, Ezra Vogel, and Shang-Jin Wei, each in their own ways, offered camaraderie, comments, encouragement, and/or wise advice. To them all, I say thanks. A special mention must be made of Liu Zhi, a fellow graduate student at Harvard who now works at the World Bank. He contributed insights and information that strengthened the analysis. Ed Steinfeld, another fellow graduate student at Harvard who now teaches at MIT's Sloan School of Management, also deserves a special thanks. He was particularly helpful in sharing with me his knowledge and experience during the publication stage of this project.

I also owe a special thanks to Nancy Hearst, librarian at Harvard's Fairbank Center for East Asian Research. Her impressive knowledge of China and of Chinese-language research materials is widely known in the United States and China. Although she may claim only to have proofread the manuscript, she made important contributions to this project by locating and providing research materials in a timely fashion even when I was overseas. Without her help, this project would have been much delayed. At the University of Michigan Press, Ellen McCarthy, Senior Editor for Social Sciences, guided me through the publication process with superb expertise and dispatch, ably assisted by Michael Kehoe, Claudia Leo, Mary Meade, and Jennifer Wisinski.

Part of the research of this study was presented to members of the American Chamber of Commerce in Beijing. For that I thank Michael Furst and Timothy Stratford. Many more friends, scholars, officials, and managers in China have also helped me generously during my research trips up and down the country. I regret that I am unable to acknowledge them individually by name out of respect for their anonymity. Nevertheless, I do want to say that I will always remain grateful to them for the time and assistance they gave me and that I have been much inspired by their commitment to helping China negotiate its transition from plan to market.

Finally, I wish to express my gratitude to the institutions that provided financial support for the project. The research was supported initially by a grant from the Andrew Mellon Foundation and subsequently by an FLAS fellowship and a grant from Harvard University's Yenching Institute. The Weatherhead Center for International Affairs at Harvard helped fund two summer research trips in China and provided both the site for much of the work on this project and a great deal of intellectual inspiration. It is difficult to imagine a more congenial or stimulating place to work, and I want to thank Jorge Dominguez, its Director, for granting me entree into this exciting community of scholars, business leaders, and government officials.

I dedicate this book to my parents for their understanding, love and confidence in me. I do not know how to give them thanks.

Introduction and Synopsis

China has been heralded as a rising economic power. Its gradual yet steady transformation from a closed command economy to a market-oriented trading nation is a story that has attracted worldwide attention. Since 1978 when economic reforms started, China has maintained an average annual GDP growth rate close to 10%, making it one of the fastest growing economies in the world.[1] More recently, even when the Asian financial crisis struck and plagued much of the region,[2] China managed to achieve a respectable GDP growth rate of 7.8% in 1998.

Over the past two decades China's foreign trade grew at an even more brisk pace, averaging over 15%, which is more than three times the world rates between 1978 and 1990 (Lardy 1994:30). China's import and export total was about US$21 billion in 1978; it was US$324 billion in 1998. This is an almost 15-fold increase in 20 years. Reflecting China's growing openness and interdependence with the world economy, the ratio of China's foreign trade to GDP expanded rapidly from 10% in 1978 to about 35% in 1998.[3]

---

1. The average yearly GDP growth rate of China in the period of 1991-96 was even higher, at 11.6%. The comparable figure for the United States was 2%. It was 3.9% for India.

2. For discussions of how the financial crisis arose and spread, and its impact on the region's economy, consider Goldstein (1998), and Radelet and Sachs (1999).

3. These figures, exceptionally high for a country with a huge domestic market, should be viewed with a degree of caution, since China's GDP is widely believed to be under-estimated. But if one is interested in trends, there seems no question that China's integration with the world economy has been deepening rapidly. According to Nicholas Lardy (1994:110-15), China today is arguably more fully integrated with the world economy than were South Korea or Taiwan at comparable stages of development. He also suggests that given its high level of FDI, China is more fully integrated with the world economy than

The rapid growth in the Chinese economy and the rapid increase in China's openness in the world economy have resulted in a very rapid increase in China's share of world exports. According to *World Development Indicators 1999* published by the World Bank, the share of China in total world exports has more than tripled since the initiation of the open-door policy, from just over 1% in 1982 to over 3% in 1998.

All at the same time the Chinese economy has operated increasingly under market conditions, rapidly displacing the pre-reform command system.[4] Now, over 90% of retail prices and over 80% of agricultural and raw materials prices are set by the market, and most sectors of industry are free from plan obligations and no longer receive subsidized inputs from the state (EAAU 1997:75-76). Average trade tariffs have fallen rapidly from over 42.9% in 1992 to 17.5% in 1998 (World Bank 1999:340). A further lowering of tariff rates and opening of key markets to foreign competition (e.g., agricultural products, banking, professional services, telecommunications) is expected as China makes the adjustments required by WTO members for accession to the World Trade Organization (WTO).[5] WTO accession is widely seen in the international business community as a major litmus test of China's commitment to becoming a true market-driven economy (Kobler 1999).

At the core of China's economic achievements is a massive influx of foreign direct investment (FDI). Indeed, FDI in China is perhaps one of the most spectacular phenomena in the country's economic reform and open-door efforts. In the initial years of reform (1979-83), China realized only US$1.8 billion in FDI, but since then FDI surged by an average yearly rate of about 40% and reached US$41.73 billion in 1996 alone. The figures for 1997 and 1998, according to the latest statistics, were both about US$45 billion, a remarkable achievement still, in light of the widespread financial turmoil that struck East and Southeast Asia in late 1997.

Japan is today. For further discussions on China's integration into the world economy, see Lardy (1994) and World Bank (1997c).

4. For a comprehensive study of the process, see Naughton (1995) and Perkins (1994).

5. For a brief description of the missions of the WTO and the implications of its membership on trade practices, see the WTO's website at <www.wto.org>.

Literally from a land of no FDI in 1978, China now hosts tens of thousands of industrial enterprises that are partially or wholly owned by foreign investors. From a tiny base in the first part of the 1980s, foreign-invested enterprises (FIEs), including joint ventures and 100% foreign-owned subsidiaries, have now become the dominant players in China's foreign trade scene. Their import and export volumes as a share of the country's total grew rapidly from less than 1% before 1982 to 48% in 1998. Time series trade statistics, including import and export breakdowns, are presented in Table 1. As the table shows, FIEs growing contribution to China's export capacity is consistent and unmistakable.

Trade benefits aside, FDI has fueled China's economy by providing capital, technology, critical managerial skills, and know-how, all of which are likely to have had a positive impact on the Chinese economy at both the macro and micro levels.[6] Even though the transfer of FDI-embodied technology, managerial skills, cultures of opportunity, and social mobility are not readily quantifiable, their contributions as an additional source of capital and employment are very tangible and indeed have become quite significant in recent years. As a share of GDP, they reached over 5% on average in the 1994-98 period; as a share of total fixed assets investment (FAI), the comparable figure was above 10% (Figure 1). By comparison, in the early 1990s FDI was only 0.2%, as a share of GDP, in the case of Korea, 2% in the case of Thailand, and 1.5% in the case of Indonesia (Yasheng Huang 1998).

All in all, from 1979 through 1998, China received some US$265 billion in actual paid-in FDI, representing more than 324,000 projects in total, and creating a huge number of job opportunities. Chinese data show that the amount of Chinese employment in FIEs rapidly rose from

---

6. Beyond the Chinese context, there are several empirical studies showing that FDI exhibits higher levels of total factor productivity than do local counterparts (Haddad and Harrison 1993; Harrison 1996; Borensztein, et al. 1995). Sectors with a higher foreign presence have a lower dispersion of productivity among all firms than do sectors with a lower foreign presence, suggesting a spillover from the foreign presence that moves domestic firms closer to the efficiency frontier (Haddad and Harrison 1993). Within the Chinese context, a preliminary empirical study suggests that FIEs, compared to domestic firms, are superior in terms of export-output ratio, capital intensity, and productivity for both capital and labor (Sun Haishun 1998: 81-99).

660,000 in 1990 to 5.4 million in 1996.[7] According to *Washington Post* (24 June 1998. A26), US affiliated firms alone in China have put as many as 250,000 Chinese employees on their payrolls. Reflecting one dimension of the positive spillover effects of FDI, "China's new business elite," as Pearson (1997) describes the emerging middle classes of coastal cities, has been growing rapidly.

Table 1: FIE Imports and Exports and Share of Country's Total, 1980-98 (US$ million)

Year	Imports & exports	% of total	Exports	% of total	Imports	% of total
1980	43	0.11	8.24	0.05	34.76	0.17
1981	143	0.33	32.35	0.15	110.65	0.51
1982	329	0.79	52.87	0.24	276.13	1.43
1983	618	1.42	330.36	1.49	287.64	1.35
1984	468	0.87	68.94	0.26	399.06	1.46
1985	2,361	3.39	296.70	1.08	2,064.30	4.89
1986	3,012	4.08	582.03	1.88	2,429.97	5.67
1987	4,330	5.60	1,208.09	3.06	3,121.91	7.90
1988	8,203	8.10	2,456.42	5.17	5,746.58	10.60
1989	13,709	12.28	4,913.20	9.35	8,795.80	15.20
1990	20,120	17.43	7,813.79	12.58	12,306.21	23.07
1991	28,954	21.35	12,047.25	16.77	16,906.75	26.50
1992	43,726	26.42	17,356.19	20.50	26,369.81	32.72
1993	67,070	34.27	25,237.17	27.50	41,832.83	40.24
1994	87,647	37.03	34,712.97	28.68	52,934.03	45.76
1995	109,818	39.10	46,876.01	31.52	62,941.99	47.66
1996	137,110	47.30	61,510.00	40.70	75,600.00	54.50
1997	152,620	46.59	74,900.00	40.99	77,720.00	54.59
1998	157,680	48.67	80,960.00	44.06	76,720.00	54.73

Source: *Zhongguo tongji zhaiyao* [A Statistical Survey of China] (various years).

7. The real number may be higher. Rosen (1998:87) observes that many FIEs today are managing Chinese employees directly through shell companies that are ostensibly independent.

Figure 1: FDI as a Share of GDP and FAI in China, 1990-98

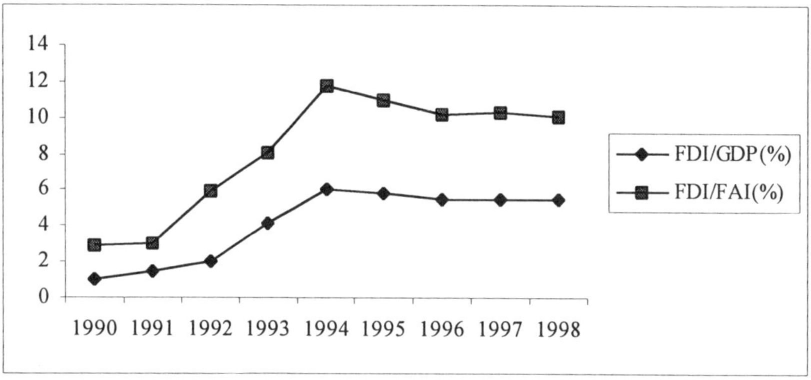

Note: In calculating FDI contributions to total fixed asset investment (FAI) I assume 70% of FDI is used for fixed investment.
Source: *Zhongguo tongji zhaiyao* [A Statistical Survey of China] (1999).

Growth trends of FDI in China were dramatic over the reform years. FDI inflows were moderate during the initial years of reform and the open door. They increased rather significantly in the latter part of the 1980s, and skyrocketed in the 1990s. The magnitude of FDI inflows in the 1990s, as exemplified by big multinationals, such as Coca-Cola, IBM, General Electric, General Motors, Motorola, Kodak, and Siemens, was astonishing. At times they accounted for close to 40% of all FDI inflows to all developing countries, making China the largest FDI recipient in the developing world, second only to the United States (Table 2).

Table 2: FDI Inflows in the World, 1985-98 (US$ billion)

	1985-1990*	1991	1992	1993	1994	1995	1996	1997	1998
World total	142	159	174	218	239	317	359	464	644
Developed world	117	115	120	139	142	206	211	273	460
US	49	23	19	44	50	61	77	109	193
Developing world	25	42	49	73	90	96	135	173	166
China	3	5	11	27	34	36	40	44	46
Share of developing world	11%	10%	22%	38%	37%	37%	30%	26%	27%

Note: * yearly averages.
Source: UNCTAD, *World Investment Report* (1997; 1999).

In the present world, in the developing and transitional economies in particular, where FDI is being actively pursued as a catalyst for development,[8] China's record of attracting FDI is very impressive. This is especially true in light of the fact that the Chinese economy was an extreme version of autarky in the pre-reform years and foreign participation in the country's economy is a phenomenon that began only two decades ago. Given so short a history, the huge FDI inflows to China during the reform era are all the more extraordinary. An obvious question arises: What is it that has been driving the growth patterns of FDI in China?

The reason for China's success in attracting FDI, it has often been argued, lies in its unique economic and cultural attributes. Those who emphasize economics often point to China's advantageous economic factors, such as its high GDP growth rates, low labor costs, and huge market size (UNCTAD 1997:92; Kraar 1994:80-82). Those who emphasize culture[9] are just as quick to point out that a significant portion of FDI that China has received comes from countries/regions that host a large overseas Chinese population. Hong Kong, Macao, Singapore, and Taiwan are notable examples.[10]

While the present study does not dispute these claims, and indeed will include both economic and cultural variables as critical

---

8. According to *Global Development Finance*, World Bank Debtor Reporting System, World Bank (1998), private capital flows now total more than four/fifth of all capital inflows to the developing and transitional economies. They amounted to US$256 billion in 1997, of which FDI accounted for close to 50% (US$120 billion). As documented by Emmott (1993), recently there has been a sea of change in developing countries' attitudes toward FDI. While MNCs were often vilified as exploiters of poor countries in the 1970s, they are now viewed as symbols of modernity and progress, such that "governments all around the world, especially in the developing countries, are queuing up to attract [them]."

9. For literature that has a cultural focus, see, for instance, Sender 1991; Tanzer 1994; Berger 1994; Oxfeld 1993; Kao 1993; Jansson 1994; Suryadinata 1995; Hamilton and Waters 1995; EAAU 1995; Ong and Nonini 1997; Huang Cen 1998.

10. For a fascinating anecdotal account of how social networks of overseas Chinese contribute to investment and economic boom, see Weidenbaum and Hughes (1996), and also see Wang Gungwu (1990), and Hamilton (1992). Another recent study that focuses on cultural factors is by Wang Hongyin (forthcoming)

contributing factors, it nonetheless diverges from, or rather goes beyond, the conventional economic and cultural perspectives. In this study, we do not take the explanatory power of economic and cultural factors for granted. Instead, as will be shown shortly, the conventional economic and cultural explanations are debilitatingly inadequate to account for the variant patterns of FDI in China if the effects of Chinese institutions, or rather the dramatic changes thereof in the reform era, are not taken seriously. Accordingly, relevant to a broader theoretical literature that looks at how political arrangements affect economic performance,[11] the current study represents an effort to go beyond economic and cultural factors to explore the connections between institutions and investments through the prism of FDI in China during the reform era.

In the rest of this introduction, we first sketch out an analytical framework designed to serve as an overall guide to the current study. We then outline the organizational structure and foci of the book. A brief note on targeted readership and sources in the study follows.

Institutions and Investments: An Analytical Framework

Flows of FDI to China, as will be documented in greater detail later in this study, display dramatic changing patterns in the reform years. Variations manifest themselves not only in space (i.e., geographical

---

11. For an illustration of this time-honored intellectual tradition, recall the *Yan Tie Lun,* or "Discourse on Salt and Iron," in Han dynasty China. This classic work documents ancient heated debates in China about how government policy affects economics. Across the Pacific, the founding fathers of the United States also wrestled with similar issues; see the *Federalist Papers* especially no. 11, by Alexander Hamilton. For a new explosion of literature in recent years on how state institutions shape expectations about economic activity and consequently affects investment, growth, and development, see, e.g., Alesina and Rodrik (1994), Barro (1991; 1994); Bates (1997b); Clark and Maxfield (1996); Cukierman, Webb, and Neyapti (1992); Frieden (1989); Grossman (1994); Hansen (1990); Katzenstein (1977); Keefer and Knack (1997); Knack and Keefer (1995); Krasner (1978); Krugman (1994); Leblang (1997); Maxfield (1997); Nordhaus (1975); North (1990); North and Weingast (1989); Olson (1993); Pastor and Sung (1995); Persson (1988); Przeworski (1991); Rama (1993); Rodrik (1989); Rogowski (1987; 1989); Root (1989); Scully (1988); Simmons (1994); Sobel (1994; 1999); Svensson (1998); Torstensson (1994); Verdier (1994).

distribution) and time (e.g., overall growth trends), but also in the mode of investment (e.g., different forms of joint ventures vis-à-vis 100% foreign-owned subsidiaries).[12] As if this picture were not already complex enough, one also finds that different modes of investment as a share of the total FDI also change dramatically over time. Clearly, if one is to systematically account for these changes, a *dynamic rather than static* analytical framework is in order. Yet, it is precisely in the face of this methodological challenge that the conventional economic and cultural approaches are at their weakest to explain the variant patterns of FDI in China *over time* during the reform years.

Let us start with a brief comment on the deficiency of culture as an explanatory variable of investment. What is culture? To the extent that we define culture to include such conditions as linguistic familiarity and kinship ties, that culture facilitates investment would seem obvious, if only because language can reduce information costs and kinship ties can mitigate opportunistic behavior (i.e., non-performance of commitments). All else being equal, there would seem to be little doubt that an overseas investor well versed in Chinese culture would be more likely to invest in China than one who is not. Not surprisingly, when an Economist Intelligence Unit survey asked FIE managers to rank the factors they felt most hampered the productivity of their operations, "language/culture" was ranked second (EIU 1997). And the Harvard Business School case on Northern Telecom's (Nortel) joint venture with Tong Guang Electronics in China underscores the importance of cultural sensitivity on the part of foreign managers. However, the problem with culture is that since it does not change measurably in the short run, say in a decade or so, we are hard-pressed to be able to use it to account for the variant patterns of FDI in China over time in the reform era.

What about economic variables? Economic variables such as GDP growth rates, market size, and low labor costs, etc. as predictors of investment behavior are also rife with both conceptual and methodological pitfalls. Take high growth rate. It is prone to the problem of endogeneity. In order words, the causal arrow between economic growth rates and levels of investment is by no means clear. Indeed, there are reasons to believe that GDP growth rates can be an

---

12. Characteristics and attendant risk implications of different modes of FDI in China will be examined in Chapter 3 of this study.

effect rather than a cause of FDI. The high growth rates in China's Special Economic Zones (SEZ) are but a case in point. The SEZs all rose as industrial centers from previously barren areas due to a huge influx of foreign investment.

Figure 2: Annual GDP Growth Rates in China, 1978-98 (constant prices)

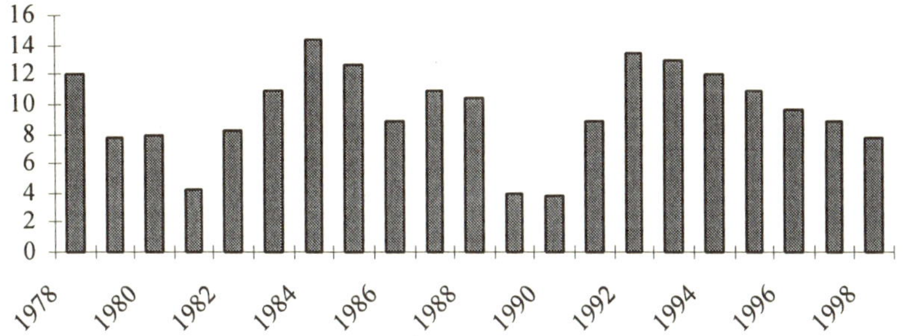

Source: *Zhongguo tongji nianjian* [China Statistical Yearbook] (various years).

Further, economic growth rates, if scrutinized *dynamically*, i.e., over time, also fail to account for the changing levels of FDI in China over the reform years. The fact is that whereas the growth rate of the Chinese economy, measured by GDP, was already high in the 1980s, relative to the 1990s (see Figure 2), the levels of FDI in the 1980s were not nearly as high as they were in the 1990s. To expand upon this point, cumulative FDI in China for 1992-94 alone amounted to 70% of the entire FDI stock in China for 1979-94. China's GDP growth rate in these years, while high, does not seem sufficient to account for the dramatic rise in FDI at the time. Conversely, the Korean experience disproves the automatic connection between GDP growth rates and levels of FDI. Amsden (1989) shows that when the Korean economy was rising rapidly in the 1970s and 1980s, the number of multinationals in Korea was smaller than in any other newly industrialized economies (NIEs).

What about market size? Market size as an explanatory variable of investment behavior often suffers from the problem of collinearity with the liberalization of exogenous policy regimes of the host country regarding market access. This is especially true in a transitional economy like that of China. Over the reform years China has moved from the Stalinist-type command model of the Mao era, to Chen Yun's "bird-cage" formula in the 1980s,[13] to Deng Xiaoping's "socialist market" economy in the early 1990s,[14] and to the recent constitutional amendment which recognizes the private sector as an important component of the country's economy.[15] During the process of transition, market size (or rather market access as far as foreign investors are concerned) is often a function of policy or institutional arrangements. This appears true even in mature and developed economies. Japan, for instance, the world's second largest economy, has a level of FDI inflows lower than that of Greece, mainly because of its high structural barriers toward foreign investors (Weinstein 1996; Lawrence 1993).

In China, the opening up of domestic markets to foreign investors has been a gradual and managed process, even though barriers have come down significantly in recent years. While we will document that process in greater detail later, suffice it here to say that whatever the size of China's domestic market may be, it was very restricted to foreign investors by exogenous policy instruments across the board during the early years of reform, and still is today in some specific sectors such as telecommunications, banking, insurance, retail and wholesale, and professional services. It is worthwhile to note, however, China has promised to gradually open these markets as well in order to satisfy the entry conditions for the World Trade Organization.

It should become sufficiently clear by now that neither GDP growth rate, nor market size, is an exogenous variable to be taken for granted. Their explanatory power may seem intuitive when looked at *statically*, i.e., at one point in time, but their explanatory power quickly diminishes once looked at *dynamically*, i.e., over time. The same is true of labor costs, although this may appear counter-intuitive at first sight. But the puzzle we must confront is this: If labor costs were so exclusive a consideration, why then did so many investors wait until the 1990s to invest in China, when China's growth rates in the 1980s

13. This can be paraphrased as a limited role for the market within the confines of planning by fiat.

14. A rough calibration of the concept is marketization without going for corresponding political decontrols.

15. The amendment was approved by the National People's Congress of China on March 15, 1999, signaling a new stage in China's efforts to reform its economy from plan to market.

were already very high and labor was eminently many times cheaper at the time? One would often hear investors say that the "time was not ripe!" But at a deeper level, many hesitant investors, in their calculations whether to "to invest, or not to invest,"[16] were, consciously or subconsciously, waiting for additional assurances and/or information about market conditions in China. Waiting, of course, incurs costs, including lost opportunities.[17] So the decision to wait does not make sense unless the costs of information and transactions exceed, or are perceived to exceed, the costs of waiting.

This in time brings us to the role of institutions. Institutions, according to Douglass North (1990:356-57), a Nobel laureate and eminent theorist of economic history, "are about the underlying rules that are the incentive structure of an economy – property rights, contracting, and credible commitment." The role of institutions is to structure human interaction. As such, different institutional arrangements have different implications for the efficiency of an economy. They can either constrain or raise transaction costs. Whether they lower or raise transaction costs "depends upon a causal complex of who gets to make decisions and the nature of the political system."[18]

The concept of transaction costs, by the way, was pioneered by another Nobel laureate Ronald Coase (1937; 1960), and developed by others, notably Oliver Williamson (1975; 1985; 1989). It encompasses the measurement costs,[19] the costs of deciding, planning, arranging, and negotiating the actions to be taken, and the terms of exchange when

---

16. My reformation of Shakespeare's "to be or not to be" to highlight a self-debating "Hamlet" in foreign investment.

17. For instance, Motorola has been a huge player in China's fast-growing paging and mobile phone market. Its success is often credited to its early decision to move to China to tap the market, when market information was not at all clear. As a senior Motorola manager reminisced, "It was very difficult in the 1980s to justify coming to China on the basis of any feasibility studies or market assessment. But in 1986 our chairman came to the Chinese market and said we needed to be in that market. We decided to go ahead. Our timing was extremely good." Cited in Yang, et al. (1999).

18. Personal communication. I am indebted to Douglass North for sharpening my understanding of the role of institutions.

19. Yoram Barzel (1982), building on the contribution of Stephen Cheung (1969), has emphasized the measurement dimension of transaction cost economics.

two or more parties do business; the costs of changing plans, renegotiating terms, and resolving disputes as changing circumstances may require; and the costs of ensuring that parties perform as agreed and property rights are protected. As Milgrom and Roberts (1990:61) have summarized, "transaction costs include anything that affects the relative performance of different ways of organizing resources and production activities." But throughout human history, as North (1990:362) has observed:

> Economic markets... are frequently very imperfect, beset by high transaction costs and defined by institutions that produce incentives that work against economic efficiency. Indeed, creating institutions that provide low costs of transacting in economic markets is the key issue to creating productive economies.

The point of departure of this study is the assumption that private investments, where current costs are incurred for future benefits, are not shaped by market forces alone. Being inherently interpersonal and intertemporal, investments are vulnerable to opportunistic behavior, including reneging, and therefore the presence of non-market institutions for the protection of property rights and the reduction of transaction costs is required. To highlight the relationship between institutions and investments, I quote Robert Bates (1997a:177-78) extensively as follows:

> Capital requires exchange over time. To form capital, people save. Withholding goods from consumption in one period, people invest, such that they can enhance their consumption in future periods. It is the prospect of rewards that motivates present sacrifices. Lying in the future, the prospective rewards are uncertain, however. Among the risks are those of non-performance, or opportunistic actions by other human beings. In the face of such risks, individuals may fail to make investments that would render them – and, indeed, all people – better off. The desire to transcend this dilemma motivates the creation of non-market institutions.

Applying the logic of neo-institutionalism,[20] our analytical framework, for the sake of conceptual clarity, starts with two extreme, albeit unrealistic, institutional models (see Figure 3). Each model has a bearing on investment behavior. One is entirely informal, defined to include such conditions as linguistic familiarity, cultural homogeneity, and kinship ties, and whose mechanism to temper opportunistic behavior can be modeled by the iterative interactions of game theory.[21] Here, reputation is a valuable asset driving performance of commitments.[22] The other is entirely formal. By it I mean formal rules, official policies, and legislation, or the concept of "abstract legal authority"[23] and "the rule of law," whose function is to provide transparency and predictability, with the attendant results of reducing transaction costs associated with *ex ante* information and haggling, and *ex post* monitoring and policing.

---

20. "Neo" as opposed to the former treatment by Karl Marx as well as by Frank Knight (1921) and John Commons (1931). Marx also dealt with institutions, or "superstructure," as he called it. But he failed to take a step further to open up the "black box," i.e., to discuss exactly how institutions affect economic activities. For a theoretical review of neo-institutionalism, see Hodgson (1998:166-92), Rutherford (1994), and Bates (1988: 387-401).

21. Game theorists generally agree that cooperation is fostered when players engage in indefinitely repeated games, so that a defector faces punishment in successive rounds. This principle is so widely recognized that one version of it is known as the folk theorem. The folk theorem holds that "always defect" is not a unique equilibrium in the repeat-play prisoner's dilemma, as it is in one-round games. For further discussion, consider Fudenberg and Maskin (1986). For how repeated games deter defection and foster cooperation in anarchical situations, see Axelrod (1984) and Taylor (1976). Specific to culture, a closed community, where personal interactions are frequent, can be modeled as a repeated game. In the language of game theory, a situation where no party can gain by making a unilateral deviation from the prescribed behavior is called a Nash equilibrium.

22. Empirical evidence that reputation played a critical role in facilitating trade among Mediterranean merchants in the 11th century is documented in Greif (1989). These merchants, who shipped goods across the Mediterranean Sea, involved the entire merchant group in ostracizing cheaters. This system made a good reputation a precious asset that merchants would go to great lengths to preserve. "Personal trust" is also a critical element in doing business in the Asian context, see Mamilton (1991).

23. Attributable to Max Weber. See Weber (1978).

Figure 3: An Illustrative Dynamic Institutional Model of Investment

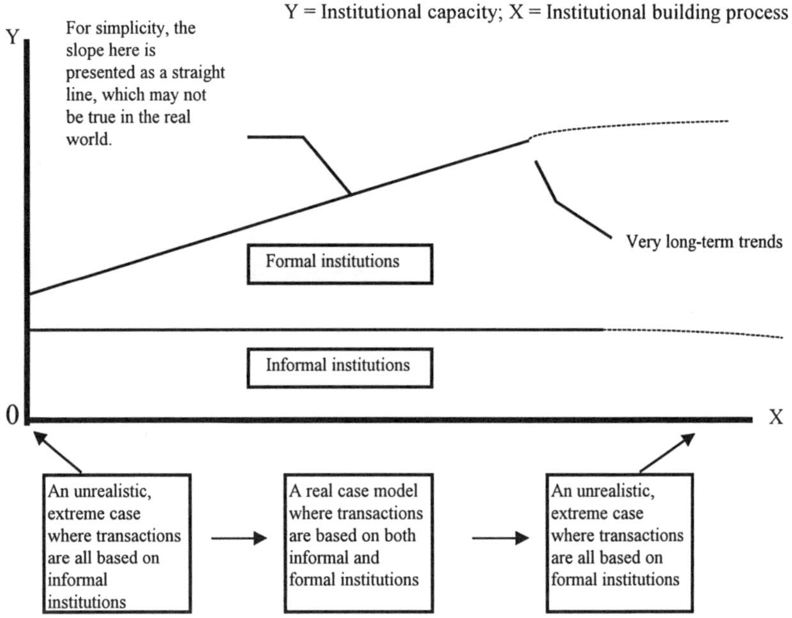

Note, however, although transactions, of which capital investment is but one kind, can conceivably take place under both models,[24] their capacity to facilitate transactions differ vastly, with the formal type far better to facilitate especially such transactions as large-scale industrial investments that are complex, interpersonal, intertemporal, and long in geographical distance. On the other hand, culture, as a facilitator of transactions, is after all limited by geographical scope, and anyway, works poorly in an impersonal context, i.e., between strangers. This difference, in turn, goes a long way in explaining why some societies industrialized ahead of others (North and Thomas 1973; Hicks 1969; Rosenberg and Birdzell 1986; Berman 1983). The industrialized

24. In the most primitive forms, human transactions could and did occur even without language. As Herodotus tells us, sign language and arm's length observation of the goods each served as a basis of these transactions. But the scope of such transactions was perforce extremely limited.

societies all developed a set of institutional arrangements, perhaps best epitomized by the concept of "the rule of law," that managed to lower the costs of exchanges and transactions over both space and time.

To be sure, when separated individually, neither of the above extreme institutional models can realistically capture the enormous richness and complexity of human interactions which are based on a mixture of formal rules and informal norms. Thus, to approximate reality better, our analytical framework, as Figure 3 illustrates, is a dynamic combination of the two extreme cases. Such a mixture better reflects the reality of China during the period of reforms, a country in rapid structural transition from plan to market,[25] but nonetheless with all of its cultural heritage instead of starting from *tabula rasa*.

Yet, in terms of institution building (the formal type), starting almost from scratch in the late 1970s, China has progressed significantly in developing the necessary legal and regulatory infrastructure, introducing many basic commercial laws and regulations essential in a modern market economy. Specific to foreign investment, the body of law now in place, both domestic and international, though by no means perfect or even entirely adequate, is impressive for a country that started with the most rudimentary laws for foreign investors only two decades ago.[26]

To understand investment behavior under such conditions, the above analytical framework will be used not only as a heuristic device in our analysis of the impact of institutions on investment behavior in the reform era. To add analytical rigor to our study, it will also be expressed formally (i.e., formal modeling) to be tested systematically against the changing patterns of FDI in China over the reform years. By definition, FDI is cross-border, long-distance operations in alien parts of the world. Many such operations are long-term, lumpy, and specific investments, which have a low salvage value for alternative uses,[27] and

---

25. Harry Harding (1987), for instance, has characterized China's reforms in the post-Mao era as a "second revolution."

26. Prior to reform, China practiced a centrally planned economy. Economic activities were primarily governed by executive orders or discretionary procedural powers. Rule-based law played a marginal role. For a brief discussion of legal history, or the lack of it, in the pre-reform era, see Fan Gang and Xin Chunying (1998).

27. For instance, when a subcontractor makes wing assemblies for a particular model of a Boeing airliner, it may invest in setting up a production

thus pose high risks under institutional uncertainty. As Lardy (1998:199) points out, "direct investors differ fundamentally from financial investors since they invest with a long time horizon and their investments are illiquid." As such, FDI represents an excellent subject matter, full of statistical data, where we can empirically test theories regarding institutional effect on economic behavior.

A principal institutional postulate is that economic development, or for that matter investment growth, is predicated upon the development of an institutional framework of laws, rules, and regulations, that are pro-competition, predictable, and transparent. Does the Chinese story of FDI represent a case of aberration or convergence with this institutional hypothesis? As the empirical findings of this study will show later, the answer is the latter, even though, at any single point in time, foreign investors may continue to be frustrated and baffled by the imperfections, and indeed at times arbitrary and shady practices, in the Chinese marketplace. Yet as a dynamic trend, China, in spite of its unique culture, seems to have largely followed the institutional logic of economic development.[28] To repeat, sustained investment growth has depended on the gradual improvement and solidification of a rule-based, market-oriented institutional framework. But that framework, to be sure, was not wished into reality overnight. It was built, one brick at a time, by trial and error, throughout the reform years. Today, gaps exist; blemishes abound; construction continues. This is the central lesson that the current study has for the reader.

---

line to make those specific assemblies. Such an investment is known as a *specific* investment because it loses much of its value outside of the specific use of providing wings to Boeing. The subcontractor does not want to make the investment unless it has some reasonable assurance that an order will be forthcoming. The concepts of asset specificity, frequency, and uncertainty as key dimensions of transactions are expounded upon by Williamson (1985). The importance of specific investments was first developed in the context of human capital theory by Becker (1964).

28. This is somewhat echoed by Guthrie (1998) who finds that the sigificance of *Guanxi,* or personal connections, has declined in China's economic transition; and also by Hodder (1996) who, in a separate study, argues against the uniqueness of overseas Chinese business practices.

Organizational Plan and Foci

The study is organized into three main parts. Each part in turn is composed of two chapters. Part I (Chapters 1 and 2), "Institutions," presents a rather detailed discussion of the evolution and the nature of China's FDI regulatory framework. Part II (Chapters 3 and 4), "Investments," discusses the various modes and patterns of FDI in China during the reform years. Part III (Chapters 5 and 6), "Evidence," sets as its central task to isolate and demonstrate a systematic link between institutional changes in China's FDI regulatory framework and the changing patterns of FDI. While the study as a whole is heavily based on statistical data-oriented analyses, the first and second parts are, on balance, more descriptive than analytical, and more qualitative than quantitative. The third part, chapter 6 in particular, by contrast, is rather analytical and at times tends to be technical. Aided by multiple regression techniques, chapter 6 aims to pin down the effects of the evolutionary dynamics of China's FDI regulatory framework on investment behavior.

Specifically, Chapter 1 examines in detail the main building blocks of China's FDI regulatory framework as it has evolved over the reform years. Presented here is a dynamic story of gradual, yet steady, improvement and liberalization of China's FDI-related laws, rules, regulations, and policies designed to attract and govern foreign participation in the country's economy. Chapter 2 focuses on the international dimension of China's current FDI regulatory framework and assesses several key aspects of the framework in international perspective. In the scheme of the study, these two chapters provide the critical background information upon which our analysis of the institutional effects on FDI will be grounded in subsequent chapters.

Chapter 3 dissects FDI in China into different modes, laying out a micro foundation for our analysis of their different characteristics with different implications for investment risks. To the extent that the evolution of China's FDI regulatory framework has a different trajectory for the different modes of FDI, this chapter constitutes our first step toward establishing a systematic relationship between institutions and investments. Chapter 4 attempts to present a comprehensive picture, both static and moving, of the variant patterns of FDI in China. After a brief overview of FDI in China on a stock basis, our investigation of the patterns of FDI moves in a flow fashion. In particular, our examination of the variant patterns of FDI proceeds in tandem with the evolutionary dynamics of China's FDI regulatory framework over the reform years. In so doing, the idea is to establish at least a *prima facie* case demonstrating that institutional changes have a systematic effect on the patterns of FDI.

Our efforts to go beyond a *prima facie* case to establish a causal link between institutions and investments begin in the Part III. In Chapter 5 we focus on China's disparate tax regimes for foreign-invested enterprises and domestic counterparts, and explain how that particular institutional arrangement had a significant impact on FDI via the demand side of investment. In the process, we will present evidence showing that the disparate treatment between FIEs and domestic firms, when coupled with the effects of fiscal decentralization in China, gave rise to what I call "abnormally high demand" for FDI. This is a unique institutional aspect of China's transitional economy, which in part explains the seemingly extraordinary surges of FDI in China during the first part of the 1990s.

To increase the analytical rigor of the study, Chapter 6 takes a step further to demonstrate the institutional effects on investment behavior by controlling for cultural and economic factors, such as market size, labor costs, labor skills, and infrastructure. In particular, we will develop a formal model, covering both the temporal (1979-96) and spatial (29 provinces) dimensions of FDI in China. Multiple regression analyses are then carried out to systematically assess the institutional effects on investment behavior under *ceteris paribus* conditions.

The empirical findings of this chapter support the central contention of the book. That is, in spite of all its imperfections, the gradual yet steady improvement of China's FDI regulatory framework over the reform years has had a *systematic* and *positive* effect on investment behavior. Seen in the broad context of China's reform endeavors, our empirical findings indicate that China has gone a long way along a continuum from a command system – where bureaucratic interference is the order of the day – to a market system that is based on the rule of law and is open to competition. China's recent efforts for accession into the WTO are but a further move along that continuum. The international community should welcome it.

Targeted Readership

This study is multidisciplinary and interdisciplinary, drawing upon concepts of business, culture, economics, law, and political science. As such, it aims to reach a number of audiences. First of all, for academic readers with an interest in neo-institutional literature in general or the relationship between law and economic development in particular, this book represents a theory-informed empirical study on that subject through the prism of FDI in China. It is an attempt to apply rigorous social science research methods to the study of China, a country immensely rich in its own culture. The findings of this book indicate that in the long run China is not immune from the institutional imperative for economic development. That is, sustained economic growth must be accompanied by painstaking efforts to systematically build up a transparent and rule-based market system.

China experts, corporate executives, and other business professionals will find the book useful as well. For one thing, the study contains a wealth of information about FDI, about FDI-related laws, regulations, and policies, and about the politics of central-local fiscal relations and their implication for foreign investment in China. For another, even though they may possess intimate knowledge about business, culture, and politics in China, such professionals sometimes lose track of the broader trends of the Chinese market and the relationship between culture, law, politics, and investment behavior that are systematically analyzed in this book.

Finally, policy makers, both in China and in the West, will find here not an anecdotal but a systematic appraisal of how well (or how poorly) China's efforts to build an attractive investment environment for foreign investment, and by extension, a rule-based, market-oriented economy, have fared over the reform years. By reading the book, I hope they will reflect upon how far China has come, and how long it still has to go. The sea of changes that has taken place in China and the effective mechanisms that have sustained healthy changes must be recognized to encourage further developments in the right direction with the right speed. While the overall assessment by this study of what China has achieved so far is a positive one, the book concludes with a caveat, indicating that daunting challenges still lie ahead for China.

A Note on Sources

For data, this study relies heavily on FDI and other economic statistics published by Chinese statistical authorities. In the case of FDI statistics, the principal sources are *Zhongguo duiwai jingji tongji nianjian* [China Foreign Economic Statistical Yearbook], and *Zhongguo duiwai jingji maoyi mianjian* [Almanac of China's Foreign Trade and Economic Relations]. For other economic statistics relating to revenue, market size, infrastructure, labor costs and labor skills, *Zhongguo tongji nianjian* [China Statistical Yearbook] and *Gaige Kaifang shiqinian de Zhongguo diqu jingji* [China Regional Economy: A Profile of 17 Years of Reform and Opening Up] are frequently consulted. These statistical books,[29] taken as a whole, constitute a rather comprehensive database, which in turn can be broken down not only on a yearly basis, but also into different provinces for systematic analysis.

Beyond these official statistical books, data are also gleaned from a wide array of materials, including journals, newspapers, and official documents, as well as research papers and publications by Chinese and Western scholars, and policy and business analysts. In addition, initial fieldwork for this study was carried out in the Summer and Fall of 1996 in Beijing, Tianjin, Nanjing, Shanghai, Guangzhou, Xiamen, and Hong Kong. I interviewed, whenever chances arose, both FIE managers and Chinese officials in charge of foreign investment. Additional trips were made in June and July in 1988 and in February and the Fall of 1999. Although the field interviews did not result in systematic data that are essential for the kind of quantitative analyses carried out in this book, they nonetheless gave me a better appreciation about some of the important motivations behind FDI, and about business practices in China, on the part of both foreign investors and Chinese partners and involved officials.

Finally, that I rely heavily on Chinese official data to carry out statistical analysis requires some comments to address an obvious concern. Are conclusions based on Chinese official statistics reliable? My answer has the following components. First, to the extent that the concern derives from a suspicion that official data may be inflated to

---

29. A list of statistical books used in the study is provided in the reference section.

highlight achievements and gloss over incompetence in an authoritarian state, my statistical analysis is little affected. The reason is that the statistical compilers, even if they wanted to manipulate the data, were not aware of the research questions that drive the current study. Second, to the extent that concern is about data inaccuracies or inconsistencies due to technical reasons such as non-standardized reporting procedures, I have taken precautions by using statistics that follow the same definitions or norms. In particular, for the regression analyses I employ statistical series that is systematic over space and time.

Furthermore, throughout the study I am consistently on the alert not to take the face value of official statistics for granted. Indeed, that I take steps to re-calibrate China's definition of FDI (and hence the FDI figures) according to international conventions in Chapter 3; and to examine the phenomenon of "round-tripping" FDI (Chinese capital moving offshore first and then re-entering as FDI) in Chapter 5 are examples of such circumspection.

Part I:

Institutions

CHAPTER 1

Evolution of China's FDI Regulatory Framework

Foreign direct investment in the People's Republic of China (PRC) is a phenomenon that has existed only in the reform era. In the pre-reform era, except for a very brief period in the 1950s,[1] the country's developmental strategy was an extreme version of autarky. Consequently when China decided to start economic reforms and the open door in the late 1970s, it had little experience about how to encourage and regulate foreign investment. There was no law to serve as a viable institutional framework to govern the participation of foreign capital in the country's economy. Viewed in this historical context, what China has achieved during the reform years in developing an institutional framework to attract and regulate foreign investment has been extraordinary.

From 1979 through 1998, China attracted from more than 150 countries/regions around the world more than US$268.64 billion in realized FDI. At the same time, since the promulgation of China's first foreign investment law in 1979, the National People's Congress (NPC) has drafted and promulgated about 270 laws designed to govern various aspects of economic life in China. This is in addition to some 700 administrative rules and regulations enacted by the State Council (Sun Shangqing and Ren Xingzhou 1997: 226-27). Some of these laws and regulations address themselves specifically to the issues of FDI.[2] In

---

1. To be sure, foreign firms operated in China since the Opium War of 1838-40. But they were all driven out after the PRC was established in 1949. Subsequently, about the only meaningful foreign economic cooperation that China had was with the former Soviet Union in the 1950s. But the relations were cut off in the early 1960s, as political relations between the two countries broke down. See Sladkovskii (1966).

2. According to the 1982 Constitution of the PRC, the notion of Chinese law includes the administrative rules and regulations published by the State

this chapter we present an overview of China's FDI regulatory framework as it has evolved over the reform years, with a focus on the legislative framework designed to encourage and regulate FDI in China.

Generally speaking, the evolution of China's FDI regulatory framework can be outlined in three phases of development. The first phase is roughly from 1979 to 1984. During this period China's efforts to promote FDI were highlighted by the promulgation in 1979 of its first joint venture law and the establishment in 1980 of four Special Economic Zones, where a plethora of preferential treatments were accorded to foreign investors.

In the second phase (1984-90), China's efforts to promote FDI intensified. There was a dramatic expansion of geographical areas open to FDI, with investment inducements starting in 1984. At the same time, China continued to improve its FDI regulatory framework. Among other highlights, it took innovative measures to remedy its rigid foreign exchange regime. It promulgated the Provisions for the Encouragement of Foreign Investment and the Law on Wholly Foreign-owned Enterprises in 1986. It also promulgated the Law on Sino-Foreign Cooperative Joint Ventures in 1988.

The opening of Shanghai Pudong New Area in 1990 marked the beginning of the third phase. China started this period by lifting its ban on foreigners from holding the position of the chairman of joint ventures, and discarding its discriminatory taxation of 100% foreign-owned subsidiaries. Following Deng Xiaoping's southern tour in 1992, a number of sectors previously off-limits to FDI were opened up. More recently, further steps have been taken to make China's FDI regulatory framework more transparent. Of late, China's efforts to enter the World Trade Organization mean that more markets will be open to foreign investors. In the sections that follow, we examine the development of China's FDI regulatory framework during the three phases outlined here in greater detail.

Council. The rules and regulations, which the State Council and subordinate ministries and commissions have been creating since 1979, constitute the bulk of the economic laws of the PRC. They represent the major part of the drafting work for the legal structure that directs and promotes the economic activities of the country.

First Period: Laying the Groundwork (1979-84)

First Foreign Investment Law

The traumatic experiences of the Great Leap Forward (1958-60) and the Cultural Revolution (1966-76) no doubt prompted Chinese leaders to blaze new paths of development. Shortly after the 3rd Plenum of the 11th Party Congress in 1978 in which reform and the open-door policy were endorsed by the post-Mao leadership,[3] China conscientiously stepped up efforts at codification of commercial laws designed to attract and regulate foreign participation in the Chinese economy (Rong Yiren 1979). The promulgation in 1979 of the Law of the PRC concerning Sino-foreign Joint Ventures, commonly known as the Equity Joint Venture Law (EJV Law), represented the beginning of such efforts.

Although the EJV Law contained a mere 15 brief articles, its significance was enormous. It signaled a reversal of China's pre-reform policy of autarky. Perhaps more importantly, as we shall see later, it is on the basis of this law that a large body of both legal and administrative rules that combine to form China's current FDI regulatory framework has gradually evolved.

Several points about the EJV Law merit attention. First of all, for a country that had until recently condemned capitalism and forbade private ownership,[4] perhaps most significant was Article 2 of the law.

---

3. The dramatic about-face can be explained in part by the trauma China suffered in the Great Leap Forward (1958-60) and again in the Cultural Revolution (1966-76), and the realization that China was outpaced by its neighbors, especially the "four little dragons," i.e., South Korea, Hong Kong, Taiwan, and Singapore. For damage done to China by the Great Leap Forward and the Cultural Revolution, see MacFarquhar (1997).

4. When the PRC was established, some 10,000 private companies existed in China. By 1956 China had transformed virtually all private businesses into joint state-private enterprises. Some individual firms were restored in the wake of the Great Leap Forward, only to be suppressed again during the Cultural Revolution. The 1975 Constitution of the PRC recognized socialist ownership only. In the reform era, however, private businesses, after a rather tentative start in early years, have developed at an impressive rate. For further discussion of the vicissitudes of private business in China, see Conner (1991). The recent 1999 constitutional amendment recognizes that the private sector is an "important component" of the country's economy.

It provided that China "permits foreign companies, enterprises, other economic entities, or individuals to incorporate themselves in the territory of China into joint ventures with Chinese companies, enterprises or other economic entities," and "the state shall not nationalize or expropriate foreign investment interest." This provision was later elevated to constitutional status when the National People's Congress amended the Chinese Constitution in 1982, reaffirming China's welcome stance toward foreign investment (Article 18).[5]

Another important point of the EJV Law was its adoption of the limited liability principle, a concept fundamental in Western corporate law, but alien to China's central planners. As China legal scholars have pointed out (Art and Gu 1995: 293), the notion that people running a business should be entitled to profits if it prospers, but should be immune from liability if it goes bankrupt, is neither intuitively appealing nor obvious. But centuries ago Western societies upheld the conviction that the benefits to society from encouraging commerce in this way would eventually outweigh the detriment to contractual claimants or even tort victims. In the cultural milieu of China, however, although attempts were made along similar lines as early as the late Qing dynasty (Xiao 1999: chapter 2), the acceptance of this principle, especially in light of the leftist politics of the Cultural Revolution, could not be taken for granted.

Finally, in contrast to some developing nations that set tight controls over ownership in fear of foreign domination of domestic industries,[6] the EJV Law was rather liberal in this aspect. While it had a floor of at least 25% of foreign equity contributions to a joint venture (JV), it set no ceilings on foreign ownership. A majority foreign ownership, up to 99%, was thus possible, without conversion conditions attached. In contrast, some countries impose such conditions whereby foreign investors are required to sell equity shares to the host country according to a specified downward ratio of equity on a pre-fixed time schedule.

---

5. For English translations of the 1982 Constitution and many other relevant Chinese laws discussed in this study, consult <www.qis.net/chinalaw/explan1.htm>.

6. Until very recently India, for instance, generally limited foreign investment to less than 50% equity ownership. See Chapter 2 for further discussion.

The above features reflected the relatively liberal nature of China's first foreign investment law, but there were restrictive and discriminatory elements. In particular, while the organizational form of a JV would follow Western business practices, i.e., the board of directors, the EJV Law forbade foreigners from holding the position of chairman of a JV, regardless of foreign equity shares. This rather discriminatory provision was to remain in effect for more than 10 years until 1990 when the EJV Law was finally amended, as China moved further to liberalize its FDI regulatory framework in the 1990s.

Whereas the EJV Law in many ways was a path-breaking piece of legislation, it is also important to point out that, strictly speaking, it was more a statement of principles than a well-defined legal code. The law was sketchy both in form and substance. Much of its wording was vague, subject to divergent interpretations. Terms on important operational issues, such as market access, taxation, foreign exchange, land use, labor management, and input sources, were either not mentioned or defined in vague terms, creating much uncertainty for foreign investors (Cohen 1982).

In taxation, although the law promised favorable treatment, it did not specify as to how and how much such treatment would be offered. In land use, while the law stipulated that land could be used as part of a JV investment when fees were paid to the state, it contained no clear answers as to in what manner and how much such fees were to be assessed. Further, while the law provided that the technology and equipment contributed by foreign investors "shall be advanced and appropriate to China's needs" (Article 5), it was silent as to what constituted "advanced" or "appropriate." As can be imagined, these and other similar points of ambiguity made the implementation of the law capricious and difficult. Presumably, they drove up both *ex ante* and *ex post* information and transaction costs, especially for those who knew little about China.

The weakness of the EJV Law is not surprising if we consider the paucity of experience on the part of Chinese leaders regarding foreign investment at the time. Chinese officials recalled that they coped by cramming through foreign investment laws of some 30 countries (Liu Xiangdong 1993: 846). Regarding operational issues, they honestly did not know, for instance, how to assess land prices, for there was no land market. Neither were they clear about what constituted advanced technology and how it could be used in a cost-effective way. Seen in this light, as Samuel Ho (1984:75) suggested, the generality and even ambiguity of the EJV Law were desirable, if only because it gave JV partners more leeway to negotiate contracts that best fitted their specific circumstances.

In retrospect, it seems clear that the EJV Law served as an enabling framework within which more specific laws and auxiliary rules were constructed, as problems were identified, experience learned and consensus gained. Indeed, such is the general *modus operandi* that has shaped what clearly has been a gradual yet steady process of "legalization" in the reform era. In other words, the legal framework governing FDI in China was not crafted overnight. Instead it may be best understood as the cumulative result of an incremental replacement of the traditional emphasis on policy and propriety with codified law and legal institutions in the reform years.[7] Chinese leaders harbored no illusions that a workable legal institution could be built from scratch in no time.

Deng Xiaoping was reported to have commented in 1978 that in law making, it was desirable to put some laws in place first, even if they were sketchy, rather than "awaiting a complete set of equipment."[8] Speaking of confusions caused by the ambiguity of the EJV Law, Xu Dixin, then Vice President of the Chinese Academy of Social Sciences, opined: "We don't have clear-cut provisions yet. Depending on circumstances there are bound to be contradictions or confusions. But we will compare different approaches, draw lessons and then formulate a unified method."[9] True to the logic of these remarks, as we shall see later, in subsequent years China continued its legislative efforts. Among the most important laws and regulations published in this period was a Detailed Implementation Act of the EJV Law issued in 1983 by the State Council.

The EJV Implementation Act was clearly an effort by China to clarify some of the critical operational issues that had been

---

7. In traditional China the Confucian concept of "*li*," or standards of social conduct, was considered far superior to narrow legalistic rules, known as "*fa*." Codified law was seen as unnecessary and abhorrent to Confucian gentlemen. During the reform era, however, this view has gradually given way to the imperatives of economic development, and a frenzy of codification has resulted. See Potter (1993).

8. *People's Daily*, Overseas Edition, 16 April 1993, p. 1.

9. *Far Eastern Economic Review*, 30 May 1980, p. 30.

insufficiently specified previously. Containing a total of 118 articles, it was both an augmentation to and a summary of the key elements of several pieces of legislation affecting FDI issued during this period. These include the PRC Income Tax Law concerning Joint Ventures, the Registration and Management of Joint Ventures, and the Regulations on Labor Management in Joint Ventures. Under the EJV Implementing Act, several important areas affecting JV operations, such as market access, management autonomy, and taxation, were given better, albeit sometimes still ambiguous, guidelines.

Regarding market access, according to the EJV Law (Article 9), a JV was "*encouraged* [emphasis added] to market its products outside of China." Although the law did not explicitly forbid a JV from selling domestically, Pearson (1991:126) observed that the ambiguous wording "encourage" made it difficult for a JV to access domestic markets. Now under the EJV Implementation Act, a JV was allowed to sell domestically as long as its products "are urgently needed by China or are import substitutes." In practice this means that while market access was still restricted, foreign investors now found it easier to receive the permission to sell their products in China (Zheng Yan'er 1985).

In management autonomy, a JV clearly enjoyed an edge over an indigenous firm. This reflected the reality that when China first started to build a legal framework for foreign investment, it proceeded with a bifurcated legal regime between foreign-invested enterprises and domestic enterprises, even though the gap has increasingly narrowed over time. At the time, however, whereas domestic firms were very much in the straight-jacket of a command economy (Li Tieying 1995), JVs were allowed at least in theory to make and implement their own production plans, set their own wage rates, and hire and fire employees. This was especially true in the Special Economic Zones where market forces, as a matter of policy experiments, were given a better chance to demonstrate their effects.

Finally, in taxation, the enterprise income tax for JVs was set at 30%, or 33% when a 3% local tax was included. This was about 20% lower than that for domestic firms.[10] There was additional tax relief if

10. Before the reform the state-owned enterprises (SOEs) in China remitted all profits to the state. Beginning in the early 1980s, the system "*li gai shui*," or tax in lieu of profit, was introduced. Under the new scheme, SOEs were divided into two main categories for tax purposes. Large- and medium-

certain conditions were met. A JV with an operational life of 10 years or more could be exempted from tax in the first 2 profit-making years, and allowed a 50% tax reduction for another 3 years. A JV in low profit sectors such as agriculture and forestry, or in economically backward areas, was eligible for a 15-30% tax reduction for 10 additional years. Moreover, if a JV were to reinvest its profits in China for at least 5 years, it could obtain a tax refund of 40% of the enterprise income tax paid on the amount reinvested.[11] The EJV Implementation Act (Article 79) also relaxed rules on income repatriation by foreign expatriates. Instead of the previous 50% limit, they could remit all of their income.

Even greater investment inducements and privileges were provided to foreign investors operating in the much-heralded Special Economic Zones in the southern coastal areas of China during the initial period.

Special Economic Zones

Another major development during the early period was the decision by Beijing to allow Guangdong and Fujian to pursue reform measures "one step ahead" of the rest of China (Vogel 1989). Specifically, in 1980 China established four Special Economic Zones. The four SEZs were Shantou, Shenzhen, and Zhuhai in Guangdong, and Xiamen in Fujian. Modeled after similar zones found elsewhere in the world and especially in Asia,[12] the establishment of the SEZs was motivated by a broad range of policy objectives.

First of all, SEZs were established to attract not only foreign capital, but also advanced foreign technology, both hardware and software. Deng Xiaoping (1983:33) made the point clear in 1980 in an interview with foreign reporters. "Technology, science and even

---

sized enterprises paid a flat tax of 55% on their profits. Small enterprises paid an eight-grade progressive tax (7-55%). For further discussions of taxation of SOEs, see Chapter 5 in this study.

11. These are based on Articles 2-6 of the Income Tax Law concerning Joint Ventures with Chinese and Foreign Investment.

12. To draw on international experience, in the early years of reform China reportedly sent research terms abroad to investigate special zones throughout the world (Chi 1981) and President Jiang Zemin, then deputy chairman of China's State Import and Export Management Commission, was on one such team (Qi Yuan 1998:12).

advanced production management, which is also a kind of science" he said, "will be useful in any society or country. We intend to acquire advanced technology, science and management skills to serve our socialist production."

Second, like other countries that set up "free trade zones" and "export processing zones" to promote export-led growth, Chinese leaders also viewed SEZs as an effective way to accelerate exports, create local employment, and generate foreign exchange.[13] A third objective was perhaps unique to China. Because SEZs were easily contained geographically, they were intended as "policy laboratories," where reformers could test policy initiatives which, if successful, could then be adopted elsewhere in China. A final aim had to do with China's goal of reunification with Hong Kong, Macao, and eventually Taiwan (Grub and Lin 1991:27).

What made SEZs special was not that FDI was not permitted elsewhere in China, for it was; but that foreign investment and other economic activity in the zones were allowed to operate under a different institutional framework from the rest of China. For instance, early in the reform era, SEZs were authorized to prepare their own investment regulations.[14] As of 1983, the Guangdong provincial government had promulgated a slew of regulations. These included the Guangdong Interim Provisions for Enterprise Registration in SEZs, the Guangdong Interim Provisions for Labor and Wage Regulations in Shenzhen SEZ, and the Guangdong Interim Provisions on Land Regulations in Shenzhen SEZ.[15]

---

13. But unlike their counterparts in other developing countries that have often limited foreign investment to small-scale assembly and processing operations, China's SEZs have also encouraged investment in major infrastructure projects such as electric power and transportation. See Stepanek (1982).

14. The central government sometimes explicitly delegates legislative power to localities to emphasize special local conditions. An example is the NPC Standing Committee's 1981 "Resolution on the Authorization of the Guangdong and Fujian Provincial People's Congresses and their Standing Committees to Enact Specific Economic Regulations for their Special Economic Zones." The only condition is that these regulations do not contradict central laws and must be reported to the Standing Committee of the NPC and the State Council.

15. Fujian drafted a similar set of regulations concerning the Xiamen SEZ. These measures include the Regulations of Xiamen Special Economic Zone on

Under the special regulatory framework of the SEZs, the local authorities in the SEZs enjoyed a considerable degree of autonomy. They had independent power to draw up development plans, organize their implementation, examine and approve investment projects, issue licenses and land-use permits, and coordinate the work of banking, taxation, customs, and frontier inspection. They were also authorized to offer a number of investment inducements not available elsewhere in China.

First of all, the enterprise income tax for all types of foreign-invested enterprises in a SEZ was set at a low of 15%, irrespective of the nature of the enterprise, manufacturing or not. This compared favorably to the 24-30% tax rate for FIEs elsewhere in the country. Second, FIEs in a SEZ engaging in services and with foreign investment exceeding US$5 million and an operating life of ten years or more was exempt from the enterprise income tax in the first profit-making year and was permitted a 50% reduction in the following two years. Moreover, whereas profit repatriation from elsewhere in China was subject to a 10% remittance tax, the SEZs imposed no such taxes. Finally, the 3% local tax was routinely waived by SEZ authorities.[16]

In spite of these investment inducements, China's FDI regulatory framework, to be sure, remained rather restrictive at the time. For one thing, locational choice was very limited, albeit not by statutory design. While the SEZs began to seek FDI by offering special policies in the form of streamlined administration and fiscal concessions, elsewhere in China the situation was not nearly as encouraging. Even though FDI was legally allowed beyond the SEZs, the investment environment as a whole was not favorable and, worse still, it was clouded in uncertainty,

---

the Registration of Enterprise, the Regulations of Xiamen Special Economc Zone on Land Use, the Regulations of Xiamen Special Economic Zone on Labor Management, and the Regulations of Xiamen Special Economic Zone on the Import of Technology. But as of 1984 they had not come into effect. In the meantime, the Xiamen SEZ followed the pattern of the regulatory framework of the Guangdong SEZs.

16. The problem for the local authorities is to determine whether a JV qualifies for preferential tax treatment. Generally speaking, for a JV to be eligible for preferential treatment, it must be registered and have a place of production and management in a SEZ. A JV which is registered in a SEZ but has real business elsewhere, is taxed under the normal laws applicable beyond the SEZs. See Ministry of Finance Notice (1983), Cai Shui Wai Zi No. 271, 9 September 1983.

especially after Chen Yun expressed doubts about the viability of the SEZs.[17] As a result, the project screening process remained complex, lengthy, and strictly controlled by Beijing.[18]

As a general rule, projects valued at over US$3 million had to be approved directly by the Ministry of Foreign Economic Relations and Trade (MOFERT),[19] although exceptions to this general rule existed. For example, the cities of Beijing and Guangzhou were authorized to approve projects valued at up to US$10 million. The SEZs, for their part, were given independent approval authority for light industrial projects up to RMB 30 million and heavy industrial projects up to RMB 50 million.[20]

The restrictive nature of China's FDI regulatory framework at the time went beyond what the law stipulated. For instance, although the EJV Law set no upper ceilings on foreign ownership, there are indications that in practice the foreign ownership of many JVs was intentionally kept to minority positions. According to one study on FDI at the time (Chu Baotai 1987), of the 14 cases included in the study, foreign ownership in 9 held a minority position. In the rest, 4 had a

---

17. Chen Yun (1986:276-77) in the early 1980s said: "Some areas in parts of... Guangdong and Fujian are experimentally implementing special economic zones (the whole province of Guangdong is not a special zone, nor is the whole province of Fujian). This is good for now, but should not be increased. Consignment processing and joint ventures are being undertaken in numerous localities; special zones are not permitted to go beyond these forms."

18. Investors first had to prepare a preliminary proposal based on their initial contacts. This proposal had to be submitted to the local government or the ministries in charge, and through them to the central government for approval. If approved, the participants could then start negotiations. A new proposal based on the negotiated agreement, together with a feasibility study, had again to be submitted to the local government, the ministries, and the central government for further approval. If passed, the participants could then start the second round of negotiations on the final contract, which then was directly submitted to the central government for final approval. Only then, did the project contract become valid. At the time this whole process usually took at least 3 months. For further details, see Lee and Ness (1986).

19. It was later renamed the Ministry of Foreign Trade and Economic Cooperation, or MOFTEC.

20. The exchange rate between the Chinese RMB and the US dollar at the time was about 1.5/1.

50:50 equity ownership ratio; there was only one case in which the foreign investors held a majority position of 60%.

Consistent with the restrictive approach to foreign ownership, although some foreign investors had expressed interest in setting up wholly foreign-owned enterprises (WFOEs),[21] their applications were routinely rejected. Indeed, in the initial years of reform and the open door, even though China demonstrated some confidence in dealing with JVs, it was much more cautious about WFOEs. As a matter of fact, prior to 1986 China did not have a national law governing WFOEs; 100% foreign-owned subsidiaries, an increasingly popular mode of FDI in China today, were permitted only on an experimental basis within the geographic confines of the SEZs.

Reflecting the incipient nature of China's FDI regulatory framework, FDI inflow was insignificant during the initial period; few WFOEs existed beyond the geographical confines of the SEZs.[22] It was only after China's FDI regulatory framework evolved into its second phase – when China opened 14 additional coastal cities in 1984 and especially after the promulgation of the WFOE Law in 1986 – that FDI started to flow to China in volumes of considerable magnitudes.

Second Period: Great Expansion (1984-90)

Spatial Expansion of FDI Policies

A salient feature of the development of China's FDI regulatory framework during the second period was the dramatic expansion, beginning in 1984, of geographical areas open to foreign investment. This included 14 coastal cities, 3 delta regions, and the whole island of Hainan. These areas in aggregate have a size of 320,000 square

---

21. One example is 3M; as early as 1981 3M tried to get permission to operate a wholly-owned subsidiary outside of the SEZs. But it did not succeed until 1984. W. R. Grace Company is another example. It started 100% ownership subsidiary negotiations in 1980, but did not get a license to operate in Shanghai until 1986. For details, see Stein (1987).

22. By 1982, FDI in the form of WFOEs in Shenzhen accounted for only 15% of total realized FDI in the zone. Many of these WFOEs were small-scale operations owned by overseas Chinese, although a few big multinational corporations, such as Sanyo Electric Co., began to establish a foothold in China. See Oborne (1986: 142).

kilometers, and a population of 160 million. Encompassing a total of 288 cities and counties, they constitute a massive belt of land mass zigzagging along China's coast, linking the Korean peninsula in the north to the South China Sea in the south.[23]

The 14 coastal open cities are, from north to south, Dalian, Qinhuangdao, Tianjin, Yantai, Qingdao, Lianyuangang, Nantong, Shanghai, Ningbo, Wenzhou, Fuzhou, Guangzhou, Zhanjiang, and Beihai. The decision to open 14 coastal cities was announced by Zhao Ziyang in May 1984, following Deng Xiaoping's inspection tour of the SEZs the same year. During his tour Deng Xiaoping endorsed SEZs by saying: "The development and experience of Shenzhen has confirmed the correctness of our policy and of establishing special economic zones."[24] As open cities, the 14 coastal cities were authorized to offer foreign investors some of the same preferential treatment hitherto available only in the SEZs.[25]

Politically, the opening of the 14 coastal cities demonstrated China's commitment to the open door. That commitment was perhaps best symbolized at the time by the glitzy chrome-and-glass Great Wall Hotel, a China-US joint venture in Beijing which opened for business in the summer of 1984. Economically, the 14 coastal cities meant a far wider latitude of location choice for foreign investors and better access to China's domestic markets. Shanghai and Tianjin, for instance, were the largest and the third largest cities in China.[26] The industrial capacity of the coastal areas as a share of the country's total is illustrated in Table I-1.

When the 14 coastal cities were opened for foreign investment, Hainan island, situated in the southernmost part of China, was also granted a high degree of economic decision-making power.[27] Although the island was still an administrative part of Guangdong province, in a speech delivered in June 1987, Deng Xiaoping unveiled a plan to

23. *People's Daily*, Overseas Edition, 21 June 1988, p. 1.

24. Cited in Zheng Jianhui (1984).

25. These incentives are contained in the "Provisional Regulations on the Reduction and Exemption of Enterprise Income Tax and Consolidated Industrial and Commercial Tax in Special Economic Zones and 14 Coastal Cities," promulgated in November 1984.

26. In 1990 the populations of Shanghai, Beijing, and Tianjin, the first three largest cities in China were 13.3; 10.9; and 8.8 million respectively.

27. *China Daily*, 26 May 1984.

elevate Hainan to a separate province and yet another SEZ in China.[28] In 1988 the island was officially granted provincial status and became the 5th and largest SEZ in China (Table I-2).[29]

Table I-1: Industrial Output of Coastal Areas and Shares of National Total (RMB billion)

	1980			1985			1990		
Jiangsu	46.8	(9.1%)	[2]	103.7	(10.7%)	[1]	276.4	(11.6%)	[1]
Shandong	34.0	(6.6%)	[4]	68.3	(7%)	[4]	220.2	(9.2%)	[2]
Guangdong	22.3	(4.3%)	[9]	53.3	(5.5%)	[6]	190.2	(8%)	[3]
Shanghai	59.9	(11.6%)	[1]	86.3	(8.9%)	[2]	163.3	(6.8%)	[4]
Liaoning	45.3	(8.8%)	[3]	77.5	(8%)	[3]	160.7	(6.7%)	[5]
Zhejiang	20.2	(3.9%)	[12]	55.1	(5.7%)	[5]	143.3	(6%)	[6]
Subtotal	228.4	(44.3%)		414.2	(42.6%)		1154.1	(48.2%)	
National Total	515.4	(100%)		971.7	(100%)		2392.4	(100%)	

Note: Percentage of national total is in parentheses. National rankings are in brackets. Value of industrial output is in historical prices.
Source: *Quanguo gesheng, zishiqu, zhixiashi lishi tongji ziliao huibian, 1949-1989* [Compendium of Historical Statistical Materials for All Provinces, Autonomous Regions, and Central Municipalities] 1990 and *Zhongguo tongji nianjian* [Statistical Yearbook of China] various years.

Table I-2: China's Five Special Economic Zones

Name	Sizes (kilometers^2)	Population	Establishment Dates
Shenzhen	327.50	1,020,000	August 1980
Zhuhai	15.60	190,000	August 1980
Shantou	52.60	60,000	August 1980
Xiamen	131.00	370,000	October 1980
Hainan	34,000.00	6,540,000	April 1988
Total	34,526.70	8,180,000	N/A

Source: *Beijing Review*, 8-14 April 1991, p. 21.

Besides the 14 coastal cities and Hainan island, in 1985 China also designated three "delta regions" for foreign investment.[30] Specifically, they are the Yangtze River Delta, Golden Triangle Delta and Pearl River Delta. The Yangtze River Delta has an area of 27,000 square kilometers, including parts of Jiangsu and Zhejiang and part of Shanghai. The Golden Triangle Delta is in Fujian. It encompasses the

28. *Beijing Review*, 24 August 1987, p. 13.

29. The decision was made by the NPC on April 3, 1988, according to *People's Daily*, 14 April 1988.

30. *China Daily*, 4 February 1985.

cities of Quanzhou, Xiamen and Zhangzhou, and is linked to the Xiamen SEZ. The Pearl River Delta lies in Guangdong. It links Shenzhen and Zhuhai SEZs with Guangzhou, creating one large open economic development zone, with a total area of 25,000 square kilometers.[31]

Geographical expansion did not stop there. It continued in 1988 to include Liaodong and Shandong peninsulas as "coastal economic open areas." Thus, by the end of 1989, the so-called "special investment areas" in China, a generic term including the SEZs, open cities, and delta regions and peninsulas, embraced close to 300 cities and counties along China's coast. They amounted to a total area of 420,000 square kilometers and a population of 280 million (Li Lanqing 1995:272). Put in international perspective, the combined size of these areas is roughly equivalent to 3 times the size of Germany; their population in aggregate is larger than that of the United States (263 million).

Table I-3: Project Approval Limits by Administrative Areas

Project approval limit	Level of approval authority
Over and including US$100 million	State Council
Over 30 but less than US$100 million	State Planning Commission and Ministry of Foreign Trade and Economic Cooperation
Up to and including US$30 million	• Provinces, Autonomous Regions, and Centrally Controlled Municipalities (Beijing, Tianjin, Shanghai and Chongqing) • Special Economic Zones • Open Coastal Cities • Cities with Independent Planning Authority • Open River and Border Cities* • Open Interior Provincial Cities*
Below and including US$10 million	Local governments below the above administrative levels

Source: Interview

* Opened after 1992.

31. Based on *China Investment Guide 1986.*

Map of China: Special Investment Areas

One effect of the dramatic expansion of the geographical areas open to foreign investment was that it made the SEZs less "special." For one thing, decentralization of project screening power now went beyond SEZs to include all the open cities. The open cities were all given independent powers to approve FDI projects up to a certain level. Shanghai, Tianjin, and Beijing, for instance, were now authorized to approve projects valued up to US$30 million. Although the approval power for other open cities was increased only to US$10 million at the time, eventually they were all raised to US$30 million, as China's FDI regulatory framework was further liberalized in the early 1990s (see Table I-3).

The decentralization of project screening power contributed to an increased enthusiasm for FDI at the local levels, and made it possible to simplify and speed up the approval process for FDI projects. While the overall picture of application efficiency was not totally clear up and down China, the situation was apparently improving in the coastal areas. In Shanghai, for instance, the time of the approval process was reportedly reduced from at least 3 months in the early 1980s to at most 45 days in the latter part of the 1980s.[32]

With the decentralization of power, the open coastal cities began to provide preferential treatment to foreign investors. Like the SEZs, the open cities were now authorized to offer a variety of investment inducements, including concessionary tax rates. However, unlike the SEZs that set a flat enterprise income tax rate of 15% for all FIEs, different tax benefits were granted to FIEs in the open cities, depending on their nature and location. Generally speaking, the dividing line was between the so-called Economic and Technological Development Zones (ETDZs)[33] and the Old Urban Districts (OUDs).

---

32. It was reported that Shanghai and Tianjin, among others, set up an information service center for foreign investors and took a variety of measures to cut back on the red-tape in a bid to attract foreign investment (*China Daily*, 15 November 1987).

33. Currently there are 34 ETDZs respectively in Beihai, Beijing, Changchun, Chongqing, Dalian, Dayawan, Dongshandao, Fuqing, Rongqiao, Fuzhou, Guangzhou, Hangzhou, Harbin, Kunshan, Lianyungang, Nansha, Nantong, Ningbo, Qingdao, Qinhuangdao, Shanghai (Caohejing, Hongqiao, Minhang), Shenyang, Tianjin, Urumqi, Weihai, Wenzhou, Wuhan, Wuhu, Xiaoshan, Yantai, Yingkou, and Zhangjiang.

Within the ETDZs, the enterprise income tax rate was 15% for production FIEs. In addition, projects valued over US$30 million and scheduled for 10 years or more could enjoy tax exemption for the first 2 profit-making years and a 50% tax reduction for another 3 years. They could also enjoy an exemption from the 3% local tax, as well as from customs tariffs on capital goods, raw materials, intermediate inputs, and office supplies imported for their own use. Finally, the 10% remittance tax was also exempted.

In the OUDs, on the other hand, the enterprise income tax for FIEs was 24%, a rate also applicable in the "delta regions." But for projects that were high-tech or knowledge-intensive, or valued over US$30 million and had a long payback period, the tax rate was 15%. Projects unable to meet the conditions for the 15% tax rate, they could be eligible for a 20% tax reduction if the investment was in priority sectors.

Finally, like in the ETDZs, FIEs in the OUDs could be exempted from the 3% local tax. But unlike in the ETDZs, FIEs in the OUDs were not allowed exemptions from the remittance tax (see Table I-4).

Table I-4: Tax Incentives for FIEs in Special Investment Areas

Locations	National Tax	Local Tax	Remittance Tax
SEZs	15% for production and non-production FIEs	Exemption possible upon application	Exemption
ETDZs	15% for production FIEs	Exemption possible upon application	Exemption
OUDs	• 24% generally • 15% for project over $30 million, or involves technology, or in energy, transport, or ports • 20% tax reduction for project involved in designated sectors*	Exemption possible upon application	No exemption or reduction

Source: The 1984 SEZs and Coastal Cities Tax Reduction and Exemption Regulations and Ministry of Finance Notice Cai Shui Wai Zi #202 (24 September 1985).

* They are machine building and electronics; metallurgical, chemical, and building materials; light industry, textiles and packaging; medical equipment and pharmaceuticals; agriculture, forestry, animal husbandry, aqua-culture, poultry raising, and related processing industries; and construction.

Foreign Exchange Remedial Measures

The energetic expansion of geographical areas open to foreign investment correlated with a steady growth of FDI in China. In the first nine months after the 14 coastal cities were opened, more than 400 contracts were signed, totaling US$880 million, which was about 1.5 times the cumulative FDI in the entire previous five years in these cities.[34] The growth trend continued by and large in the second part of the 1980s. In 1986, however, there was a sharp drop in FDI. Contracted FDI declined from US$5.935 billion in 1985 to US$3.332 billion in 1986; actual FDI also slowed down measurably. While analysts attributed the decline to a variety of causes,[35] probably the greatest culprit, as many have argued (McKenzie 1990:114-30; Lardy 1987:36; World Bank 1988:256), was the problem associated with China's rigid foreign exchange system, i.e., the non-convertibility of the Chinese local currency, the renminbi (RMB).

Foreign exchange (FX) is a critical issue for many FIEs, because they require a regular source of it to pay charges denominated in foreign currency, such as imported capital goods, raw materials, loans, and expatriate salaries. In China, FX transactions are controlled by the State Administration of Foreign Exchange (SAFE) and its local branches. Prior to 1986, FX issues were governed by the Provisional Regulations on Foreign Exchange Control[36] and the Foreign Exchange Implementation Act.[37] Under that system, FIEs enjoyed different and somewhat more favorable treatment than their Chinese counterparts.[38]

---

34. *Beijing Review*, 10 December 1984, p. 16.

35. Many reported that profits were less than anticipated and these were being further reduced by rapidly rising costs, especially of accommodations and office space. Others complained of low productivity and lack of motivation in the work force, and of excessive red-tape and bureaucratic interference. See Gelatt (1986: 28-31).

36. Promulgated by the State Council in December 1980.

37. Published by the State Administration of Foreign Exchange Control in August 1983.

38. FIEs were allowed to have their own FX accounts with the Bank of China. Domestic firms were not allowed to have such accounts, although this restriction has been relaxed in the 1990s. Further, whereas FIEs could retain foreign currencies for their own use, domestic firms were required to sell them to the state; whereas domestic firms were required to secure government

But in principle they were expected to balance their own FX accounts through exports. Little assistance, therefore, was available to them, if they expanded their business scope beyond what was originally envisioned and specified in contracts, or if they failed to reach export targets.[39]

The stringent FX regulatory regime bred problems just as quickly as the number of FIEs in China grew. The problem was especially acute for those FIEs that depended on imported sources of supplies or whose products aimed primarily at domestic markets.[40] To the dismay of foreign investors, even when they were able to sell their products successfully on domestic markets, they were not so successful in converting RMB into hard currency and thus unable to repatriate profits and to pay for importation of supplies. The problem became exacerbated when China incurred billions of dollars of trade deficits in 1985 and the country's foreign exchange reserves plummeted by 38% in the first 6 months of 1986.[41] Mired in a FX crisis, many FIEs were reportedly forced to halt operations temporarily or to withdraw altogether.[42]

---

approval before they could spend FX, FIEs were not subject to such restrictions.

39. The government was willing to help only insofar as FX needs were clearly specified in the contracts that the government had had a chance to examine. But even this was not guaranteed when China was short of FX, as it was in 1985.

40. For example, when VW started its operations in Shanghai in the early 1980s, to ensure quality it had to import all the kits needed to produce the "Santana." This was possible only when the government promised that money earned in RMB could be converted into hard currency to buy imported parts. See Bennett and Thurow (1984:37).

41. Over the reform years, while China has by and large enjoyed a favorable trade balance, it incurred a trade deficit of RMB 13 billion in 1985. This prompted the government to tighten import controls, bringing about a 70% reduction in the trade deficit and an increase of US$4.7 billion in foreign exchange reserves in 1987.

42. A much publicized case involved Beijing Jeep Corporation, a joint venture with American Motors Corporation (the latter later sold its equity to Chrysler). At one point, the firm was deeply mired in foreign exchange problems. It was only after a high-level lobbying effort by the US that the Chinese government decided to provide additional foreign exchange to the venture. For a fascinating account of the case, see Mann (1989).

In response to the difficulties that investors faced in balancing their FX accounts, in 1986 China took a number of innovative measures, mostly contained in the Foreign Exchange Balance Act[43] and the Provision for the Encouragement of Foreign Investment, or better known as the "22 Articles."[44] Although the FX Balance Act reiterated the need for FIEs to balance their own FX accounts through exports, it contained substantive measures whereby FIEs could generate FX. Specifically, it required Chinese local governments to assist in arranging for domestic firms to enter into import substitution arrangements with FIEs. In this way, foreign currencies originally earmarked for imports by Chinese firms could end up buying import substitutes produced by FIEs. Another measure was to allow FIEs to purchase domestic products in RMB for sale on international markets to earn foreign currencies. Finally, FIEs were also permitted to balance FX among related firms established by the same foreign investor, although in practice this last measure was not applicable to many because at the time there were few FIEs with a holding company structure (Zeichner 1987: 402).

Additional measures of assistance were contained in the "22 Articles." To promote FDI, the "22 Articles" contained deeper tax cuts for "technology advanced" or "export oriented" enterprises (or TAEs and EOEs). Under the "22 Articles," FIEs classified as TAEs were eligible for a three-year extension of a 50% enterprise income tax reduction, subject to a minimum reduced tax rate of 10%. On the expiry of the ordinary tax holidays, FIEs qualified as EOEs, i.e., with an export ratio of more than 70% in a given year, were eligible for a 50% reduction in the enterprise income tax in that year, subject to a minimum reduced tax rate of 10%.

In addition to such tax relief, now all FIEs were given yet another means to balance FX. Specifically, they were allowed to negotiate with other FIEs to adjust their FX surpluses and deficits at a rate agreed upon by both parties at the newly established Foreign Exchange Adjustment Centers, or the so-called swap centers. Indeed, the establishment of swap centers to facilitate the operations of FIEs was another major institutional development in China's FDI regulatory framework in the second part of the 1980s.

---

43. Promulgated by the State Council in January 1986.

44. So dubbed because the provision, promulgated by the State Council in October 1986, contains 22 articles.

Starting in Shenzhen and Shanghai, FX swap centers soon mushroomed wherein FIEs could trade RMB and FX.[45] By 1990 about 90 swap centers had been established (Davis and Yi 1992:14-16). Taken together, these centers served to reallocate a very impressive 20% of all FX earnings in China (Lardy 1992a: 81). The operating rules for swap centers tended to differ somewhat from one city to another and the rate at which foreign exchange was traded was generally higher than the official quotes (but lower than the black market rates).[46] Such variations notwithstanding, the swap system seems to have worked reasonably well for FIEs to solve FX headaches.

According to one survey report, after the inception of the swap system, the onus of balancing foreign exchange – once arguably the most thorny issue facing many FIEs in China – became less of a burden.[47] In another study (Wu Chao 1991:177), the ratio between the number of those FIEs able to maintain a favorable FX balance and the total number of FIEs in Fujian increased rapidly from 21.5% in 1985 to 73.3% in 1988. This is not surprising, given that FX for all FIEs in China showed a favorable balance of payments since 1988 (see Table I-5).

More recently, further progress was registered on the FX front. In 1994 China abolished the use of FX certificates, allowing FIEs to convert RMB directly into foreign currencies against a managed floating rate, initially about RMB 8.7 to US$1.00.[48] In July 1996 China decided to allow FIEs to buy and sell FX in designated banks for trade and services, loan payments, and profit repatriation. In December 1996 China formally achieved convertibility on current account transactions. Capital account transactions, however, remain controlled, even though

---

45. For a detailed account of how swap centers operate, consider Chodosh (1991:415-29).

46. In 1988, according to Davis and Yi (1992:14), the swap market rate was almost twice the official rate. Also, a service fee was charged at 0.15% of each transaction, ad valorem in RMB, with upper and lower ceilings set at 100,000 RMB and 10 RMB. MOFTEC (1993: 238).

47. The survey was conducted by the US-China Business Council in 1991. The report concluded that although some bureaucratic obstacles still remained, the situation of balancing foreign exchange had improved since the late 1980s. See Frisbie (1992:15).

48. *People's Daily*, Overseas Edition, 20 January 1995.

Chinese leaders have repeatedly said that their goal is to make the RMB fully convertible.

Table I-5: Foreign Exchange Balance of FIEs, 1987-95

Year	Balance (US$ million)
1987	-0.1
1988	4.1
1989	11.4
1990	10.1
1991	16.5
1992	24.2
1993	60.6
1994*	31.2
1995	49.2

Note: * April-November 1994.
Source: MOFTEC, cited in Wang Luolin, ed., (1997). *Zhongguo waishang touzi baogao* [Report on Foreign Investment in China], p. 8.

Under the present system, the regulatory control on FX transactions by FIEs depends on whether the transaction is a current account item or a capital account item. Current account items refer to ordinary transactions within the context of international receipts and payments, including proceeds from trade, labor services, unilateral transfers, etc. Capital account items refer to items of an increase or decrease in debt and equity due to the inflow or outflow of capital, including direct investment, all forms of loans, investment in securities, etc. In the case of a current account transaction, an FIE can purchase and sell foreign currency through designated banks without the prior approval of the State Administration of Foreign Exchange. In the case of a capital account transaction, however, prior approval from the SAFE must be obtained.

The principal features of exchange control that remain in China today include:

- Foreign exchange borrowing is required to be registered with the SAFE;
- Export proceeds or receipts from sources outside of China must be transferred into China;
- FIEs may open a foreign exchange account with a bank abroad with the approval of the SAFE.

Legalizing Wholly Foreign-Owned Enterprises

In the early 1980s China allowed a small but growing number of foreign investors to establish wholly foreign-owned enterprises on an experimental basis, first in the SEZs and then in the open cities. By the end of 1985 a total of 120 WFOEs reportedly had been established, of which 104 were located in the SEZs and 16 in Beijing, Shanghai, Guangzhou, and Changsha.[49] However, the WFOE Law was not promulgated until April 1986. As was the case with EJVs where a time gap of four years existed between the promulgation of the EJV Law and its Implementation Act, the WFOE Implementation Act, likewise, was not enacted until four years later.[50] As a result, there was a lengthy period of uncertainty, especially before 1986, during which WFOEs operated in China on a rather *ad hoc* basis and were treated differently in different locales. This apparently deterred foreign investors (Torbert 1986:50-53).

To legitimize WFOEs by promulgating a national WFOE Law was a break from Marxist orthodoxy. It was an institutional breakthrough in China's FDI regulatory framework. China thus became the first socialist country to publish a national law that allowed foreign capitalist firms on its soil alongside its state enterprises (Fang and Tang 1988:156). Ideological justification for the breakthrough was not immediately available; but it finally came in October 1987 when the 13th Party Congress propagated a novel, neo-Marxist theory. The theory claimed that China was in a "primary stage of socialism," which was said to have begun in the 1950s and was expected to last one hundred years thereafter. In this stage, said Zhao Ziyang, then the Party's General Secretary, "whatever is conducive to the growth [of the productive forces] is in keeping with the fundamental interests of the people and is therefore needed by socialism and allowed to exist"(cited in Baum 1994:140). Presumably, by bringing capital and technology to China, the WFOEs passed muster.

The WFOE Law defined a wholly foreign-owned enterprise as a limited liability company established in China with capital contributed exclusively by foreign investors. It provided that the property rights of WFOEs be protected by the state (Article 4) and foreign investors could remit profits out of China and were entitled to any funds which

49. *Beijing Review*, 5 May 1986, p. 6.

50. Promulgated in December 1990.

might be left over if a WFOE were to be liquidated (Article 19). The law contained a special clause (Article 5) that explicitly prohibited the state from nationalizing or expropriating WFOEs.

Compared to JVs, WFOEs faced greater sectoral restrictions and performance requirements. WFOEs were prohibited from operating in such sectors as the media; retail and wholesale; and telecommunications. Public utilities, transportation, real estate, trusts, and leasing were restricted sectors for WFOEs. "Restricted" sectors meant that to operate in those sectors foreign investors needed direct approval from the central government. For a WFOE to be approved it "must" employ advanced technology, develop new products, or produce import substitutes, or else have an export ratio of over 50%. By comparison, JVs were only "*encouraged*" to employ advanced technology or engage in export-oriented production. The term "encourage" is flexible and does not constitute a legal requirement.

When the WFOE Law was first published in 1986, there were no explicit tax concessions for WFOEs. WFOEs were required to pay taxes in accordance with the Foreign Enterprise Income Tax Law of 1982. Under that law, the enterprise income tax for WFOEs was charged at a progressive rate, from 20% on income at RMB 250,000 to 40% on income over RMB1 million. A local tax surcharge of 10% was also chargeable, bringing the total rate to a maximum of 50%. As a result, except for very small operations, WFOEs generally paid higher taxes than JVs.

The tax discrimination was consistently objected to by foreign investors, which perhaps explains at least in part the relatively small proportion of FDI in China in the mode of WFOE before 1990. In 1989 proposals were reportedly submitted to the NPC to end the discriminatory tax treatment toward WFOEs.[51] The proposals, however, did not pass until April 1991 when China promulgated the Foreign Investment Enterprise and Foreign Enterprise Income Tax Law, commonly known as the Unified Tax Law. Table 1-6 summarizes the key elements of the Unified Tax Law. As it shows, the new law treated all forms of FDI (i.e., EJVs, contractual joint venture CJVs, and WFOEs) equally for tax purposes.[52] In the meantime, the 1989

51. *People's Daily*, 21 December 1990.

52. In addition to WFOEs, CJVs are still another major form of FDI in China. While the CJV as a mode of FDI will be elaborated upon in the next chapter, suffice it here to say that a CJV is more flexible than an equity joint

Tiananmen events took place. For a moment it seemed that China would close its doors to foreign investment. But that prospect did not materialize.

Table I-6: Key Elements of China's Unified Tax Law

	FIE	FE with establishment in China	FE without establishment in China
Taxable income source	Worldwide	China only	China only
National tax	30% generally; 15% in SEZs and ETDZs; 24% in OUDs (15% if in energy, ports, ortransport)	30% generally; 15% in SEZs and ETDZs; 24% in OUDs	20% withholding tax (may be reduced under double tax treaty or by concession)
Local tax	3% (reduction and exemption possible)	3% (reduction and exemption possible)	
Under the Unified Tax Law, taxation of corporate entities depends on whether the entity is a Foreign Investment Enterprise or a Foreign Enterprise (FE). FIEs, including EJVs, CJVs, and WFOEs, refer to entities that are legally incorporated in China, and thus are Chinese legal entities; FEs are not Chinese legal entities, but have establishments or places in China and are engaged in production or business operations.			

Source: *Foreign Investment Enterprise and Foreign Enterprise Income Law and its Implementation Act.*

Third Period: Further Liberalization (Post-Tiananmen)

Shanghai Pudong New Area

If the 1989 Tiananmen events had caused doubts on the part of foreign investors about whether or not China would continue to pursue reform and the open door, their jitters were somewhat eased in 1990. Less than a year after Tiananmen, instead of turning inward, China moved to open up further. The first such move came in the spring of 1990 when China decided to open Pudong in Shanghai for foreign investment. Perhaps the most decisive force behind this decision was China's desire not to be seen as diverting its course of reforms in the wake of

---

venture and has a business structure somewhat akin to a strategic partnership. Before the CJV Law was published in 1988, China treated CJVs on the pattern of the EJV Law of 1979.

Tiananmen. Policy makers with respect to the opening of Pudong were reportedly "lightened and encouraged" by Deng Xiaoping's remark that "the country must be courageous and accomplish new things to show to the world that we stick to the open policy."[53]

Pudong New Area, connected to Shanghai proper by highways and cross-river tunnels, is a triangular area surrounded by the Huangpu and Yangtze rivers and Hangzhou bay. It has an area of 350 square kilometers and a population of 1.1 million. By developing Pudong, the goal was to turn greater Shanghai into an international hub of finance and trade, or the New York of China, so that it could serve as a catalyst for the development of the whole Yangtze River Valley. The valley, which includes major cities such as Nanjing, Wuhan, and Chongqing, is home to roughly 400 million people and its combined agricultural and industrial output accounts for about 40% of the country's total.[54]

The Shanghai Pudong New Area offers preferential treatments to foreign investors similar to those found in the SEZs. Production FIEs and FIEs engaged in energy or transport construction projects in this area pay an enterprise income tax of 15%. FIEs with an operating life of more than 15 years and engaged in the construction of energy or transport projects are eligible for a five-year enterprise income tax exemption starting from the first profit-making year and a 50% reduction in the following five years. In addition to SEZ-like preferential policies, accompanying the opening of Pudong was a steady relaxation of sectoral restrictions on FDI.

One of the important sectors to first undergo liberalization was banking. Chinese leaders realized that it was impossible to revitalize Shanghai as China's premier financial center any time soon without the modeling effect of foreign banks, and that Shanghai itself would not be able to attract enough capital for the development of Pudong.[55] It was against this backdrop that in September 1990 the Shanghai Regulatory Measures relating to Foreign Financial Institutions and Joint Chinese-Foreign Financial Institutions (the Shanghai Financial Measures) came out.

---

53. *People's Daily*, Overseas Edition, 1 October 1991.

54. The description here is based on CERD Consultants Ltd. 1991.

55. For the 1991-1995 period, reportedly the Shanghai government planned to inject 20 billion RMB into Pudong, which was only 40% of the estimated total of 50 billion RMB needed for infrastructure investment. See *Ta Kung Pao*, 24 March 1992, p. 3.

The Shanghai Financial Measures, for the first time, allowed foreign banks to start branching operations beyond the geographical confines of the SEZs.[56] The effect was swift. Almost immediately 30 foreign banks applied for permission and the first six approvals were announced in early 1991.[57] This liberalization, in retrospect, was the harbinger of a proliferation of foreign banks in many other major cities in China. In the wake of the publication of the Shanghai Financial Measures, other provincial and city officials reportedly were all clamoring for permission from Beijing to tap foreign capital by allowing the presence of foreign banks and financial institutions in their jurisdictions.[58]

As a result, the number of foreign banks and financial institutions increased rapidly in the 1990s, and foreign insurance companies also made their debut in China at the time. In September 1992 American International Group (AIG) won approval to establish a branch in Shanghai. It was followed by Japan's Tokyo Marine and Fire Insurance Company which set up its Shanghai office in July 1994. In 1995 the State Council designated Guangzhou as another city for foreign insurance business. AIG again was allowed to open two more branch offices there engaged respectively in life and property insurance services. In December 1995 Kyoritsu Co., a Japanese insurance brokerage firm, opened its first representative office in Shanghai. In late 1996 Swiss Winterthur Insurance (Asia) Co. was also allowed to operate in Shanghai. In the same year, Zhong Hong Life Insurance Co., the first joint venture insurance company in China (with a Canadian life insurance firm) was formed in Shanghai.[59]

By the end of 1996, a total of 156 foreign banks and financial institutions had opened branch offices in China and the number of

56. As was the case with the WFOEs, foreign banks had been accepted only on an experimental basis within SEZs under the 1985 SEZ Foreign Bank Regulations. In 1985-90, 31 foreign banks established branches or subsidiaries in the SEZs. The first foreign bank to open a branch in the SEZ was the Hong Kong and Shanghai Banking Co. (*Beijing Review*, 27 January-2 February 1992, p. 24).

57. Of the 6, 2 were US banks (CitiBank; Bank of America), 2 were Japanese banks (Industrial Bank of Japan; Sanwan), and 2 were French banks (Banque Indosuez; Credit Lyonnais). Pomfret (1992).

58. *Asian Wall Street Journal Weekly*, 3 August 1992, p. 1.

59. Data here are from Sun Shangqing and Ren Xingzhou (1997:141-42).

representative offices of foreign banks reached 528 (Wang Luolin 1997:314). In Shanghai alone, 30 foreign financial institutions reportedly had set up branches by the end of 1994, some 20 of which ranking among the 50 largest in the world.[60] In Beijing China's first JV investment bank was established between China's Construction Bank and Morgan Stanley Co. in August 1995. By late 1996, assets of foreign-invested banks (including financial institutions) amounted to US$28 billion. This accounted for 3% of the total capital of the entire banking industry in China.[61] These banks were making loans totaling US$17.55 billion, with savings deposits reaching US$3.81 billion, of which 86% were domestically generated.

The rapid expansion of foreign banking activity in China was apparently facilitated by the Regulatory Provisions on Foreign Financial Institutions issued in January 1994.[62] The new provisions clarified rules to be applied to a greater geographical scope on the basis of both the SEZ Foreign Bank Regulations and the Shanghai Financial Measures. Note that the rapid rise of assets, loans, and savings of foreign-invested banks was especially evident in and after 1994 (see Figure I-1).

Under the current regulatory framework, foreign financial institutions are allowed to establish representative offices in open cities where they can engage in "liaison" services, or other services not directly related to profit making, such as conducting market surveys and collecting business information. If they operate their branch offices in the SEZs or the State Council-designated cities such as Dalian, Fuzhou, Guangzhou, Qingdao, Nanjing, Ningbo, Shanghai, and Tianjin,[63] they can also engage directly in business, including limited RMB deposit taking.[64] Financial institutions located in these cities with

60. *China Business Journal*, 17 November 1994.

61. This is about the same as that in the US in the early 1970s. In 1973, for instance, foreign asset holdings as a share of the assets of all US banks was 3.8%, although they stood at 21.2% in 1990. See Graham and Krugman (1991:29).

62. *People's Daily*, Overseas Edition, 4 March 1994.

63. In August 1994 China added to the list another 11 cities, i.e., Beijing, Shenyang, Shijiazhuang, Xi'an, Chengdu, Chongqing, Wuhan, Hefei, Hangzhou, Suzhou, and Kunming. Wang Luolin (1997:315).

64. In principle, foreign banks are so far not allowed to transact in RMB. They can, however, with approval, accept limited RMB deposits from FIEs and

foreign investment valued over US$10 million and with an operating life of ten years or more may pay the enterprise income tax at 15% on their foreign currency business. Such financial institutions may be eligible for a one-year enterprise income tax exemption, starting with the first profit-making year, and a 50% reduction in the next two years. These reduced tax rates do not apply to RMB currency trading which will be subject to enterprise income tax at 30%.

Figure I-1: Assets, Loans and Savings of Foreign-Invested Banks, 1991-96 (US$ billion)

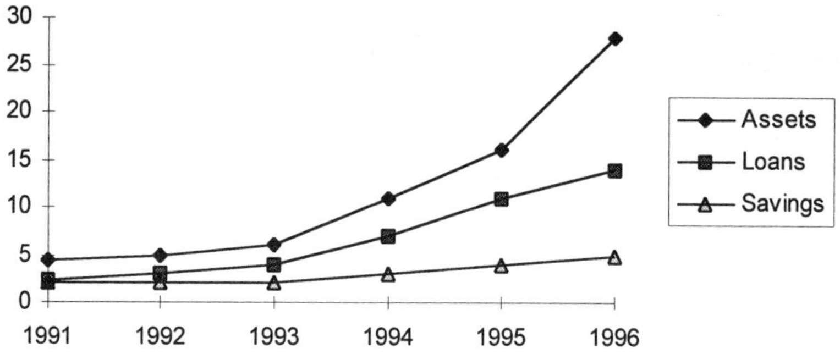

Note: Figure for 1996 is up to October of that year.
Source: *Zhongguo renmin yinhang tongji jikan* [Bank of China Statistics Quarterly] (various years).

To establish a 100% foreign-owned banking subsidiary in China, the applicant has to meet two basic pre-conditions. First, it must have maintained a representative office in China for at least three years prior to application. Second, it must have total assets of more than US$10 billion.[65]

Another important sector that was allowed a significant degree of liberalization was real estate. In May 1990, a month after Pudong was declared open, the State Council issued the Interim Measures for Land Investment, Development, and Management by Foreign Businesses

---

from local state or collective enterprises where RMB deposits are the portion of a loan from foreign banks that has not been spent.

65. The minimum registered capital required of a foreign-owned bank or a JV bank is 300 million RMB, and 200 million RMB for other financial firms. The paid-in capital must be more than 50% of the registered capital. See Xie Zhao Hua Lushi Shiwusuo (1995:53-4).

(Foreign Business Land Development Measures), which were applicable in the SEZs and coastal open cities, including the Pudong New Area. The Foreign Business Land Development Measures allowed the transfer and re-transfer of usage rights of land in China and large-scale land development schemes by foreign investors. This represented a new breakthrough in China's FDI regulatory framework with respect to foreign participation in land development projects.

Until then China had prohibited the leasing or any form of transfer of land except for the land used by JVs in accordance with special land-use legislation. According to China's 1982 Constitution (Article 10), "no organization or individual may appropriate, buy, sell, or lease land or otherwise engage in the transfer of land." This absolute ban was lifted with the adoption of the amendments to the 1982 Constitution and the Foreign Business Land Development Measures in 1990.[66] The lifting of the prohibition of foreign participation in land development, very much like the banking industry, had an immediate effect on the pattern of FDI in China.

In Shanghai, according to one study (Tian Gang 1996:173), the real estate share of total FDI in the service sector increased rapidly from 20% in 1990 to 76% in 1993. Following the lead of Shanghai, the number of provinces, including centrally administered municipalities, that engaged in land lease to foreign real estate developers reportedly expanded to 17 by 1992 and, total area committed to such leasing to foreign investors for development was more than 2,500 hectares.[67] In the first half of 1993 alone, an astonishing US$9.5 billion of FDI poured into real estate development throughout China, which was more than 16% of the total FDI committed in the period.[68] In retrospect, the momentum of these rapid developments was clearly spurred by Deng Xiaoping's now famous tour of South China in 1992.

---

66. The constitutional amendments deleted the phrase "or lease land" and provided the "right to the use of land may be transferred according to law." The maximum periods for land lease are 70 years for residential use; 50 years for industrial use; 50 years for educational, cultural, and sport facility purposes; and 40 years for commercial, tourism, and recreational use. See Liu Xiangdong (1993:901).

67. *People's Daily*, Overseas Edition, 26 June 1992.

68. Xinhua Overseas News Service, 24 August 1993, Lexis/Nexis, File: China.

Deng Xiaoping's Southern Tour

Deng Xiaoping, whose visit to Shenzhen in 1984 served to boost SEZs, again made a similar inspection tour of Wuchang, Shenzhen, Zhuhai and Shanghai in early 1992. The background of the trip was that in the wake of the collapse of the former Soviet Union conservative forces in China were using the "peaceful evolution" shibboleth in an effort to slow down China's reforms.[69] To counter the rise of conservative forces, at each stop of his tour Deng Xiaoping exhorted the country to speed up reform and open up further. "For a large, developing country like ours, the economic growth rate must be a bit faster," he said. "Reform and opening require bold moves and courageous experiments and must not proceed like a woman with bound feet." To drive home his support for speeding up economic reforms, he challenged Guangdong to catch up with the "four little dragons" within 20 years.[70]

Deng Xiaoping's remarks had electrifying effects. In May 1992 the Communist Party Politburo adopted Document No. 4, entitled, "The CCP Central Çommittee's Opinions on Expediting Reform, Opening Wider to the Outside World, and Working to Raise the Economy to a New Level in a Better and Quicker Way."(See Appendix I for summary points.) The document, reportedly drafted under Zhu Rongji, now China's Premier, marked a new stage in China's reform and open-door policy. The new tide was further reinforced at the 14th Party Congress of October the same year, during which Jiang Zemin, the Party's General Secretary, declared for the first time that the goal of China's reforms was to establish a "socialist *market* [emphasis added] economy."[71]

One important element contained in Document No. 4 was a new round of relaxation on FDI in high value-added service industries. Accordingly, Beijing, Dalian, Guangzhou, Qingdao, Shanghai, Tianjin

---

69. "Peaceful evolution" was the term used by US Secretary of State John Foster Dulles to describe the strategic objective of "containment" against China. The idea is that the socialist system will eventually be subverted by peaceful, i.e., economic, means.

70. Deng Xiaoping, "Zai Wuchang, Shenzhen, Zhuhai dengdi de tanhua yaodian," in Deng Xiaoping (1993: 370). A full text of his talks can also be found in FBIS-CHI-92-050 March 13, 1992.

71. "Political Report" to the 14th Party Congress in FBIS-CHI, 13 October 1992, 23-43.

and the SEZs were authorized to experiment with FDI in retail and tourism (in addition to banking and real estate discussed previously). In China, the service sectors had previously been monopolized by state-owned enterprises for both political and economic reasons. Politically, banking and insurance, for instance, are considered to be arterial industries that have a great impact on the national economy. Economically, retail and wholesale, for instance, are highly profitable. Thus, the opening of these tertiary industries signaled yet another significant FDI policy development from a previously single focus on manufacturing to a now double-pronged emphasis on both industrial production and high value-added tertiary sectors.

Accordingly, new service sectors, such as retail and tourism, have been gradually opened to foreign investors on an experimental basis since 1992. Yaohan International, a Hong Kong-based Japanese firm, was the first retailer to win approval in 1992 to join hands with Shanghai Number One Department Store to build a huge complex in Pudong. Subsequently, the number of foreign-invested shopping centers approved directly by the central government reached 14 in 1995 (Chen Wenjin 1996:33). China currently allows a maximum of 22 foreign investments in JV retail department stores. Of the total, 15 have been approved and 4 have begun business. In addition, in 1996 two JV chain stores were allowed to operate in China. China's first JV tourism company, with a minority-stake of Japanese and Hong Kong investment, was approved in December 1996.

Chinese officials admitted that international pressure, especially from bilateral negotiations with the United States regarding China's accession to the WTO, figured prominently in China's decision to open the service sectors to foreign investment. But they also became increasingly aware that the demonstration effect of foreign companies (e.g., management style that comes with FDI) was essential to upgrade the dilapidated services industry in China. As one official commented: "Machines may be brought in upgrading manufacturing capacities; good services, however, have to be learned through demonstrations."[72] It seems that in the near future China may continue to be reluctant for WFOEs to participate in many service sectors, but there lacks no domestic momentum nor rationale to push for more JV projects in the services industry.

---

72. Interview.

Another key dimension of the liberalization of China's FDI regulatory framework, also envisioned in Document No. 4, was the geographical opening of China's interior for foreign trade and investment. Under the so-called strategy "to open the areas along the borders, along the (Yangtze) River, and along the coast," China moved quickly to open 21 additional cities along the Yangtze River and in the northeast, and authorized them to set up their own development zones, either in the form of New and High Tech Zones (NHTZs)[73] or Economic and Technology Development Zones (ETDZs). As of 1996, 14 border cities (including counties) in the southwest, northwest, north and northeast were also declared open; the number of the ETDZs increased from the previous 14 to 34; and all provincial capitals were now authorized to offer SEZ-like preferential policies.

In addition, nationwide a total of 52 NHTZs, 13 bonded trade zones, and 11 tourism zones were established, offering a range of preferential policies to foreign investment (see Table I-7). All in all, these "open investment areas" covered a total of 354 cities and counties, and had a combined size of some 550,000 square kilometers populated by 330 million people (Li Lanqing 1995:274).

Table I-7: Development Zones and Preferential Policies in China

Zone categories	#	Key elements of preferential policies
Economic and Technology Development Zones	34	National tax of 15% for production FIEs; 3% local tax may be exempted
New & High Tech Zones	52	National tax of 15% for high or new technology FIEs; 3% local tax may be exempted
Bonded Free Trade Zones	13	FIEs engaged in processing and assembly for export pay tax at 15%; no tariff within the designated zones
Open Border Cities	14	National tax of 24% for production FIEs; 3% local tax may be exempted
National Tourism Zones	11	National tax of 24% for production FIEs; 3% local tax may be exempted

Source: Li Lanqing, ed. (1995). *Zhongguo liyong waizi jichu zhishi*, [Essential Information on China's Utilization of Foreign Investment], pp. 290-304.

73. The first NHTZ was established in Beijing in 1988. In terms of special incentives to foreign investors, NHTZs are similar to ETDZs.

Recent Developments

China's high growth rates placed enormous stress on its basic infrastructure. To sustain growth, the World Bank (1995:4) estimates that in 1995-2004 China will need to invest US$744 billion in electric power, telecommunications, transportation, and water and sanitation infrastructure. In order to help smooth out infrastructure bottlenecks, China recently began to look for new ways to encourage foreign investment in infrastructure projects. Shifting foreign investment to infrastructure projects away from export-oriented industries presents challenges, however, because projects in the road, rail, and power sectors usually have long payback periods. As such, infrastructure projects pose high risks to foreign investors, especially if there is no ready source of foreign exchange.

But obstacles to foreign involvement in infrastructure projects have gradually been removed in China in recent years. For instance, China's has recently decided to allow current account convertibility including debt servicing. This goes a long way toward alleviating the problem of financing for infrastructure projects. In addition, China also offers fiscal inducements for FDI in long-term infrastructure projects. FDI engaged in harbor or wharf construction may pay the enterprise income tax at 15%. Alternatively, if the operating life of a project is not less than 15 years, foreign investors may apply for a 5-year tax holiday, starting from the first profit-making year, and a 50% tax reduction for 5 additional years.

Perhaps more important than tax relief, to accommodate FDI in infrastructure projects, China has begun to experiment with foreign participation on a build-operate-transfer (BOT) basis. Under the BOT formula, foreign investors are permitted to build, say, a highway, operate it for a certain period for capital recuperation, and then transfer it to the host country. The Guangxi Laibing Power Plant B project reportedly began in 1986. It was perhaps China's first BOT project (Chen Jinghua 1996: 237). Another example is the Shandong Rizhao Power Project, a 700-megawatt coal-fired facility that will cost US$625 million to be paid off over a decade (Fang 1997:29-31).

More recently, another important step China has taken to improve its FDI regulatory framework is the publication of the Regulations for

Guiding the Direction of Foreign Investment (FDI Guideline). The FDI Guideline was approved by the State Council and issued jointly by the State Planning Commission (SPC), the State Economic and Trade Commission (SETC), and the Ministry of Foreign Trade and Economic Cooperation, indicating enormous inter-agency coordination. Prior to the first appearance of this document in 1995 (it was revised in late 1997), sectoral investment priorities were often treated as "*neibu,*" i.e., information only for the eyes of bureaucrats, but not readily available to foreign investors. The FDI Guideline presented to foreign investors for the first time a detailed sectoral road map, including whether WFOEs or JVs were preferred or required, under four categories of projects: encouraged, restricted, prohibited, and permitted.

In encouraged sectors, such as improvement of the ecological environment, investors can expect a warm welcome, face fewer performance requirements, and enjoy higher managerial control and greater tax incentives. In restricted sectors, such as production of washing machines or refrigerators where the market is already crowded, projects require central-level approval, and investors are expected to justify the project by demonstrating some advantage to China. Prohibited areas include sectors that either have security implications (e.g., air traffic controls or electric power grids), or are politically sensitive (e.g., radio and TV broadcasting) or culturally repugnant (e.g., prostitution). Finally, the permitted category is a neutral catchall for areas not covered by the other three categories.

The promulgation of the FDI Guideline signals that the period of China's FDI policy experimentation, which started in the SEZs in the early years of the reform, is winding down. After almost two decades of "crossing the river by groping for stepping stones," a phrase that Chinese often use to describe the incremental approach of their reform endeavor, China's FDI regulatory framework has matured considerably. It seems that China has finally become confident and clear, broadly speaking, about which sectors ought to be closed off to foreign participation and which should be thrown wide open. By translating ad hoc policy into written commitments in the form of the FDI Guideline, one important objective is to temper the arbitrary and capricious character of the screening process and to make China's FDI regulatory framework more predictable and transparent.[74]

---

74. Interview.

In late 1995, the Chinese government announced that it would begin to initiate another round of tax reforms for foreign-invested enterprises, as a first step toward integrating what still remained a bifurcated system of tax treatments between FIEs and domestic firms. The new tax system gradually replaced all kinds of preferential tax treatments to FIEs with a flat 30% national corporate tax, plus local taxes. Exemptions on equipment imports by FIEs would also be abolished. The new reform was accompanied by a series of other measures, including reductions of tariff rates and elimination of many import and export quotas and controls. These measures, aimed at creating a level playing field for both FIEs and domestic firms, were part of China's efforts for entry into the World Trade Organization, a topic to be further discussed in the next chapter.

Concluding Remarks

In this chapter we have reviewed the incremental, yet steady, improvement of China's FDI regulatory framework. We have noted that while China's FDI regulatory framework has now become increasingly sophisticated and transparent, statutory and regulatory ambiguity abounded in the early years of reform and receded only gradually over time. In retrospect, it seems that there was a salutatory element in the ambiguity as the building process of China's FDI regulatory framework unfolds in the reform era.

After all, when the reforms started in the late 1970s, there was no strong ideological consensus among Chinese leaders about to how far and how fast the reforms should go, and the leaders had little experience in crafting a legal institution necessary for the proper functioning of a market economy. In this light, deliberate ambiguity perhaps served as a vehicle for the reformers to learn from experience and eventually to push FDI policy experiments beyond points of reversal. All the while, when the process by trial and error continued, foreign investment was given a chance to demonstrate its benefits to the Chinese economy. In this virtuous circle, important milestones, one after another, erected in China's FDI regulatory framework, and, as we will demonstrate in greater statistical detail in Part II of this study, foreign investors began to feel sufficiently protected to find China's marketplace attractive for their investments.

Appendix I: Summary Points of Central Committee Document No. 4, 1992

CCP Central Committee Document No. 4 (1992)

"Party Central Committee's Opinions on Expediting Reform, Opening Wider to the Outside World, and Working to Raise the Economy to a New Level in a Better and Quicker Way"

- With the development of Pudong in Shanghai serving as the dragon head, further develop Wuhu, Jiujiang, Wuhan, Yueyang, and Chongqing along the Yangtze River, and adopt the same policies toward them as those applied in the coastal open cities.
- Gradually open cities along the borders to the outside world to form a peripheral opening pattern. Apart from the four cities including Heihe, open another nine cities and counties in southwest and northeast China to the outside world; Pingxing and Dongxing in Guangxi; Hekou county, Wanding and Ruili counties in Yunnan, Yili, Tacheng and Bole in Xinjiang; and Erenhot in Inner Mongolia.
- To actively promote border trade with neighboring countries and adopt relevant policies for open cities in Harbin, Changchun, Huhehot, Urumqi, Kunming, and Nanning.
- To continue to run well the Special Economic Zones and coastal open cities and open zones and boldly make use of foreign funds and introduce technologies.
- To select a port city in every special economic zone, as well as in Shandong, Jiangsu, Zhejiang, and Fujian, for the establishment of a bonded zone.
- To strengthen the association between coastal and inland areas and the influence of the former on the latter and to give full play to the role of Guangxi as a thoroughfare in southwest China. To accelerate the pace of opening up in the inland areas and, in the projects using foreign funds, to implement the relevant policies for the coastal open cities in the capitals of the inland provinces and regions.
- To implement the policy combining the preferential measures for certain regions with those for certain industries, expand the spheres for opening up to the outside world, find more ways to make use of foreign funds and funds from Hong Kong, Macao, and Taiwan. All major projects and high and new technological projects, which have been approved by the state and which are in conformity with industrial policy, irrespective of their localities, can enjoy the preferential policies for the development zones. The spheres for directly using foreign funds should be gradually extended to finance, trade, commerce, communications, tourism, and tertiary industry through experiments.
- To allow the approved establishment of one or two foreign-funded banks and foreign-invested retail firms in certain cities and to allow Shanghai to run a foreign-invested insurance company on a trial basis.

Source: Hong Kong Ta Kung Pao, 18 June 1992, in FBIS-CHI-92-118, 19 June 1992.

CHAPTER 2

International Perspectives

When China's leaders decided to reform their economy and open their doors to the outside world in 1978, they recognized that legal construction would be necessary. But while their legal expertise was short, their memories were long about "extraterritoriality," a system imposed on China in the wake of the Opium War of 1838-40. It shielded foreigners from Chinese jurisdiction and legitimized foreign encroachment that eventually contributed to the dismantling of the country around the turn of the 20th century (Fairbank 1983: 167-71). To be aware of this historical background is important to appreciate the pace of China's legal developments in the reform era.

As documented in the previous chapter, legal norms and institutions, many recognizably Western in principle, have evolved only gradually, and sometimes hesitantly, in the reform years. But after two decades of reform, an reasonably well-operating system of law has now more or less been cobbled together. The building process includes the gradual replacement of personal pronouncements by party leaders with publicly available laws and regulations, the establishment of commercial courts to adjudicate civil disputes, and the expansion of law schools to train lawyers, judges, and legislators. Reflecting the growing importance of law as an institution in China in the reform era, the development of the legal profession has been significant. While the number of lawyers and law firms in 1979 was 212 and 79 respectively, it grew quickly to about 40,000 and 3,600 in 1993 and reached more than 100,000 and 8,000 in 1997. So far, the Ministry of Justice has approved 67 representative offices of foreign law firms in China, and 26 branches of Hong Kong law firms. In 1993-98, 111,000 persons were admitted to the bar. It was estimated that by the end of 2000, there will be 150,000 lawyers in China and 250,000-300,000 by 2010.[1]

Specific to FDI, as documented in Chapter 1, a rather comprehensive set of laws covering all major modes of investment (e.g., EJVs, CJVs, and WFOEs) had been put in place in China by the early 1990s. This has been reinforced by a host of auxiliary rules and regulations aimed to clarify operational issues. At the same time, China has opened up, or relaxed conditions for, a growing range of new sectors previously off-limits to foreign investment. Moreover, what started as policy experiments in the geographical confines of the SEZs has now been diffused from coastal regions into the interior. In this chapter we continue our discussion of China's FDI regulatory framework but focus on its international dimension. In the process we assess several key aspects of the current framework in an international perspective.

Investment Protection and Dispute Resolution

Chinese leaders recognize that unless foreign investors feel that their investments are sufficiently protected they will not invest in significant ways; and that capricious policy swings resulting from personal idiosyncrasies need to be tempered by legislative deliberativeness so as to provide stability and continuity in an era of change. This is especially true for a country in transition where prediction is anything but easy. Reflecting this recognition, for instance, China has decided to set term limits on high officials, and the NPC, formerly known as a mere "rubber stamp," has shown increasing signs of independence in recent years. (Mufson 1995: A21; Fan Gang and Xin Chunying 1998: 15).

However, while the development of a domestic legal institution is necessary to boost the confidence of foreign investors, it is not a sufficient condition. A fundamental question that a cross-national investor has to ponder is: Why should I trust the commitments of a foreign sovereign who in theory is not answerable to me? This problem is especially acute for large investment projects involving large sunk capital, and thus vulnerable to the "hostage effect," or the so-called

1. Wang Yu, "Lawyers' Profession: Promising 'Sunshine Industry,'" *Fazhi ribao*, 12 November 1998.

"hold-up problem" in business jargon.[2] Such vulnerability on the part of the foreign investor can be highlighted by Raymond Vernon's "obsolescing bargain" model (1971). According to Vernon, before the investment is sunk, risk and uncertainty are high and the potential investor should be able to extract from the host country quite favorable terms to compensate for both. But as risk and uncertainty dissipate after the project proves successful and as other potential investors emerge on the scene, the host country finds itself in a position to renegotiate the initial terms, even though it does not resort to outright nationalization or expropriation.[3]

Given the "structural vulnerability" arising from the power asymmetry between a sovereign (i.e., the Chinese state) and a foreign private investor, it would seem logical that in order to increase the security of a private foreign investment, sovereign discretion must be put in check. As Shepsle (1991:246) argues, "discretion" after all, "is the enemy of optimality, commitment its ally."[4] In this regard, the evidence is compelling that China has been following the logical imperative. Specifically, as we will discuss shortly, to enhance its creditworthiness, China has entered into a sophisticated web of international institutional guarantees, at both bilateral and multilateral levels, which greatly increase the cost that China will have to pay should it renege on its international commitments.

As early as 1980 China signed the Investment Incentive Agreement with the United States. In so doing, China undertook to abide by the principle of subrogation, whereby the US government, through its Overseas Private Investment Corporation (OPIC), would acquire the right of an aggrieved private company into a government-to-government dispute. This, in turn, permitted OPIC to extend political

---

2. A general business problem in which each party to a contract worries about being forced to accept disadvantageous terms later, after it has sunk an investment. Williamson (1975: 1985) and Klein, Crawford, and Alchian (1978) were among the first scholars to emphasize and elaborate on the importance of the hold-up problem for an analysis of business institutions and practices.

3. The importance of the general issue of commitment and renegotiation, both in contracting and in other institutions, has been repeatedly emphasized by Tirole (1988).

4. A similar maxim is attributed to Joseph Schumpeter: "The maximal exploitation of present possibilities may often be an obstacle to the maximal creation of new possibilities." Cited in Elster (1971:10).

risk insurance to private US investment in China. Through such mechanisms, the dilemma of power asymmetry is reduced, if not swept away completely. Throughout the 1980s OPIC had an active China program. As of 1990, its political risk insurance portfolio in China included 31 US investments valued a total of US$300 million. In the aftermath of the Tiananmen events in 1989, however, the US suspended the OPIC China program.

Another mechanism that similarly checks sovereign discretion is a bilateral investment protection treaty (BIT). BIT agreements almost invariably contain provisions about the reciprocal granting of most-favored-nation (MFN) status, safeguards against expropriation and nationalization, freedom of capital repatriation, and dispute resolution through international arbitration tribunals. These, for example, include the American Arbitration Association <www.adr.org>, the Arbitration Institute of the Stockholm Chamber of Commerce <www.chamber.se>, the Hong Kong International Arbitration Center <www.hkiac.org>, and the Court of Arbitration of the International Chamber of Commerce <www.iccwbo.org>.[5] Since its first BIT agreement with Sweden in 1982, China has concluded BIT agreements with more than three dozen countries, including all major capital-exporting countries, except the United States.[6]

Bilateral treaty guarantees aside, still another measure of assurance has to do with the enforcement of foreign arbitral awards. A "foreign" award is one made outside the territory of the country in which recognition or enforcement is sought (Redfern and Hunter 1991:448). As can be imagined, enforcement of such an award can be a complex matter, if the process is not governed by treaty obligations. To facilitate the enforcement of foreign arbitral awards, thus boosting the confidence of foreign investors, in 1987 China acceded to the United Nations Convention on the Recognition and Enforcement of Foreign Arbitral Awards (New York Convention). As a signatory to the New

---

5. Until recently, arbitration in the Court of Arbitration of the International Chamber of Commerce (ICC) was discouraged because mainland China was not a member of the ICC, while Taiwan has been. With China's acceptance into the ICC in 1994, its reluctance to submit to the ICC has been diminished.

6. Presumably because efforts to conclude a BIT agreement have been hampered by the annual debate on China's MFN status in the US Congress, since BIT would have to reciprocate MFN status.

York Convention, China is under treaty obligations to honor foreign arbitral awards.[7]

China's enforcement record so far indicates that China is serious about its international arbitration obligations. One case, however, may raise some questions. For almost a year starting in late 1993, a US firm tried unsuccessfully to seek enforcement of a Stockholm arbitral award with a local court in Shanghai. It was only through the intervention of Beijing that the Shanghai court eventually accepted the case and ruled in favor of the US firm.[8] A Chinese official suggested that local officials did not have the right training to deal with matters of international law.[9] But the truth may have a deeper institutional cause: Since the ruling would be against a local SOE, local authorities had less incentive to abide by treaty obligations than Beijing. Such tensions indicate that the decentralization of power in the reform era, generally applauded by foreign observers of China, may not necessarily work in favor of foreign investment, or for the same matter, of the protection of intellectual property rights, to be discussed in the next section.

China's multilateral commitments bearing on foreign investment include other dimensions. One good example is the Multinational Investment Guarantee Agency (MIGA), a World Bank organization which provides political risk insurance for private foreign investors in emerging markets <www.miga.org>. By joining MIGA in 1988 China committed itself to the principle of subrogation at a multilateral level. This was a step forward from the same principle but only on a bilateral plane.

Now, absent the OPIC China program, US firms can avail themselves of the MIGA program. MIGA provides political risk insurance via contracts of guarantee for foreign equity and related debt investments. In addition to covering losses from currency inconvertibility, expropriation, and war and civil disturbances, it can insure investors against host-country breaches of contract if the investor is denied an appropriate forum to adjudicate its claim or denied the right to enforce a favorable judgment regarding the breach.

---

7. For a detailed analysis of the enforcement mechanism in China under the New York Convention, see Schulberg (1989).

8. Revpower Ltd. v. Shanghai Far East Aerial Tech. Import and Export Corp. Interview.

9. Interview.

Because "developing countries often rely on continued financial support from the World Bank to support their development strategies," Benoit (1996:48) has observed that the World Bank occupies "a relatively strong position to address and resolve with host governments disputes regarding government actions which might adversely affect the project." As of January 1997, the MIGA portfolio in China included 18 contracts of guarantee in 11 projects, valued at over US$63.44 million; many were long-term infrastructure projects (Feng Yushu 1997:13).

Moreover, in 1990 China signed the Convention on the Settlement of Investment Disputes between States and the Nationals of Other States (Washington Convention). Under the Washington Convention, the arbitration procedures of the International Center for the Settlement of Investment Disputes (ICSID) are now available for the resolution of disputes between private foreign investors and the Chinese government. Until then China had rejected the notion that a government representing a sovereign state could directly be sued for disputes by a private foreign national. Now this hard version of sovereignty has been softened, at least in the commercial realm.

For dispute resolutions, foreign investors can now avail themselves of international arbitration tribunals, or they can also use Chinese arbitration courts. China's own arbitration regime remains bifurcated. As such, the domestic arbitration system governs settlement of economic disputes among Chinese individuals and firms. On the other hand, international arbitration of disputes that involve a "foreign element" is largely the purview of the China International Economic and Trade Arbitration Commission (CIETAC) and, to a lesser extent, the China Maritime Arbitration Commission (CMAC). To make use of CIETAC services, parties to a contract can either stipulate in the contract to resolve disputes at CIETAC or jointly submit in writing to the commission after a conflict arises. CIETAC findings are binding and not subject to appeal by either side, at least in theory.

When first resurrected in the 1980s after decades of hiatus, CIETAC and CMAC were derided for their partiality. In order to inspire foreign confidence in the impartiality of the work of these commissions, China has allowed prominent foreign nationals to sit on the commissions. By the early 1990s, whereas the panel of CMAC arbitrators included 66 Chinese and 1 foreigner; that of CIETAC, which handled over 95% of international arbitration cases in China was composed of 291 arbitrators, of whom 88 (30%) were foreigners. In addition, foreign laws have been made applicable in China to arbitrate disputes so long as the arbitration clause in the contract so stipulates. China's Arbitration Law, for instance, which became effective in September 1995, is basically an amalgam of provisions from international experts and norms set by the UNCITRAL Model Law on International Commercial Arbitration (Cheng Dejun, et al., 1995:18, 297).

Has China's arbitration regime evolved to such an extent that it is able to work impartially and effectively in solving disputes? Those interviewed were generally optimistic and positive, even though some raised concerns about enforcement risks. Since CIETAC has no independent power of enforcement, plaintiffs have to apply to the local Intermediate People's Court in the jurisdiction of the losing party to enforce the commission's decisions. While the Intermediate People's Court is not supposed to obstruct the commission's findings, cases have been reported where some judges, finding "fraud" in original contract terms, blocked or even reversed CIETAC decisions. As can be imaged, such flip-flops implicitly raise the transaction costs of doing business in China. But do these cases represent a worsening trend or are they simply isolated incidents in what is, on balance, an improving system?

Relevant statistics suggest that the latter is the case. Table II-1 presents the annual number of cases processed by CIETAC and CMAC in 1990-94,[10] along with those by other well-known international arbitration tribunals. As shown in the table, China's arbitration tribunals have rapidly become some of the busiest in the world. Consider the fact that arbitration services in China are not free (see Table II-2 for fee schedules), it seems reasonable to conclude that China's arbitration courts have inspired a growing level of confidence among foreign investors. To conclude otherwise would have to create a forced paradox. That is, why would a growing number of "rational" investors resort to a system if that system has an overall poor, non-improving record, given that the use of that system may incur additional costs in the form of arbitration fees, not to mention the necessary time involved in the process.

---

10. For trends in the late 1980s, see Brahm (1989:13-14).

Table II-1: Ranking of Major International Arbitration Bodies by Number of New Cases

	1990	Rank	1991	Rank	1992	Rank	1993	1994
AAA	224	2	319	2	252	3	--	--
CIETAC/ CMAC	184/ 10	3	274/ 8	3	267 /14	2	486/ 8	829/ --
HKIAC	54	4	94	4	185	4	--	--
ICC	365	1	333	1	337	1	--	--
LCIA	--	--	--	--	75	5	--	--
SCC	35	5	62	5	63	6	--	--

Note: Roughly 80% of the cases submitted to the CMAC are commenced by foreign parties. The comparable figure for the CIETAC is about 50%.
AAA= American Arbitration Association; HKIAC= Hong Kong International Arbitration Center; ICC=International Chamber of Commerce; LCIA=London Court of International Arbitration; SCC= Arbitration Institute of the Stockholm Chamber of Commerce.
Source: Cheng Dejun, ed. (1995), *International Arbitration in the PRC*, pp. 22-23.

Table II-2: Arbitration Fee Schedule by CIETAC

Amount of Claim (RMB)	Amount of Fee (RMB)
1,000,000 or less	4% of the claimed amount, minimum 20,000
1,000,000 to 5,000,000	40,000 plus 3% of the excess over 1,000,000
5,000,000 to 10,000,000	160,000 plus 2% of the excess over 5,000,000
10,000,000 to 50,000,000	260,000 plus 1% of the excess over 10,000,000
50,000,000 or more	660,000 plus 0.5% of the excess over 50,000,000

Note: When a claimant applies for arbitration case is charged an additional 10,000 RMB as a registration fee. If the amount of the claim is not specified at the time of application, arbitration fees are determined by the secretariat of the CIETAC.
Source: *Addendum to the 1994 CIETAC Rules.*

Intellectual Property Rights Protection

Transfer of advanced foreign technology, both the hard and soft type, has been an essential ingredient in China's efforts to promote FDI since 1979. That aim was made quite explicit in China's first foreign investment law of 1979 and especially in the "22 Articles" of 1986, which made a point of promoting high-tech or knowledge-intensive projects. Again, in 1995 the FDI Guideline also stated explicitly that approval preferences would be extended to firms that transfer sophisticated technology.

But from the perspectives of foreign investors, advanced technology, both the soft and hard kind, constitutes their firm-specific assets that make them competitive in the market in the first place. While they may be ready to transfer technology as part and parcel of FDI, they have to maintain a competitive edge over rival firms, both real and potential, in order to be successful in the host country.[11] Thus, if the development of an intellectual property and technology protection regime does not keep up with the needs of foreign investors, China risks discouraging rather than encouraging FDI.

However, embedded in a culture where "to steal a book is an elegant offense,"[12] not surprisingly, China's efforts in the protection of intellectual property rights (IPR) were slow in coming in the 1980s. Although China promulgated a trademark law in 1982 and a patent law in 1984, the scope and terms for the protection of intangible property (copyrights, patents, trademarks, etc.) in these laws fell short of international standards. In the 1990s, however, as China's integration with the world economy deepened, international pressure was mounting for China to strengthen its IPR regime, and it is no secret that in recent years China has moved to increase IPR protection in part because of pressure from the US.

To begin, it took the arm-twisting of a Super 301 investigation by the US, coupled with the threat of trade sanctions, to gain Chinese agreement to align its IPR regime with international norms and standards (Shirk 1994:79). In 1992 China signed an IPR Memorandum of Understanding (MOU) with the US, whereby China pledged to improve its IPR protection regime. Subsequently China followed through on its commitments by revising its patent law, which enlarged the scope of patent protection to cover pharmaceutical and chemical inventions, and extended the protection terms to 20 years. China also amended its trademark law with new provisions for the protection of service marks and well-known marks, and included special regulations for criminal prosecution for trademark infringement.

---

11. Points relating to the importance of firm-specific assets for operations in foreign countries are further discussed in Chapter 6.

12. For a fascinating discussion of China's historical experience with copyrights, patents and trademarks, and related issues, consider Alford (1995).

Also related to IPR protection, in 1993 China promulgated the Law against Unfair Competition. Under the law, unfair competition is defined to include acts that violate "commercial secrets," which in turn are defined to include technical and operational information not available to the public. Sanctions for violations include civil remedies such as damages, administrative sanctions such as fines, and criminal penalties for "serious violations." However, because the law is relatively new and untested, many FIEs in China in practice continued to rely upon confidentiality and non-competition clauses in contracts to protect business or technical information.[13] This, incidentally, is a fairly standard way of business practice in places like Hong Kong and the US.

Along with progress in domestic legislation, efforts were also made to improve the country's IPR protection regime at both the bilateral and multilateral levels. In October 1992 China acceded to both the Berne Convention for the Protection of Literary and Artistic Works and the Universal Copyright Convention. In April 1993 China joined the Geneva Phonogram Convention. Under the Berne Convention, China explicitly recognized computer software as a literary work to be protected for 50 years without mandatory registration requirements. In addition, China has reached bilateral agreements on mutual protection of intellectual property with major industrialized countries such as the US, EC, Switzerland, and Japan (Foreign Investment Administration, MOFTEC 1994:14-15). Other IPR-related international treaties to which China has become a party include the Madrid Trademark Convention and the Paris Convention for the Protection of Industrial Property.[14]

In an effort to put teeth into the laws, China established IPR tribunals in Beijing, Shanghai, Guangzhou, Shenzhen, Xiamen, and Haikou to adjudicate cases of violations of trademarks, copyrights, and patents.[15] These legal institutions provided judicial means for foreign firms to police and penalize IPR violations. At the same time, Beijing also ordered local governments to conduct a series of raids against CD pirates. As an indication of the seriousness of such efforts, a

---

13. Interview.

14. Much of the information in this paragraph is based on Peter Feng (1997).

15. *China Daily*, 29 March 1994.

Guangdong official said that several CD factories there were ordered to close down, even though that inflicted significant damage to a local township economy.[16]

Washington seems to have been generally pleased with Beijing's recent efforts at IPR protection. In 1997 the International Intellectual Property Alliance no longer targeted China as a priority for US foreign policy (Holden 1997). The Clinton administration noted that China had taken "significant steps to crack down on piracy" by closing 37 illegal CD factories between May 1996 and March 1997.[17] In 1997 there was a report that Chinese courts had sentenced IPR violators to lengthy prison terms.[18] Anecdotal evidence suggests that the business climate in China had become so chilly for illegal companies that many factories had reportedly left China for Singapore, Taiwan, Macao, and Hong Kong.[19]

Indeed, at the policy level at least, China has been as compliant on IPR issues as anyone could expect, and has won praise from Arpad Bogsch, the Director General of the World Intellectual Property Organization (WIPO): "It is remarkable that China has made such rapid progress in a short time."[20] But actual IPR enforcement in China either through judicial or administrative means remains problematic, from the standpoint of foreign companies, especially US software developers. According to a US estimate (Goldstein 1994), the US lost US$827 million worth of software programs in 1993 to Chinese piracy of CDs. While there is no denying that piracy is a problem in China, that estimate seems to be exaggerated. The problem derives from assumptions of an inelastic demand curve. That is, given an upward price change (from a low "pirate" price in China to a high "normal" price in the US), demand for CDs in China, measured in number, would remain constant, which is of course highly unlikely. The estimate also fails to consider a very likely scenario whereby "cheap" CDs may have generated additional demand for CD-related hardware

---

16. Interview.

17. *National Trade Estimate Report for the People's Republic of China.*

18. *New York Times,* 17 April 1997.

19. *Wall Street Journal,* 22 August 1997, 19 September 1997.

20. *Beijing Review*, 17 February 1992. For a historical perspective on the development of IPR protection in the US, consider Clark (1960); in Europe, Nimmer (1978) and Rosenberg (1983).

such as computers, and thus may have increased US sales of these products. Further, to put the problem in international perspective, based on industry estimates, US losses in Japan due to piracy have been almost double those in China. Piracy in the US itself causes the greatest losses for US industries (Gomez 1997).

Chinese central officials, while expressing their commitment to IPR protection, attributed the intractability of the piracy problem to the enormous asymmetry between their still limited (albeit growing) legal and administrative capacity and the country's "vast territory and large population."[21] But the problem apparently has a deeper institutional cause. As China observers have noted (Simone 1992; Shirk 1994), some of the lucrative businesses were sponsored by powerful local and ministry officials, including the military which ran a vast commercial network in the reform years. Such being the case, central anti-piracy authorities often lacked the political clout to enforce IPR protection laws evenly and vigorously up and down the country. Senior Chinese leaders have become increasingly cognizant of the institutional sources of such conflicts, as evidenced by China's latest efforts to cut off the umbilical cord between the military and its commercial enterprises.[22]

Special Policy Enclaves

While FDI has been increasingly recognized as a catalyst for growth by bringing to the host country capital, effective management, marketing, and technology to improve productivity, there is also a long history of criticism of multinational corporations (Grieo 1986; Cardoso and Dornbusch 1989; and Gillis, et al. 1996). Much of it centers on the possibility that foreign investors will thwart the host country's efforts to constrain socially undesirable practices – such as pollution regulations or health, safety, and minimum wage requirements. Thus, in their efforts to promote FDI while attempting to contain its possible negative influence, an important policy instrument that many developing countries have used is to set up policy enclaves. They are

---

21. Xinhua News Agency, 28 January 1994

22. For reports on recent developments, see "Out of Business," *Far Eastern Economic Review,* 6 August, 1998, pp. 68-69; "China's army gives up business," *The Economist*, 8 May 1999: p. 34. For an investigation of the military's commercial activities, see Mulvenson (1998).

variably called "free trade zones," "export processing zones," "special industrial estates," or, in the case of China, "Special Economic Zones," in the southernmost parts of the country.

Table II-3: Special Zones in Selected Countries

COUNTRY	ZONE NAME/SIZE (SQUARE MILES)
China	Hainan Island (13,104.00); Shenzhen (126.20); Xiamen (50.50); Zhuhai (46.60); Shantou (20.30)
Indonesia	Batam Island (14.10); Jakarta/Tanjung Priok (0.13)
Malaysia	Prai (0.64); Pulau Jerajak (0.63); Pennang/Bayan Lepas (0.47); Sungei Way – Subang (0.22); Senai (0.15); Melaka/Batu Berendam (0.08); Kang (0.08); Telok Panglima Garang (0.08)
Philippines	Central Luzon/Bataan (1.31); Central Visayas/Mactan (0.45); Northern Luzon/Baguio (0.24)
Singapore	All industrial areas (33.90)
Taiwan	Nantze (0.34); Kaohsiung (0.26); Taichung (0.09)
Thailand	Lard Krabang (0.11)

Note: Zone size in parentheses.
Sources: *Beijing Review*, 8-14 April 1991; Spinanger, (1983) "Economic Activity Zones: Objectives and Impact: Some Evidence from Asia."

The precise functions of these special zones may vary somewhat across countries;[23] the commonality they all share is to encourage foreign capital by bundling together many concessions from the host country's prevailing taxes, tariffs, labor regulations, etc., which the host government does not wish, or is unready, to repeal outright. According to a United Nations source, by 1989, over 200 such zones had been established in the developing world, and over 50 more were planned.[24] The efficacy of these special policy enclaves is indicated by the recent Asian successes with export-led growth and the reorientation of countries in Latin America and elsewhere toward the penetration of

23. For an extensive international inquiry, see Frobel and Kreye (1980).
24. United Nations (1991).

external markets. Ranis and Schive (1985:55-137) reported that Taiwan's export processing zones successfully mobilized FDI to play an important catalytic role in the transition from import competing to export-oriented industrialization.

To the extent that empirical research has found that the acreage of these special zones is a significant determinant of the distribution of FDI in Caribbean countries (Woodward and Rolfe 1993: 121-44), it makes sense to compare the geographical size of the special zones of various countries. In this aspect, China is simply unmatchable by other countries. As Table II-3 shows, China's Hainan SEZ, which assumed the administrative status of a province in 1988, is by a very huge margin the largest special zone in the world. Even Shantou SEZ, the smallest zone in China, is many times larger than those in other developing countries.

Beyond acreage, it is important to note that foreign investors in the special zones of many developing countries are not permitted to sell their products in the domestic markets of the host country. By contrast, in China, many FIEs in the SEZs, availing themselves of the low labor costs (relative to those of their own country) as well as many policy-specific advantages (e.g., low taxes and concessionary tariff rates), are producing goods not just for export but also for China's domestic markets. Because there are many policy-specific advantages that are not available to indigenous firms, FIEs in China in many ways enjoy super-national treatment, the depth of which in aggregate is very significant. For tariffs, for instance, Naughton (1996) reports that imports into China under concessionary terms amounted to 30% of the total imports in 1988; the figure increased to more than 60% by the mid-1990s. Policy-specific advantages exclusively accorded to FIEs have deep implications on the demand side of FDI in China, a topic we will explore in more depth in Chapter 5.

Capital and Profits Repatriation

The freedom to remit profits and dividends and to repatriate capital is a critical element of an attractive climate for foreign investment. One way to measure the liberalization of a host country's FDI regulatory framework is thus to measure the degree of restrictions the host country imposes on profit and capital repatriation by foreign investors. While no country in the world today seems to have adopted outright policies to prohibit the repatriation of profits and capital, many attempt to discourage capital outflows by imposing remittance taxes, and these tax rates vary across countries. Without attempting a comprehensive survey, a few examples for illustrative purposes follow.

In Vietnam, for instance, a progressive rate of 5-10% is imposed on profit remittances, depending on the foreign equity ratio and the size of investment (Wu Yi 1995:21). Brazil uses a more complicated system and imposes more stringent conditions. The remittance of profits and repatriation of capital are subject to authorization by the central bank. In addition, there generally is a levy of a 25% withholding tax on remittances and when remittances exceed an average of 12% a year of registered capital and reinvestment for a period of 3 years, the excess is taxed at a supplementary rate of 40-60% (Rosenn 1991:39; Chitrakar 1994:48). In China, although the general remittance tax is 10% for joint ventures, in the vast regions of China's special investment areas such as the SEZs and ETDZs, the remittance tax is routinely waived. In the case of WFOEs, no tax is levied on profit remittances.

To be sure, while the legal encumbrance on profit remittances in China seems to be minimal, the real impediment, one could argue, lies in the non-convertibility of China's local currency, the renminbi. On that score, presumably the impediment was indeed great in the 1980s, and especially prior to 1986, that is, before China made substantial institutional innovations, such as the swap centers, to ameliorate the problems faced by many FIEs in balancing their FX accounts. But in the 1990s and especially since January 1994 when China decided to do away with its foreign exchange certificates and introduced current account convertibility to FIEs, the impediment has practically become insignificant (Rosen 1998: 67). The capital account, as mentioned in the previous chapter, continues to be restricted, pending further reforms in China's banking industry. Ironically, that restriction probably helped China stave off the contagion of the Asian financial crisis. According to a senior Ministry of Finance official, China originally planned to achieve full foreign exchange convertibility by 2000.[25] In light of the Asian financial crisis, however, the timetable for reaching this objective has apparently been readjusted.

25. Interview.

Performance Requirements and Ownership Controls

Performance requirements refer to stipulations, such as export ratios, technology transfer, and local content, to which foreign investors must agree in order for their investments to be approved by the host government. The imposition of such requirements reflects the host government's belief that without government intervention foreign investors would not automatically further the country's developmental objectives, e.g., to stimulate export-led growth, enhance "industrial deepening," or multiply "backward linkages" in the hope of creating a reasonably vibrant, productive, and, ultimately, competitive indigenous industrial base. From the perspective of foreign investors, however, performance requirements are often seen as barriers to investment, since they are often configured with the different levels of ownership that the host government allows foreign investors.

Restrictions on foreign ownership are not necessarily unique to developing countries. They exist in developed countries as well. In the United States, for instance, a few federally regulated industries, such as domestic air transport, production and utilization of nuclear energy, and domestic maritime transport, are strictly restricted to FDI for national security reasons. In broadcasting and telecommunications, foreign-controlled enterprises may not own more than 20% equity, unless the Federal Communications Commission grants an exception (Wilkins 1989). But generally speaking, foreign ownership controls in developing countries are far more extensive than those in developed countries, and they are often imposed in combination with performance requirements in the form of export ratios and/or technology transfer.

In Indonesia and Singapore, foreign equity shares in retail projects, for instance, are restricted to less than 50%. In South Korea, even though no restrictions are imposed on technology-intensive projects, foreign investors are not allowed to invest more than 50% equity shares in labor-intensive projects. In India, nationalist sentiments have long kept foreign investors from holding majority shares. Although the upper limits of foreign equity ownership have recently increased to 51%, Indian law provides that for foreign citizens to qualify for majority ownership, they must produce goods entirely for export (Chitrakar 1994:53). In Malaysia, foreign equity ownership is pegged to a progressive export ratio. In the case of an export ratio of less than 20%, foreign equity ownership is limited to 30%. If the export ratio reaches 50%; foreign equity ownership is allowed up to 50%. 100% foreign equity ownership is only allowed for those with an export ratio of over 80% (Liu Guoping 1993:23-24). In Thailand, like in India, 100% foreign ownership is allowed only if the firm exports 100% of its products (Steven 1990:282; Chitraker 1994:44).

In China, on the other hand, according to the amended version of the joint venture law of 1990, there are no upper ceilings on foreign equity ownership of joint ventures. Foreign investors can thus own up to 99% equity shares with no statutory obligations to export, even though they may face informal pressure to include export performance targets during the project review and screening process. But since such performance targets for joint ventures are without statutory basis, Rosen reports (1998:65-66) that as a negotiation tactic some joint ventures agreed to soft export targets in order to get "carrots" and to avoid a "stick," thereby accomplishing their negotiating goals with relative ease. In practice, performance requirements are rarely enforced for joint ventures in China.

In the case of 100% foreign equity ownership, China does impose performance requirements as a matter of law. The Detailed Implementation Act of the WFOE Law (Article 3) stipulates that WFOEs must use advanced technology, design new products, produce import-substitutes, *or* export 50% of the output value of their products. But these statutory performance requirements are not imposed vigorously. Field interviews with both Chinese officials in charge of FDI and FIE managers indicate that in practice while higher-level Chinese authorities were serious about imposing performance requirements, local officials often displayed collusive behavior with foreign investors, helping the FIEs within their jurisdictions to circumvent performance requirements.[26]

The reason why they did so is two-fold and straightforward. First, because local officials were often evaluated for promotions by how much FDI they brought to the local economy,[27] quality criteria were

26. Interview.

27. This evaluation criterion has changed since the mid-1990s when a new dual-track tax system was introduced. Under the new system, the tax is divided into central and local portions, similar to the division between the state and federal taxes in the US. Such being the case, higher-level officials care less about the amount of FDI than about the amount of revenue local officials can generate. Interview.

thus frequently circumvented in favor of quantity. Second, because it is difficult to define what exactly constitutes advanced technology, new products, or import-substitutes, export targets can easily be avoided for WFOEs by generously interpreting import substitution, new product design, or high-technology manufacturing. Indeed, the tendency of local officials to undermine the gate-keeping intentions of central authorities prompted many FIE managers to characterize China as being more open to 100% foreign-owned subsidiaries than Japan or South Korea, where central bureaucrats wield more control over local behavior. Supplementing the anecdotal evidence gleaned from interviews,[28] a high and rapidly growing share of WFOEs vis-à-vis FIE joint ventures, i.e., over 24% of all FDI projects in China by the end of 1996, was a good indication of the lax conditions China imposes as performance requirements on 100% foreign-owned subsidiaries.

Tax Relief and Other Incentives

Offering tax breaks and other fiscal incentives is a common practice to which host governments frequently resort to attract new business and industrial investment. This is so even though early studies (Reuber 1973; Lim 1983:207-212; O'Sullivan 1985:28-35; Cable and Persaud 1987) did not conclusively demonstrate the efficacy of the incentive package as the FDI locational determinant. Reuber (1973:129), for instance, noted in his survey study: "It is evident that incentives are of some importance. On the other hand, most firms are acutely aware of the difficulties posed by such incentives and frequently assert that they are reluctant to undertake projects that are heavily dependent for their success upon the incentives provided by the host country."

More recently, however, with sophisticated research designs, empirical studies (Wells 1986; Hines 1996) show that locational grants, tax holidays, and reduced tax rates do, in short, play a role in multinational corporate choice among locations for investment. A detailed Harvard Business School case study (Harvard Business School

---

28. In a recent study based on extensive interview information, Rosen (1998:216) concludes that "China's technology regimes are not always strictly enforced. Generally, technology transfer obligations are negotiable."

1993) finds that General Motors used locational incentives and subsidies as a tiebreaker in choosing alternative sites in Europe. Not surprisingly then, one observes that beginning in the early 1980s there was a rapid expansion in the use of fiscal incentives and subsidies in both developed and developing countries. This trend has escalated since then (OECD 1992, 1996; UNCTAD 1999).

In the United States, for instance, between 1977 and 1984, the number of states offering corporate tax exemptions to investors increased from 21 to 28. The number of states offering incentives for establishing plants in areas of high unemployment grew from 17 to 24, and the number of states offering state financing aid for expansion of existing plants grew from 29 to 37. All in all, various incentive programs amounted to more than US$20 billion annually (Council of State Governments 1989; Schweke, Risk, and Dabson 1994).

Similar trends of attracting business by offering tax and other fiscal incentives were observed in Europe. In a survey of nine regional incentive programs in Europe in 1981, Yuill and Allen (1981) found that all countries included in the survey provided capital grants and interest-rate subsidies, four provided tax concessions, and four provided labor-related subsidies. The largest grants amounted to 60% of the cost of the project. Moreover, over time the focus of these incentive programs shifted from a predominant concern with keeping firms and jobs to attracting new business, in particular foreign investment. This is evidenced by recent surveys, showing that 86% of all domestic support programs are available to foreign investors willing to establish domestic affiliates (Moran 1998:96).

The escalation of locational subsidies in the developed countries over the past two decades has presumably left the developing countries at a further disadvantage to attract FDI. Under competitive pressure, many developing countries in their pursuit of foreign investment have to hold out an impressive array of locational grants, subsidies, tax breaks, and other incentives to foreign investors. They have to do so in spite of their meager financial resources. To understand the forces that drive such world-wide phenomena of bidding for investment, one easy way is to draw upon the logic of the "prisoner's dilemma" game: In this game the "prisoner" is the host country. Absent central coordination, host countries have to engage in competitive bidding, since in isolation any single country would easily be out-advantaged by not bidding. This is so even though competitive bidding would eventually arrive at a

Pareto inferior solution, a condition that would leave all host countries worse off than if no bidding had occurred.[29]

Thus, according to the United Nations Center on Transnational Corporations (UNCTC 1991:6; 1985:22), many developing countries seem to have been inextricably locked into a spiral of expanding tax and other fiscal incentives to foreign investors. In 1977-87, concessionary tax rates and other fiscal incentives were in fact the most frequent policy announcements by host governments in their attempt to promote foreign investment. Concurrent interviews with host government officials demonstrated that they had considerable knowledge of investment inducement packages offered elsewhere, and they believed that they could not reduce their packages to attract foreign firms without losing substantial FDI (Guisinger 1985; 1989).

Table II-4: Investment-Related Regulatory Changes around the World

	1991	1992	1993	1994	1995	1996	1997	1998
# of countries that introduced investment regulatory changes	35	43	57	49	64	65	76	60
# of regulatory changes	82	79	102	110	112	114	151	145
of which:								
More favorable to FDI[a]	80	79	101	108	106	98	135	136
Less favorable to FDI[b]	2	-	1	2	6	16	16	9

Source: UNCTAD, (1999), *World Investment Report 1999: Foreign Direct Investment and the Challenge of Development,* Table IV. 1, p. 115.
a: including liberalizing changes or changes aimed at strengthening market functioning, as well as increased incentives.
b: including changes aimed at increasing control as well as reducing incentives.

The *World Investment Report* 1999 reported that the trends toward the liberalization of regulatory regimes for FDI, including promotional measures of low tax rates and other fiscal incentives, continued in the 1990s. Out of 145 regulatory changes relating to FDI made in 1998 by 60 countries, 136, or 94%, were in the direction of creating more

29. The competitive bidding in our case is in the form of offering tax concessions or fiscal subsidies. Apparently it has normative implications on the overall welfare of the host countries. But this is beyond the scope of the current study.

favorable conditions for FDI. This is largely the pattern throughout the 1990s (Table II-4).

Table II-5: Preferential Tax Treatment of Selected Countries

Country	Tax rate	Tax exemption and reduction
China	15-30% depending on industry and geographical location	Exemption for first 2 profit-making years; 50% reduction for another 3 years. Additional 10 years of 15-30% tax reduction for those located in economically backward areas, or engaged in agriculture, forestry, or animal husbandry
Brazil	48%	10 year exemption only for those located in economically backward areas
India	progressive rate of 30-40%	5 year exemption possible for that portion of profits that is no more than 7.5% of investment capital
Malaysia	40%	2-5 year exemption
Philippines	35%	n/a
Singapore	40%	5 year exemption; 50% reduction for another 3 years
South Korea	25-40% depending on industry	5 year exemption; 50% reduction for another 3 years
Taiwan	22-35% depending on industry	5 year exemption
Thailand	35-40%	3-8 year exemption
Vietnam	15-25% depending on industry	Exemption for first 2 profit-making years; 50% reduction for another 2 years

Sources: *Guoji shichang* [International Market] no. 9, 1989; SGV & Co. (1982), *Doing Business in the Philippines*; *Economic Bulletin for Asia and Pacific*, vol. 27, no. 2; Hang Thi-Thu Le, (1993), "Foreign Investment Policies in Vietnam and Thailand." Arif Hava Oegroseno, (1992), "Foreign Investment Inflows in Indonesia Compared to Malaysia and Thailand." Deok Il Seo, (1991) "Foreign Investment Policy in Korea." Keith Rosennv (1991), *Foreign Investment in Brazil.* Wu Yi, ed., (1995 b,c), *Trade and Investment Guide: Latin America/India.*

In this respect, China is no exception. Table II-5 contains an illustrative and comparative picture of concessionary tax terms to foreign investors offered by China, Brazil, India, Malaysia, the Philippines, Singapore, South Korea, Taiwan, Thailand, and Vietnam.

As the table indicates, China's outlays of tax concessions seem more generous than the other countries included in the comparison.

But the true picture of China's concessionary tax terms and other fiscal incentives is more than Table II-5 conveys. In China, although the general national enterprise income tax rate for FIEs is 30%, in its vast special investment areas, such as the SEZs and coastal open cities where the bulk of FDI in China concentrates, the enterprise income tax for FIEs is 15-24%. This compares favorably with other countries. With respect to tax exemptions and reductions, although at first glance China seems to offer fewer tax holidays than many countries included in our comparison, in reality the length of the tax holidays for FIEs in China also compares favorably with that of other countries.

The reason is that unlike other countries where the number of tax holidays begins to tick off once the project is put into operation, in China tax holidays are not counted until after an FIE begins to reap profits. A sweeter deal still, China also allows loss carryovers. Specifically, net losses incurred by FIEs may be carried forward for a period up to five years (Wang Chunping 1996:111). Consequently, as Xin Ming (1995:26) noted, there can be a considerable number of years, especially in long-term investment projects, before tax holidays even begin to be counted.

It is also important to note that in countries such as Brazil, India, Malaysia, Singapore, South Korea, Taiwan, and Thailand, preferential fiscal treatment granted to foreign investment is also given to domestic investors.[30] Indeed, in some cases – Brazil and India in particular – preferential policies on the whole are biased in favor of domestic firms more than foreign investors. In China, by contrast, because of the transitional nature of its economy, FIEs enjoy a wide range of incentives and privileges, many of which are off-limits to domestic firms. These include preferential tax treatments, import and export rights, access to foreign exchange, expensive duty-free imports, and managerial autonomy. This was especially true before 1994 – the year when China finally decided to lower the tax rate for domestic firms from the previous 55% to 33%, which still is the maximum tax rate for FIEs. These policy-specific advantages enjoyed exclusively by FIEs, as we will elaborate upon further in Part III, give rise to what I call

30. For Brazil, see Rosenn (1991); for India, see *Financial Times*, 2, 27, 28 and 30 July 1991.

"abnormally high demand" for FDI in China. This in turn helps to shed light on the huge flows of FDI to China in the early 1990s.

Finally, to evaluate the efficacy of tax incentives on foreign investment, we need to look into another international dimension, i.e., bilateral tax treaties aimed at avoiding double taxation between FDI home and host countries. For without these treaties, FIEs would face the prospect of double taxation, which, in turn, would likely affect their investment decisions. Even with the treaties, some investors might still be prevented from enjoying some, or even all, of the benefits of the tax concessions offered by the host country, depending on which one of the following two tax models is employed by the home country.

There are two basic models to avoid double taxation according to the Model Income Tax Treaties of the OECD and the United Nations: the exemption model or the credit model.[31] The exemption model is a straightforward system. Under this model, the home country, either by domestic legislation or by bilateral agreement, simply exempts taxation on incomes generated by an FIE in the host country, although the degree of exemption may vary from country to country. Countries that employ this system include many European countries such as France, Holland, and Germany (Liu Changgen 1996:206).

The credit model, on the other hand, is a more complex system. Under this model, the home country gives a credit for whatever income tax an FIE has paid to the host country. Complications arise, however, under this system, if and when the home country allows only taxes *actually* paid to the host country to be credited. In such a case, even if tax concessions are available in the host country, the investor does not benefit from them, because the taxes thus "spared" in the host countries still have to be paid by the investor, but, this time, to the treasury of his home country.

The way for the host country to avoid such a diminishing effect is to write into its treaties a "tax-sparing" provision which allows taxes "spared" by the host country to be credited by the home country. China has successfully negotiated into all of its bilateral tax treaties a "tax-sparing" provision, save that with the United States. Countries with which China has tax treaties are listed in Table II-6. As a policy, the US has uniformly refused to include a "tax-sparing" provision in its tax treaties with any country, on the grounds that it violates the principle of

31. Van Read (1990).

capital export neutrality since it would favor foreign investment over domestic investment. Such being the case, US affiliates do not benefit from the tax concessions offered by China, and indeed, by any country, in the form of exemptions, reductions, and/or refunds.

Table II-6: Double Tax Treaties

Armenia	France	Macedonia	Slovenia
Australia	Germany	Malaysia	Spain
Austria	Hong Kong SAR	Malta	Sudan
Bangladesh	Hungary	Mauritius	Sweden
Belarus	Iceland	Mongolia	Switzerland
Belgium	India	Netherlands	Thailand
Brazil	Israel	New Zealand	Turkey
Bulgaria	Italy	Norway	Ukraine
Canada	Jamaica	Pakistan	United Arab Emirates
Croatia	Japan	Papua New Guinea	United Kingdom
Cyprus	Korea	Poland	United States
Czech Republic	Kuwait	Romania	Uzbekistan
Denmark	Latvia	Russia	Vietnam
Egypt	Lithuania	Singapore	White Russia
Finland	Luxembourg	Slovakia	Yugoslavia

The WTO Bid

The key multilateral economic institutions that constitute the global economic regime include the World Bank, and International Monetary Fund (IMF), and the General Agreement on Tariffs and Trade (GATT) and its successor, the World Trade Organization. The latest example of China's willingness for greater integration into the global economic regime is perhaps best illustrated by the agreement on November 15, 1999 with the US on China's terms for accession to the WTO. The agreement has been a full 13 years in the making.[32] It demonstrates China's increasing readiness to play by the "rules of the game" of international standards.

The agreement called for China to open up further a wide range of markets to foreign participation, including politically sensitive

32. In July 1986 China applied to the GATT to resume its status as an original contracting party. For more discussions on China's efforts in this regard, see Jacobson and Oksenberg (1990).

industries, such as banking, insurance, telecommunications, and the Internet. In return, the US must grant China the status of normal trade relations (NTR) on a permanent basis, which would guarantee Chinese goods the same low-tariff access to US markets as products from nearly every other nation. This is to conform to the most-favored nation treatment, one of the cornerstones of the WTO, which now has 135 members. Although China must still conclude bilateral agreements with the European Union (EU), among others, before entering the WTO, full accession has been widely predicted in 2000.

The final details of China's WTO accession package will not be known until agreement has been reached with all members of the Working Party, and approved by the members of the WTO. However, it seems likely that the November 1999 offers to the US will form the basis for the final agreement. (Partial details of the market opening measures of this agreement are in Appendix II).

A critical concession China has made is the opening of its agricultural markets. Although technically separate from the November deal, China has agreed to lift the ban on Northwest wheat, along with citrus, beef and poultry from other parts of the US, and to reduce tariffs to an average of 14.5-15%. In that range, because China's agricultural prices are much higher than international levels for many non-labor intensive products, there will be significant surges in foreign imports to China such as corn, cotton, citrus, soybeans, wheat, etc., all big-ticket items in the US.

In financial sectors, China's current geographic restrictions on foreign banking activity to a few select cities will be eliminated within 5 years of accession. Foreign banks will be allowed to offer services in local currency to Chinese firms within 2 years of accession, and to Chinese households within 5 years. In the insurance industry, similar geographic limits will be dropped within 3 years. Foreign firms can own up to 50% equity in life insurance and 51% in non-life insurance immediately upon accession. Two years afterwards, 100% foreign-owned subsidiaries in non-life insurance will be allowed. Group, health and pension insurance will be opened to foreign insurers within 5 years. Securities, like insurance, are another infant industry in China. But they, too, will be opened to foreign competition, pursuant to the WTO's Financial Services Agreement (FSA). Specifically, a 33% stake will be allowed to foreign firms in securities fund management ventures immediately upon accession, rising up to 49% within 3 years.

In telecommunications, once within the orbit of the WTO's Basic Telecoms Agreement (BTA), current state monopolies in this industry will wane. Foreign phone companies, now restricted to equipment sales, will be able to own up to 33% of equity share in basic telecom services and 49% in valued-added businesses upon China's accession. The proportion will rise to 50% in 2 years. Similarly, all aspects of the Internet, including both Internet Service Providers (ISP) and Internet Content Providers (ICP) are to be liberalized for foreign investment at the same rate as other telecom services.

WTO membership will commit China to a fixed-date schedule over a 6-year period for abolishing quotas, slashing tariffs, discarding restrictions and a host of other barriers. China has agreed to phase out most non-tariff barriers (NTB), such as quotas and subsidies by 2002. Average industrial tariffs, standing at 24.6% in 1997, are scheduled to fall to 9.4% in 2005. For cars, the rates will go down from the current 100-80% to 25% by July 2006. Tariffs on information technology (IT) equipment, which average 13.3% at present, will be eliminated by 2005. In addition, within 3 years of accession, foreign investors will enjoy import rights, distribution rights, service rights, and the freedom to conduct a host of auxiliary activities key to a modern enterprise. Currently, save for the goods that they produce by themselves in China, foreign firms have to operate through Chinese state-controlled intermediaries.

Moreover, for foreign investors averse to forced technology transfers and weak protection of intellectual property rights, the prospects also bode well. WTO membership will require China to further strengthen its IPR protection regime, as mandated by the rules of the Trade-Related Intellectual Property Rights (TRIPS), the most comprehensive and stringent multilateral IPR protection agreement. Forced technology transfers, along with local content requirements and foreign exchange balancing restrictions, will also have to be removed under the rules of the Trade-Related Investment Measures (TRIMS).

In short, it seems safe to say that, regardless of the final details of China's accession to the WTO, China has obliged itself to working toward a more transparent and consistent system of rules and regulations regarding foreign trade and investment.

Concluding Remarks

In this chapter we have reviewed some international dimensions of China's FDI regulatory framework. We started with a puzzle posed by the apparent power asymmetry between a sovereign state and a private foreign investor, i.e., why should a foreign private investor trust a foreign sovereign state that it will honor commitments when in theory it is not answerable to him?

We found that to boost the confidence of foreign investors, China has undeniably limited its sovereign discretion by entering into a network of international guarantees, so that the cost for China will be higher should it choose to renege on its international commitments. Such restraint mechanisms are exemplified by the principle of subrogation, whereby a foreign government or an international organization can acquire the rights of the aggrieved private investor, thus turning a dispute between a private investor and a sovereign state into a government-to-government dispute.

To further inspire foreign confidence, China has also allowed foreign nationals to sit on its arbitration tribunals. About one-third of the arbitors of the CIETAC, which handles most of the arbitration cases in China, are non-PRC citizens. Such moves invoke the image of the far-sighted Ulysses who ties himself to the mast in order to elude the siren's call, symbolizing the rule of law and delegation of power (Elster 1979). The idea, in the parlance of international relations theory, is to demonstrate one's seriousness of honoring commitments by showing that one has bound his own hands (and indeed the hands of his successors as well) to enforce one's promises (Schelling 1966).

Investment inducement, ownership control, and performance requirements – all important topics in assessing investment conditions in host countries today – are also addressed in this chapter. Our examination suggests that in all these areas, China's current FDI regulatory framework is quite liberal in an international perspective. In fact, China imposes no explicit statutory performance requirements for joint ventures. Mandatory requirements, in the form of technology transfer or export ratios, are germane only to 100% foreign-owned subsidiaries. But even in that area, we found that in practice performance requirements are less onerous than generally thought.

For instance, export ratios can be relaxed or altogether avoided by generously interpreting the exemptions for FIEs engaged in import substitution. As Rosen reports in a recent study based on interviews (1998:66), the WFOE law provides ample latitude for such an interpretation, and only one other ingredient is needed: sympathetic local authorities hungry for FDI and willing to cooperate. If we look ahead, China's accession to the WTO will not only mean a wider range of markets to foreign participation. It also will mean that foreign investors will be given national treatment, and that local content requirements, technology transfer requirements, and foreign exchange balancing requirements will be history soon.

Finally, around the world, the past two decades have witnessed many countries, including developed economies, engaged in a competitive bidding war in terms of offering a plethora of fiscal and regulatory incentives to induce FDI. In this respect, China's outlays of investment incentives are comparable, if not more generous.[33] To make sure that fiscal incentives accrue to individual foreign investors and not merely to the coffers of foreign governments, China has successfully negotiated into all of its double tax treaties (except the one with the US) a "tax sparing" provision to avoid diluting the effects of fiscal incentives. Particularly important for us to note is the fact that due to the transitional nature of the Chinese economy, in many areas China has offered considerable fiscal, monetary, and operational incentives to FIEs but not to indigenous firms. This is an institutional aspect unique to China, which has implications on the demand side of FDI in China, a topic we will explore in more depth in Chapter 5 of this study.

33. Indeed, some have argued that the Chinese tax regime is more liberal than many other FDI host countries, and this has led to high levels of FDI flows to China. See Dean (1988).

Appendix II: Partial Details of China's Market Opening Measures under the WTO

Sector	Timetable
Banking	
-- Geographic restrictions to be eliminated	Within 5 years of accession
-- Local currency business with Chinese companies to be allowed	Within 2 years of accession
-- Local currency business with Chinese individuals to be allowed	Within 5 years of accession
Insurance	
-- Geographic limitations to be eliminated	Within 3 years of accession
-- Group, health, and pension insurance to be opened to foreign insurers	Within 5 years of accession
-- Life insurance to be opened to 50% of foreign equity share	Upon accession
-- Non-life insurance to be opened to foreign insurance branches, majority-held, and eventually wholly-owned operations	Branching and 51% foreign ownership permitted upon accession; wholly-owned subsidiaries within 2 years
-- Reinsurance to be fully opened to foreign insurers	Upon accession
Telecommunications	
Foreign investment in telecommunications networks to be allowed	49% foreign ownership in all services, including the Internet sector, upon accession; 50% foreign ownership in value-added paging services within 2 years of accession; 50% foreign ownership in mobile telecoms within 5 years; 49% foreign ownership of international and domestic services within 6 years

Source: The White House Office of Public Liaison, Posted on the US-China Business Council's website: <www.uschina.org/public/99115a.html>.

Part II:

Investments

CHAPTER 3

Principal Modes of FDI in China

The principal objectives of the next two chapters that make up Part II of this study are to document, examine, and analyze the overall trends and patterns of FDI in China. By trends I mean the year-by-year upward (or downward) flows of FDI into China during the reform years. By patterns I refer to the source, sectoral composition, geographical distribution, and ownership structure of FDI. To document the overall trends and patterns of FDI is a critical precondition for our systematic assessment of institutional effects on investment behavior. To have some sense of the parameters of an overall picture of FDI in China on both a stock and flow basis would serve us well in interpreting the results of our regression analyses of the institutional effects on investment – an integral part of our investigation to be carried out later in this study.

In this chapter, we set out to accomplish the tasks outlined here by first examining the different modes of FDI in China, e.g., WFOEs, EJVs, and CJVs. In doing so, our aim is to arrive at a better appreciation of the different risk (or benefit) implications of different modes of investment from the standpoint of foreign investors. Moreover, to the extent that the evolution of China's FDI regulatory framework has a different trajectory for different modes of FDI, as documented in Chapter 1, an understanding of the intricate legal and regulatory requirements of different investment modalities becomes a prerequisite for analyzing institutional effects on investment behavior. We begin this chapter by defining foreign direct investment according to commonly accepted international standards.

Defining Foreign Direct Investment

Foreign direct investment is a particular type of foreign capital. As such it does not include loan capital provided by international organizations, foreign governments, or private commercial banks. Nor does it automatically include portfolio investment such as bonds and stocks purchased by foreigners.[1] What makes investment "direct" as opposed to other forms of foreign capital is the concept of managerial control over an enterprise in which foreign capital participates. As Charles Kindleberger (1969) pointed out, foreign *direct* investment is essentially about *transfer of control* rather than movement of capital per se [emphasis added]. In a similar vein, the International Monetary Fund defines FDI as "investment that is made to acquire a lasting interest in an enterprise operating in an economy other than that of the investor, the investor's purpose being to have an effective voice in the management of the enterprise"(IMF 1977).

As we can see, while the first part of the above definition establishes "foreign" as opposed to "domestic" investment, the second part says what constitutes "direct" as opposed to "indirect" foreign investment. It underscores the key ingredient of managerial controls.

Consistent with the IMF definition, the US Department of Commerce, for instance, defines foreign investment as "direct" when a

---

1. Stock markets in China, as an alternative way to attract foreign investment, are a phenomenon of more recent vintage, and are beyond the scope of the current study. Suffice it here to note that in the early 1990s, China started institutional building on that front by setting up two separate stock markets, the so-called A-share and B-share markets. Whereas A-shares are sold and traded exclusively to Chinese citizens, B-shares, which are listed in the Shanghai and Shenzhen Stock Markets, are available to foreigners. The idea of devising this bifurcated system was to insulate the nascent A-share market from international market volatility, given that the relatively small volume and size of the Chinese market would be easily subject to manipulations by large international funds. Later, shares available to foreigners were also expanded to include H-shares and S-shares (also known as "red chips") issued by Chinese state-run enterprises and sold on the Hong Kong and Singapore Stock Markets, and N shares (also known as American Depository Receipts [ADRs]) listed in New York. Normally, foreign investors eager to invest in China have found H-shares or N-shares more attractive vehicles than B-shares which are listed in the Shanghai and Shenzhen markets. In Shanghai and Shenzhen markets, accounting and regulatory standards are believed to fall short of international standards and there is less liquidity, especially before 1994, because Chinese currency is not yet totally convertible. Generally speaking, it is much easier for foreign currency to enter than to exit China, given China's current foreign exchange control regime.

foreign investor has acquired an equity share of 10% or more in a domestic enterprise (Graham and Krugman 1991:9). As can be imagined, a "portfolio investment" through stock markets can become "direct investment" when its magnitude passes an artificially-set threshold of equity ownership ratio. In the US, that trigger is set at 10%. Although the threshold criteria are a matter of judgment and they vary somewhat from country to country,[2] they nevertheless underscore the idea that the foreign investor must have a sufficiently large share of equity so that s/he will have a considerable degree of influence. Or, in the words of the IMF, an investor must have "an effective voice" in the management of the enterprise in which his/her capital participates.

For supplemental funds, sophisticated technology, managerial expertise, and/or critical know-how, most countries in the world permit several different forms of foreign capital participation in domestic enterprises. While some of these activities are thought of as FDI, others are not. In China, Chinese official statistics indicate that FDI is more broadly delineated than in commonly accepted standards. According to Chinese official publications, seven different modes of foreign capital participation are subsumed under the rubric of FDI. They include not only equity joint ventures, contractual joint ventures, wholly foreign-owned enterprises, and joint development projects (JDP). They also embrace compensation trade (CT), processing and assembly (PA), and international leasing (IL) (Liu Xiangdong 1993:338).

While the former categories (i.e., EJV, CJV, WFOE, and JDP) are more or less FDI in the normal international usage of the term, the latter ones (CT and PA) are not necessarily so. The reason is that, as we elaborate later in this chapter, CT, PA, or IL involve very little in terms of managerial control by foreign investors. As such, they are often recognized outside of China merely as different forms of trade. CT, for example, has been widely used in developing countries as a means to save scarce foreign exchange when trading with developed countries, but is not usually regarded as *direct* foreign investment.

The present study, to be consistent with the normal international definition of FDI, will focus primarily on EJV, CJV, and WFOE. Taken together, these modes of investment are commonly referred to in Chinese publications as "*sanzi*" or "three kinds of capital," enterprises.

---

2. In Canada and other countries, the rate is higher than 10%, generally from 14-21%. See Rugman (1985:9).

Notwithstanding such a focus, it would be worth our while also to briefly discuss other forms of investment activities in China as well, not only because when we turn to Chinese official FDI statistics we can interpret them more precisely. More importantly, for our purposes, a discussion of these other forms of investment will shed additional light on institutional effects on investment behavior.

Equity Joint Ventures

Equity joint ventures are arguably the most important mode of FDI in China. As a share of all modes of FDI on a stock basis, they are the largest foreign investment so far. In the initial years of the open door in particular, China considered EJVs to be the preferred mode of FDI, believing that they would not only be most effective in bringing foreign capital, technology, and managerial skills, but they would also allow a considerable degree of control over domestic enterprises (Pearson 1991:80). Reflecting the importance that China attaches to EJV mode of investment, the promulgation of the law to govern EJVs predated all other modes of foreign investment. The legal framework for EJVs is based primarily on the Law of the PRC on Joint Ventures Using Chinese and Foreign Investment promulgated in July 1979 (revised in 1990), and its Detailed Implementation Act promulgated in September 1983.

Under the current Chinese legal framework, an EJV is defined as a limited liability company incorporated and registered in China with capital contributions from both Chinese and foreign parties. It is treated as a distinct *Chinese* legal person subject in all aspects to Chinese laws and administrative procedures, unless domestic legal provisions contravene the international treaties that China has signed. The 1991 revision of China's Civil Procedure Law (Part 4) provides that if domestic law contravenes international obligations, the treaty provisions shall override domestic provisions, except to the extent that such treaties contain provisions to which China has made reservations.

According to the General Principles of China's Civil Law of 1986 (Article 37), to be qualified as a distinct legal person, several conditions must be met. First, the business entity must be established through due legal procedures. Second, it must possess property or funds separate from the state. Third, it must have its own name, organizational structure, and premises. Finally, it must have the ability to bear civil liability independently.

Table III-1: EJV Capitalization Requirements in China (US$)

TOTAL INVESTMENT	MINIMUM REGISTERED CAPITAL
-- Up to 3 million	70% of total investment
-- More than 3 million and up to 10 million	50% of total investment
-- More than 3 but less than 4.2 million	2.1 million
-- More than 10 million and up to 30 million	40% of total investment
-- More than 10 million but less than 12.5 million	5 million
-- More than 30 million	1/3 of total investment
-- More than 30 but less than 36 million	12 million
TOTAL REGISTERED CAPITAL	**MANDATORY PAYMENT SCHEDULES**
-- If paid in lump sum	Within 6 months of issue of business license
-- If paid in installments	1st installment of no less than 15% in 3 months
-- 500,000 or under	Within 1 year
-- 500,000 to 1 million	Within 1.5 years
-- 1 to 3 million	Within 2 years
-- 3 to 10 million	Within 3 years
-- More than 10 million	Subject to approval authority

Source: Provisional Regulations Regarding the Ratios of Registered Capital to Total Investment in Chinese-Foreign Equity Joint Ventures (issued by SAIC in 1987).

An EJV, by definition, is formed by the injection of capital contributions by both Chinese and foreign partners. All parties to the venture share profits and losses in proportion to their equity contributions. The *total equity* of the venture is expressed as the total *registered capital.* The *concept of registered capital* refers to the amount of capital subscribed by all the parties to the venture and registered with the State Administration of Industry and Commerce (SAIC) at the time when the venture is formally established. This is to be distinguished from the *concept of total investment*, which includes not only the total registered capital but also *external borrowings.* Under current Chinese law, capitalization requirements for an EJV, or the legal debt-equity ratios, depend on the size of the total investment. The same is true of the mandatory capital payment schedules. The specifics of these requirements are contained in Table III-1.

To establish an EJV, equity contributions may come in the form of cash, machinery, buildings, intellectual property, critical managerial know-how, and other types of transferable proprietary interests. In practice, the foreign party usually contributes cash (in hard currency), advanced technology, and managerial know-how. Note, however, according to China's Company Law of 1993, the value of the technology component cannot exceed 20% of the registered capital of a limited liability company, including EJVs, unless an EJV is qualified as a TAE, or technologically advanced enterprise, under the "22 Articles," discussed in Chapter 1. The Chinese party usually provides cash (in local currency), land-use rights,[3] factory buildings, and facilities. While the EJV Law sets a minimal foreign equity contribution of 25%, there is no upper limit. The foreign party can thus contribute up to 100%, in which case an EJV becomes a wholly foreign-owned enterprise, which in turn is governed by a separate set of laws.

Note that in China the 25% minimal foreign equity threshold is higher than, say, that of the US, which is 10%. The ostensible purpose, from the standpoint of the Chinese government, is to preclude "fake" FDI from enjoying the preferential treatment given exclusively to FIEs. However, from the point of view of foreign investors, a 25% equity stake in a joint venture in China may not necessarily guarantee having an "effective voice in the management of the enterprise." The reason is that, as Huang (1999:2) has observed, most Chinese joint venture partners are state-owned enterprises (SOE) whose shares are not traded in open markets and thus have a high level of concentration.

An EJV is required to establish a board of directors. The board composition is usually determined with reference to the ratio of the equity contributions. Before 1990, however, foreigners were legally barred from holding the position of chairman. With the 1990 amendments to the 1979 EJV Law, the current law has lifted this

---

3. The Chinese party can only contribute "purchased," but not "allocated," land-use rights. In other words, it must first convert the allocated land-use rights through payment of a land use fee to the authorized land administration department.

prohibition. Now the chairman of board, or the general manager and deputy general managers, may be either Chinese or foreign. In practice, if the chairman is a foreigner, the deputy chairman is usually a Chinese, or vice versa.

Current Chinese law sets no explicit legal restrictions on the duration of an EJV, except in some service industries such as real estate and land development or in projects of natural resource extraction.[4] The exact duration of an EJV is largely a matter of negotiations between the joint venture partners. Once a term expires, it can be extended by agreement of the parties involved. Otherwise, upon expiration, the EJV law requires that the assets of an EJV be liquidated and apportioned among all the parties to the venture according to their respective equity contributions, assuming that the EJV has fulfilled its debt obligations to all third parties in the first place.[5]

Before 1990 an EJV was not legally permitted to contract out operational controls to any third parties. But after 1990 that restriction has been relaxed. According to the Regulations on Contracting for EJV Operations (issued jointly by the MOFTEC and SAIC in 1990), an EJV now can contract out its operational controls to a third party, as long as it satisfies the following conditions. First, the venture must be involved in an industry that is encouraged by the state. Second, the original partners to the venture must have already paid in all equity capital. Third, the venture must have operational or managerial problems. Finally, the third party itself must be a legal person in the same industry as the EJV, and it must have existed for a minimum of three years.

To establish an EJV, generally speaking, the potential partners must first obtain *preliminary approval* from the overseeing authority responsible for the Chinese partner, under the authority of the Ministry of Foreign Trade and Economic Cooperation, or another ministry in charge of the industry in question, or its local subsidiaries. Specifically, this step involves the submission of an *initial project proposal* including a *preliminary feasibility study* and background materials on

---

4. The maximum periods for land lease are 70 years for residential use; 50 years for educational, cultural, and sport facility use; and 40 years for commercial, tourist, and recreational use.

5. According to Article 203 of the PRC Civil Procedure Law, creditors shall enjoy priority rights over the proceeds from secured property.

the foreign partner. After preliminary approval is secured, serious negotiations between the Chinese and foreign parties can proceed. At this stage the parties must prepare a *formal feasibility study* to be circulated to the relevant government departments overseeing the project, such as the Bureaus of City Planning, Environmental Protection, Labor, and Foreign Exchange. If the formal feasibility study passes muster, the parties can then negotiate for a *contract* and *articles of association*, which in turn must be approved by the MOFTEC (or its local subsidiaries) before it issues a *certificate of approval*. With that certificate, the partners can then apply for a *business license* from the State Administration of Industry and Commerce or its local subsidiaries. The license formally establishes the venture and provides it with legal status.[6]

The first EJV in China to receive a business license from the SAIC was the Beijing Air Catering Company (Du Xianzhong 1995:18). Other early high profile FDI projects in the mode of EJV included Beijing Jianguo Hotel (HK), China Schindler Elevator (Switzerland), Beijing Jeep Corporation (US), China Tianjin Otis Elevator (US), Tianjin China Oksuka Pharmaceutical Company (Japan), Shanghai Volkswagen (Germany), Shanghai Yaohua Pilington Glass (UK), Fujian Hitachi Television (Japan), and Tianjin Sino-French Winery, whose brand name is "Dynasty." In 1998 EJV on approval basis covered about 45% of total FDI inflows in China.

Contractual Joint Ventures

Contractual joint ventures are another mode of FDI in China. They appeared at the same time as EJVs, after China's first Joint Venture Law was promulgated in 1979. In fact, CJVs were the dominant mode during the early years. Initially there was no separate law governing this mode of investment. CJVs were dealt with largely by applying the laws and regulations promulgated for EJVs. This was possible, and indeed feasible, primarily because CJVs and EJVs, in spite of their many differences, after all are both *joint* ventures, as opposed to wholly foreign-owned enterprises. So at least ideologically there was no additional hurdle for China to overcome. In April 1988 the CJV Law

6. The discussion here is based on Lee and Ness (1986).

was promulgated. The CJV Law Implementation Act was promulgated in September 1995.

CJVs are less ambitious ventures used mostly for lower value-added export-processing operations. More than anything else, a salient characteristic of this mode of investment is flexibility. First of all, a CJV faces less stringent legal requirements. Unlike an EJV, a CJV does not have to be a distinct Chinese legal person. It is up to the joint venture partners to decide whether the cooperative undertaking should take the form of a separate business entity (a distinct legal person) or should be a loose arrangement such as a strategic partnership, in which case each party maintains its own identity.

The corporate structure of a CJV is also flexible. One option is to establish a board of directors. Another is to form a joint committee made up of representatives of the parties involved. A third way is simply to entrust the daily managerial tasks to a third party. By comparison, before 1990, neither the second nor the third option was available for EJVs. As of 1990, however, the last option has become available to EJVs, but with several qualifications, as we discussed above.

Again relative to an EJV, a joint venture in the mode of CJV enjoys more freedom in terms of financing. Capital contributions to a CJV may come in the form of cash, buildings, facilities, machinery, industrial property rights, or trade-marks. But they may also be in the form of natural resource rights and labor, which is not permitted for an EJV. Further, if investment involves non-cash contributions, the non-cash components do not necessarily have to be factored into the equity equation of a CJV, as is mandatory for an EJV. Consequently, for CJVs there is no accurate equity ratio to be used as a reference for sharing profits. Profit distribution is a matter of negotiation between partners to be finalized in contracts. Further still, there is no minimum foreign equity requirement for a CJV. By contrast, an EJV requires at least 25% foreign equity. Finally, as Table III-1 above shows, there are strict legal requirements of capital payment schedules for an EJV. By contrast, for a joint venture in the mode of a CJV, it is up to the joint venture partners to negotiate such terms in the contracts.

In practice, the Chinese party to a CJV often contributes land-use rights and existing facilities. The foreign party contributes all other necessary components of the joint venture. As Liang Shibin (1993:310) reports, since a profit-sharing scheme does not have to be exactly according to the ratio of capital contributions, in many CJV contracts a *larger* (relative to the equity contribution) share of profits is assigned to the foreign party in the early years of operation to insure a *quicker* return to the foreign party. Such schemes are often aided by accelerated depreciation on fixed assets.[7] On the other hand, to compensate for the delay in sharing its "due" share of profits, the Chinese party is given the total assets without liquidation when a CJV expires. This actually is legally required by the CJV Law.

The flexible features in corporate structure, financing, and profit-sharing schemes of the CJV mode have implications on investment behavior. As can be imagined, if one is to invest at all in an environment where protection of property rights is, or perceived to be, tenuous, the CJV mode of investment would be the logical choice. The reason is straightforward: Short-term behavior would be best accommodated under this mode of investment. Given its flexibility in capitalization (e.g., there is no 25% minimal foreign equity requirement) and profit-sharing (i.e., profit-sharing does not have to be done according to equity contributions), the CJV mode allows the foreign investor to set up a joint venture with a smaller amount of investment for a quicker return and therefore with a smaller risk, relative to an EJV. Further, if the foreign investor, for one reason or another, cannot devote full time to the running of the joint venture but has someone in the host country he can trust, say a friend or relative, the CJV mode again is the logical choice. As we discussed above, a CJV is very flexible in terms of organization, and is legally permitted to entrust management tasks to a third party.

Based on the above discussion of the intricate legal requirements and organizational features of CJVs and EJVs as different modes of FDI, we can generate several hypotheses bearing on the strategic choice of investment vehicles under institutional uncertainties. First, we would expect, *ceteris paribus*, overseas Chinese investors, many of whom are used to family-based corporate structures, are more likely to

---

7. Wear and tear allowances are granted on fixed assets and other capital assets. Generally China allows the straight-line method of depreciation. Minimum depreciation periods for different kinds of fixed assets are specified as follows: 20 years for premises, buildings, and structures; 10 years for trains, ships, machinery, and other production materials; and 5 years for electronic equipment, means of transport other than trains, and ships, appliances, tools, and furniture, etc.

employ the CJV mode, because a CJV, unlike an EJV, has no legal or regulatory hurdles to overcome in transferring the managerial tasks of the joint venture to a third party. In other words, in the CJV mode, if the investor cannot devote full time to the daily running of his business, he can easily entrust the managerial tasks to the hands of his relatives or personal friends.

Second, an EJV has to be a distinct Chinese legal person, whereas a CJV does not. If China's FDI regulatory framework is immature, non-transparent, and unreliable, we would expect, *ceteris paribus*, a larger share of CJV, relative to EJV. The reason is straightforward: Who wants to be a distinct Chinese legal person subject in all aspects to Chinese laws and administrative procedures if the legal framework in China is very unreliable? Conversely, however, if institutional uncertainties in China recede, we would expect a smaller share of CJV, relative to EJV. After all, there is a big disincentive in the CJV mode from the point of view of foreign investors. Recall that the total assets of a CJV are legally required to revert to the Chinese side, lock, stock, and barrel. In short, we would expect that the share of CJV, relative to EJV, and, for that matter, WFOE to be discussed next, is inversely related to the maturity of China's FDI regulatory framework. To the extent that we argue that China's FDI regulatory framework has matured over the reform years, we would expect that the share of CJV, relative to other modes of FDI, to be larger in the initial years of reforms and smaller in the later years. As we will see shortly, these predictions have strong empirical support.

First of all, without a doubt, CJVs are especially popular among overseas Chinese investors, thus validating our first hypothesis. The tourism-related businesses dominated by Hong Kong investors, for instance, often take the CJV format. Wu Chao (1991:112) reports that investment in the CJV mode took as much as 82% of all contracted FDI in 1979-83 in Guangdong and the CJV mode was indeed the choice of investment among overseas Chinese investors. A Guangdong official in charge of foreign investment also confirmed that the daily managerial tasks of joint ventures in the CJV mode were routinely run by relatives and personal friends of overseas Chinese investors.[8]

8. Interview.

Figure III-1: Different Modes of FDI as a Share of the Total by Contract Numbers, 1979-98

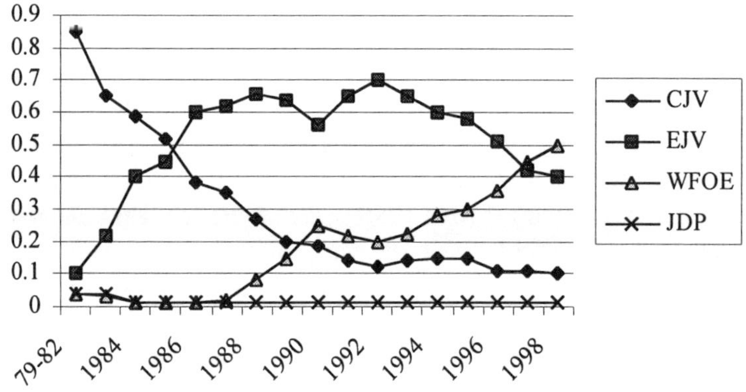

Source: *Zhongguo duiwai jingji nianjian* [China Foreign Economic Statistical Yearbook] (various years); *Zhongguo duiwai maoyi nianjian* [Almanac of China's Foreign Trade and Economic Relations] (various years).

The second hypothesis is also partially borne out by statistical evidence. Figure III-1 contains data on approved FDI project numbers broken down by different modes of investment as a share of total. As the figure shows, the share of CJV, relative to other modes of FDI, declined very steadily and consistently over the years, from over 80% in the early 1980s to only about 10% in the 1990s. This part of the story seems amply clear. What needs to be further introduced is evidence pointing to an improvement in China's FDI regulatory framework over time. Part of that evidence was documented in the previous two chapters of this study. But we will deal with this in a more rigorous and systematic fashion in subsequent chapters. For the time being, let us move on to another mode of investment in China, i.e., 100% foreign-owned subsidiaries.

Wholly Foreign-Owned Enterprises

Although China's first joint venture law specifies a minimum of 25% of foreign equity stake, it sets no upper limits. This implies a theoretical possibility for the setting up of wholly foreign-owned enterprises even at the beginning of China's open-door policy. In reality, however, initially the WFOE mode was not permitted except as policy experiments within the geographical confines of the SEZs, and the extension of this mode to the rest of China occurred only in the mid-1980s. The Chinese legal framework governing the WFOE mode is primarily set forth in the Law of the PRC on Wholly Foreign-Owned Enterprises promulgated in April 1986 and its Detailed Implementation Act enacted in December 1990. Under the framework, a WFOE is treated as a distinct *Chinese* legal person subject in all aspects to Chinese laws and administrative procedures (WFOE Law, Article 8). It is defined as a limited liability company incorporated in China with capital solely contributed by foreign investors. The liability of the firm is limited to the extent of the total registered capital.

Compared to CJVs or EJVs, a crucial advantage of WFOEs has to do with the protection of proprietary assets which in many ways makes multinational corporations (MNCs) competitive in the first place.[9] Another has to do with managerial autonomy, including wage and employment decisions. This is to be contrasted with the management control pitfall that joint ventures have had to face, especially in the 1980s. The widely known story of the Beijing Jeep venture was strewn with contentious wrangling between joint venture partners regarding employment levels and bonus distributions that nearly sank the business (Mann 1989). Even today, because many local partners in JVs are state-owned enterprises, a sector overflowing with redundant workers,[10] many FIE managers interviewed reported that forced overstaffing continued as a major concern for JVs, even though they

---

9. For a theoretical expounding of how proprietary assets, also referred to sometimes as "intangible assets," "firm-specific assets," and "monopolistic advantages," give the MNC a competitive advantage, see Caves (1996:3-5) and Chapter 6 of this study.

10. A World Bank survey of 142 SOEs in 1994, for example, found 60% of the firms had redundant workers, exceeding 10% of their labor force; one-third of the firms reported a labor redundancy exceeding 20%. See World Bank (1994a:19).

also admitted that overall the severity of the problem had been decreasing over time.

But, on the other hand, to set up and run a WFOE, the foreign investor has to face a distinct set of problems not shared by JVs. For one thing, WFOEs face greater sectoral restrictions. In a number of sectors the WFOE mode is either prohibited by the Investment Guideline or automatically requires approval by the central authorities. For another, a WFOE has to satisfy statutory performance requirements: either a high export ratio (greater than 50% annually), or an advantaged level of technology. These requirements are theoretically nonnegotiable, even though, as we noted in the previous chapter, they are not enforced rigorously in practice. In any event, the requirements seem less burdensome than usually assumed, because in many cases the very reason that the WFOE mode is chosen is because the investor has advanced technology and/or international market outlets that he does not want to share through a JV.

Finally, a crucial disadvantage that a WFOE faces is the absence of the benefits that a local partner can provide to a JV in at least two respects. First, the foreign investor is unable to count on an experienced local partner to get local market intelligence, deal with local public relations, and/or work on the bureaucracy, thus increasing information and transaction costs.[11] Second, the foreign investor has to make all the lumpy site-specific investments (such as land and buildings), some of which can otherwise be provided by a local partner, and will therefore expose himself to greater risks under institutional uncertainty. As Williamson (1985) has cautioned, fixed and site-specific investments, unlike mobile general investments which can remain close to the same value in alternative uses, often have a salvage value significantly below their value at the site. In plain language, you can't take your wares and leave, without suffering great losses.

Based on the above discussion of the inherent features of the WFOE mode, we can generate the following hypotheses. If an investment environment is opaque and unreliable, and capricious, we

11. Quite a number of FIE managers whom I interviewed identified the need for reliable information and good public relations work as a crucial reason why partnering with a favored Chinese entity is very important in China. They also noted, however, that as more consulting firms and public relations firms have begun to emerge in China in recent years, the need for a "permanent partner," i.e., a JV partner, has become less crucial.

would expect that the foreign investor would be less likely to choose the WFOE mode of investment, relative to JV formats, because in JV formats, the foreign investor has the additional wherewithal – land, buildings, and information provided by the local partner – to hedge against risks associated with institutional uncertainty. Conversely, if institutional uncertainty recedes, such that property rights are sufficiently protected and information becomes transparent and reliable, we would expect that more foreign investors choose the WFOE mode, relative to the JV formats. Do these hypotheses have empirical support?

The answer is positive. Again, as Figure III-1 shows, after a very tentative appearance in the first part of the 1980s, the share of the WFOE mode, relative to other modes of FDI, began to rise after 1986, the year the WFOE Law was promulgated. Surpassing that of CJVs in 1990, the share of WFOEs continued to grow in importance in the 1990s, and has been rapidly closing the gap with that of EJVs, thanks at least in part to the improving institutional framework in China regarding FDI. Recall from the previous chapters that by the early 1990s China's FDI regulatory framework had been both improved and liberalized considerably. Specific to 100% foreign-owned subsidiaries, the Detailed Implementation Act of the WFOE Law and the Unified Tax Law, which treats WFOEs equally as other modes of investment for tax purposes, were both put in place in the early 1990s.

Joint Development Projects

Joint development projects refer to a particular type of cooperative efforts between Chinese and foreign parties to explore and develop natural resources such as mineral, gas, and, most noticeably, offshore oil. To help meet a growing energy demand as China launched its ambitious modernization program at the end of the 1970s,[12] China early on established a separate regulatory framework governing JDPs, the

---

12. Chinese planners were well aware that bottlenecks in the energy sector had slowed down the overall industrial growth potentials of the country. According to the State Planning Commission, the industrial output lost in a recent (unspecified) year owing to idle capacity due to energy shortages was more than RMB70 billion. This represented about 12% of total industrial output at the time. See Li Guang'an and Wei Liqun (1982:10).

principal elements of which were set forth in the 1982 Regulations of the PRC on the Exploitation of Offshore Petroleum Resources in Cooperation with Foreign Enterprises. In 1993, China also promulgated the Regulations of the PRC on Chinese-Foreign Cooperation in the Development of Continental Petroleum Resources, thus completing the circle with respect to rules governing natural resource extraction projects, both offshore and onshore.

Under the Chinese regulatory framework, a JDP proceeds in two stages. During the first stage, the foreign party normally enters into a JDP through a competitive bidding process, and is solely responsible for all of the risks involved in the initial stage of geophysical surveying and exploration. During the second stage, i.e., after resources are found to be profitably extractable and marketable, both the Chinese and foreign parties mutually assume risks and profits according to a negotiated formula which often takes into account the initial exploration costs, development expenses, and allocable profits. The Chinese equity position in a JDP in the second stage is usually 51%, and a JDP contract frequently lasts for 20 years, with 5 years for the first stage and 15 years for the second stage.

In several aspects, a JDP is similar to the CJV mode. First, like a CJV, a JDP is often structured in ways akin to a strategic partnership where each party maintains its own identity. As such, the cooperative undertaking does not necessarily constitute a distinct Chinese legal person. Second, similar to a CJV, profit-sharing between/among parties to a JDP does not necessarily follow equity ratios. It is effectuated essentially according to whatever is spelled out in the JDP contract. Third, in a JDP, "profits" are usually distributed in the form of specified shares of the physical output of the venture, which again is not unusual for a CJV. Typically, in offshore oil projects for instance, while the Chinese party may use its share of oil for domestic purposes, the foreign party may sell its share on international markets.

But the similarities with the CJV mode stop here. JDPs have fundamentally different characteristics from other modes of FDI. Basically they are projects where the host country yields part of its sovereign possessions over natural resources in exchange for the large start-up funds that the host country itself cannot afford. As such, as Moran (1998:141) has observed, they have often stirred up strong nationalist sentiments. Fears about loss of sovereignty, exploitation, gunboat diplomacy, and foreign intervention go back to the 19th century and earlier (Lipson 1985; Rodman 1988; Mckern 1993).

Because FDI in the JDP mode involves sensitive questions about foreign ownership of subsoil rights and about loss of control over exhaustible resources, little wonder that China does not treat JDPs just like any other mode of FDI. As mentioned above, there is a separate regulatory framework governing the JDP mode and foreign investors in JDPs are usually not allowed to hold a majority equity position. Note in particular that China proceeded with *offshore* projects first, presumably because, like policy experiments in the SEZs, the potential political ramifications of *offshore* (as opposed to *onshore*) projects could be contained more easily. Only after more than a decade of the open door did China become more confident and finally allow foreign participation in *onshore* projects.

From the perspective of foreign investors, JDPs represent particularly risky investments. JDPs normally involve a huge amount of up-front capital and a long payback period. As such, they suffer from the "hostage effect" associated with large sunk capital, and unlike with small investments, foreign investors cannot easily threaten to withdraw. Consequently, these projects normally require extensive political-risk insurance, including expropriation, war, civil disturbance, and contract frustration, covered through an elaborate institutional network of bilateral or multinational treaties (Brownlees 1997). China's acceptance of the principle of subrogation on both bilateral and multilateral planes, as we discussed in Chapter 2, is, to a large extent, to facilitate such political risk insurance coverage.

As the above discussion of the special features of JDPs demonstrates, there are serious constraints on both the supply and demand side of the equation of FDI in the JDP mode. Little wonder that, again as Figure III-1 shows, compared to other modes of FDI, the number of JDPs is low. During the 1980s some 45 foreign oil companies were involved in the search for Chinese offshore oil. Between 1982 and 1992 foreign companies spent some US$2.25 billion on oil exploration and US$814 million on oil development in China (US Department of Energy 1995). Johnson reports (1999), however, that despite relatively good luck in finding oil and gas, most of the finds were small and not commercially viable. As a result, while foreign interest in offshore oil development has waned, there has been new interest in onshore exploration such as in the Tarim Basin in Xinjiang.

Occidental Petroleum and Atlantic Richfield are examples of FDI in the JDP mode. Occidental Petroleum has an onshore JDP in China. It is involved in an open-pit coal mine with the Antaibao, or Pingshuo, mine in Shanxi province, with an investment estimated at US$175 million. This is roughly 100 times larger than the average scale of FDI projects in China. The project required many years of negotiation. Once the contract was signed in 1985, it was another five years before any coal was produced. In the meantime, international coal prices fell from US$52/ton to below US$32/ton. In 1991 Occidental decided to pull out of the deal. For its part, Atlantic Richfield is involved in developing offshore gas fields in the South China Sea, with a total investment estimated at US$170 million.

Other Forms of Investment

Compensation Trade

Compensation trade, also known as counter-trade, refers broadly to any transaction involving the purchase by a domestic enterprise of foreign capital equipment and/or technology with repayment *not in cash but in kind*. As such, CT effectively circumvents the thorny problem of foreign exchange shortages that many developing nations suffer from. In China, CT is an especially popular form of business cooperation between Hong Kong and Chinese enterprises located in nearby Guangdong and Fujian provinces. This is so primarily because of geographical proximity, which, if for no other reason, can cut down on transportation costs significantly.

In its pure form, CT is essentially a loan transaction. The loan principal, consisting of the agreed purchase price of the equipment or technology, is to be repaid by the Chinese party in installments of the goods manufactured directly with the equipment purchased. In addition, an interest factor is usually built in and is paid in kind as well. This pure form of CT is known as *direct* compensation trade, because payment in this form is made with goods produced *directly* with the new equipment. Variations of this pure form exist and are usually lumped together under the rubric of *indirect* CT. One such variation is, for instance, for the Chinese party to use the new equipment to produce goods which are in short supply domestically and to pay the foreign party with raw materials or other types of manufactured goods that the foreign party can sell internationally. A hybrid arrangement is also possible where payment is made in part with goods produced directly with the new equipment, and in part with raw materials or other types of manufactured goods.

But be it in direct or indirect forms, CT usually does not involve the setting up by the foreign party of an "establishment" in China. Consequently, the foreign party is not involved in the management of the enterprise. Given these features, CT offers a relatively low-risk avenue for the foreign party to access the relatively cheap natural and labor resources of China. From the Chinese perspective, a key attraction of CT is the importation of advanced machinery or technology without incurring foreign exchange costs, even though there is little to be gained from the foreign party in terms of critical managerial know-how. Although in some cases the maker of the machinery may also supply some managerial assistance, this is not usually a major feature of CT arrangements. As a result, CT does not qualify as FDI in the normal international usage of the term. The same is also true of processing and assembly, and international leasing, to be discussed briefly next.

Processing and Assembly

Processing and assembly may be regarded as a variant of CT, in that payment to the foreign party is also made *in kind*, which effectively frees such business arrangements from the onus of balancing foreign exchange. Under PA, the foreign party typically supplies machinery, designs, components, and, sometimes, raw materials and the Chinese party assembles or processes these according to the specifications and quality requirements of the foreign party. The foreign party receives the finished products and in return the Chinese party is paid a processing fee, from which the installment price of the machinery and so on may be deducted.

PA is also a popular form of business arrangement between firms located in Hong Kong and neighboring Guangdong provinces especially in such labor-intensive industries as garments, toys, footwear, and umbrellas. As is the case of CT, under PA the foreign party will not normally set up an "establishment" in China, nor will it be involved in the management of the enterprise. Therefore, there is very little that the Chinese party can get in terms of sophisticated managerial expertise. Notwithstanding this, from the perspective of the Chinese party, the value of the machinery, equipment, and/or, sometimes, technical assistance supplied by the foreign party is treated as foreign capital absorbed by the host country.

International Leasing

International leasing is still another means whereby domestic firms acquire capital goods and machinery from foreign suppliers. Sometimes IL takes the form of operational leasing, but usually financial leasing is employed. In operational leasing, which typically involves expensive construction equipment, the lessor loans the equipment to the lessee for a certain time and fee that are typically specified in the lease contract, and upon expiration of that contract, the lessee returns the equipment to the lessor. In financial leasing, normally the lessor arranges to raise (usually through financial institutions) for the lessee whatever funds necessary to purchase the equipment specified in the lease contract, and leases it to the lessee. Upon expiration of contract, every aspect of the ownership rights of the equipment is transferred to the lessee after the lessee has made all payment obligations to the lessor. A good example of equipment acquired by a Chinese party from abroad through financial leasing is commercial aircraft. In 1981-96, China's civil aviation industry acquired a total of 322 aircraft from foreign countries by way of IL with a total outlay of US$11.8 billion. Of this fleet, 241 planes were through financial leasing and 81 through operational leasing (Wang Luolin 1997: 312).

Normally, Chinese enterprises seeking to purchase machinery directly do so by means of CT or PA arrangements. Leasing transactions, it seems, are almost invariably conducted through leasing companies set up especially for that purpose. According to one source (Li Lanqing 1995:95), by 1994, 35 such companies were established with foreign capital in China, and altogether they were involved in leasing transactions of capital goods to domestic enterprises worth a total of US$5 billion. Notable among the companies in China which are involved in leasing businesses are China International Trust and Investment Company, Beijing Machinery and Electric Equipment

Company, China Oriental Leasing Company (a joint firm with Japanese capital), China Leasing Company. At the local level, Qingdao Leasing Company and Guangzhou International Company are examples (Xu Jinhe 1995:88).

Emerging New Modes

CJVs, EJVs, and WFOEs together represent an overwhelming majority of all FIEs in China. Reflecting the growing needs and complexity of foreign business operations in China, in recent years China has begun to experiment with a variety of new foreign investment structures, or variants of the CJV, EJV, and WFOE modes. A Partnership Law passed in early 1997 is being gradually implemented (Clark, Howson, and Qiao 1997). The law is expected to facilitate the establishment of joint ventures, especially in legal, accounting, information, consulting, and other services sectors. China's Company Law of 1993 has made it possible for some foreign firms to open branches more easily.[13] Joint stock companies, holding companies, and joint trading companies are all forms of corporate structures being explored, albeit cautiously. These emerging forms of corporate structures reflect the growing sophistication of China's market-oriented economy, and the changing orientation of Chinese leaders – increasingly outward – as China has further aligned itself with the world economy in the latter part of the 1990s.

Concluding Remarks

Of the major modes of foreign capital flows into China that we have discussed in this chapter, EJV, CJV, WFOE, and JDP qualify as FDI in the normal international usage of the term, because these modes, more or less, involve the injection of managerial expertise or managerial control by the foreign party over the enterprise. On the other hand, CT,

---

13. The law provides for two basic types of shareholding companies: limited liability companies and limited liability stock companies. The former can be established when there are 2-50 shareholders, in which case the entity is a wholly state-owned limited liability company. Limited liability stock companies may, but are not required to, sell shares to the public. These shares may or may not be listed, i.e., traded, on the Shanghai or Shenzhen stock markets.

PA, and IL, which are often lumped together as "other types" of foreign investment in Chinese statistics, outside of China are not normally thought of as FDI. For none of these "other types" represents an interest on the part of the foreign investor to have, in the words of the IMF, "an effective voice over the enterprise."

Table III-2: Potential Benefits of Different Modes of Foreign Capital to China

Mode	*Managerial expertise*	*Foreign capital*	*Foreign technology*	*International marketing*	*FX balance*
EJV	Yes	Yes	Yes	Yes	No
CJV	Yes	Yes	Yes	Yes	No
WFOE	Yes	Yes	Yes	Yes	No
JDP	Yes	Yes	Yes	Yes	Yes
CT	No	Weak	Yes	Yes	Yes
PA	No	Weak	Yes	Yes	Yes
IL	No	Weak	Yes	No	No

Source: Adapted from World Bank (1988), *China: External Trade and Capital*, p. 250

Figure III-2: Compensation Trade, Processing & Assembly, and International Leasing as a Share of FDI, 1979-98 (contract value)

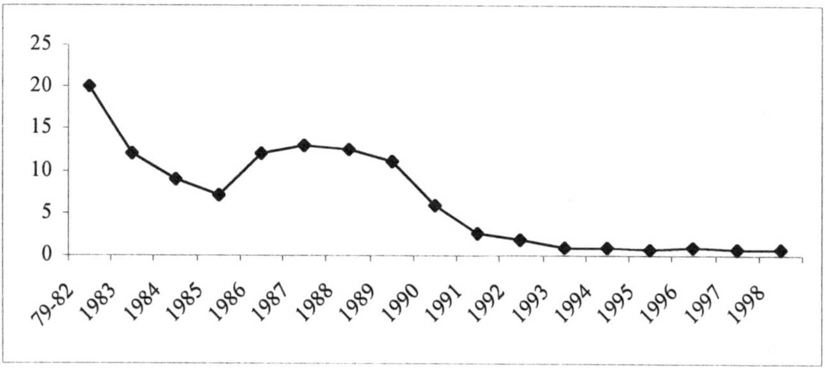

Sources: *Zhongguo duiwai jingji nianjian* [China Foreign Economic Statistical Yearbook] (various years); *Zhongguo duiwai maoyi nianjian* [Almanac of China's Foreign Trade and Economic Relations] (various years).

Notwithstanding the definitional difference, each of the above formats of foreign capital, whether or not normally thought of as FDI, does share some of the important characteristics of FDI, albeit in some cases only in very small degrees. For instance, they all involve varying degrees of technology transfer, foreign capital, and some other investable resources. Table III-2 summarizes the potential benefits which may accrue from the inherent features of these various modes of foreign capital to China.

How inflated may Chinese statistics on FDI be if the values of these "other types" of investment, i.e., CT, PA, and IL, are not excluded? According to my computations based on Chinese official publications, from 1979 through 1996, on yearly average China attracted about US$440 million in contract value of CT, PA, and IL. This was about 7% of total FDI inflows. This seemingly high average percentage, however, is largely a function of the very significant portion of these "other types" of investment during the initial years. It was, for instance, close to 20% in 1979-82, as is shown in Figure III-2. In subsequent years, however, the combined share of these "other types" dwindled rapidly to almost a negligible level in the 1990s. A temporary upward movement in the mid-1980s can probably be best interpreted to suggest the negative impact of the foreign exchange crisis around 1986 on those *bona fide* modes of FDI. For none of the *bona fide* investment modes, as is indicated in column 2 of Table III-2, has a built-in mechanism to balance foreign exchange automatically. By contrast, the very design of CT and PA is to free these arrangements from foreign exchange snarls.

There is one more implication we need to underscore from the trend of these "other types" of investment vis-à-vis the *bona fide* modes of FDI in China over time. Their general downward movement as a share of FDI lends *prima facie* support to our general argument that investment behavior is systematically related to the institutional framework of China's FDI regulatory regime. Given the incipient nature of China's FDI regulatory framework in the early 1980s, and the relatively low-risk nature of these "other types" of investment activities,[14] it is only natural that the share of these "other types" of investment was larger in earlier rather than in later years. Having made this point, in the next chapter we will leave CT, PA, and IL out of the picture, and turn instead to conduct a close investigation of the trends

---

14. Admittedly, IL is by no means a low-risk arrangement. But arguably, in part because it is not a low-risk arrangement, it represents only a tiny share in the total outlay of foreign investment in China. For instance, as a share of all "other types" of investment, which in turn is only about 1 percent of all FDI in China in the 1990s, it was only 6%, 12%, and 12% in 1991, 1992 and 1993 respectively.

and patterns of the *bona fide* modes of FDI in China, i.e., EJV, CJV, WFOE, and JDP.

CHAPTER 4

Trends and Patterns of FDI

There were neither wholly nor partially foreign-owned enterprises in the PRC in the pre-reform era. Chinese leaders used to take pride in this fact. Indeed, even disaster-relief aid volunteered by foreign governments and international organizations was shunned.[1] In 1979, in a dramatic shift in foreign economic policy China ended its long-standing prohibition of foreign investment by publishing its first foreign investment law. Since then, after a tentative start initially, FDI flows to China have been growing in ways that few expected. Relying primarily on official Chinese statistical publications, supplemented by other existing independent studies, in this chapter we will attempt to provide a comprehensive picture of the trends and patterns of FDI in China during the reform years. Our examination will proceed first on a stock basis and then in a flow fashion.

FDI Stock in Aggregate

To begin our examination of the trends and patterns of FDI in China, several technical notes on FDI data are in order here. First, by FDI stock, we mean the cumulative amount of FDI at a given point in time. This is to be contrasted with FDI flow figures, which refer to the amount of FDI received by a host country during a given period of time. Second, unless otherwise noted, data used in this chapter do not include compensation trade, processing and assembly, and international leasing, for reasons that we discussed in Chapter 3.

---

1. This point is perhaps best illustrated by the Chinese government's decline of foreign aid in the wake of the catastrophic earthquake which hit Tangshan, a coal-mining city in north China in 1976, killing more than 240,000 people and leaving more than 160,000 injured. See Fang Weizhong (1984:568).

Finally, Chinese statistics typically report two types of FDI data, i.e., the *actual amount* (also known as the realized, utilized, or arrived amount), and the *contract amount* (also known as the approved, pledged, or committed amount). Whereas the actual amount is the quantity of FDI that has actually arrived at a given time, the contract amount refers to the amount of FDI that the investor *plans* to invest at the time when the project contract is approved. However, as can be imagined, the planned total investment may not arrive in one lump sum; it may come in installments over a period of time. Consequently, there is usually a time lag between the two sets of data. Depending on the research question, we need to employ the different data appropriately. To illustrate, if what needs to be seen is the immediate reaction on the part of foreign investors to a policy change related to investment, the contract figures obviously are a better measure than the actual amount.

The general contours of FDI stock in China for the period from 1979 through 1998 are presented in Table IV-1. As we can see, by the end of 1998 China attracted a total of 324,195 FDI projects, of which 191,122 (or 58%) were EJVs, 86,952 (or 27%) were WFOEs, 45,861 (or 14%) were CJVs, and 158 (less than 1%) were JDPs. These FDI projects represented a total US$571.7 billion of pledged investment, of which some US$255.4 billion (or 45%) were EJVs, US$177.3 billion (or 31%) were WFOEs, US$133.2 (or 23%) were CJVs, and US$5.28 billion (or less than 1%) were JDPs. The average size of these projects was US$1.76 million. More specifically, it was US$1.34 million for EJVs; US$2.04 million for WFOEs; US$2.90 million for CJVs, and US$33.4 million for JDPs.

Two points of explanation are in order regarding the relative size of the different modes of FDI in China. First, the exceptionally large size of JDPs reflects the very special nature of this particular mode of FDI. Natural resource projects, such as oil exploration, both onshore and offshore, normally require a huge amount of up-front capital commitment. Actual expenses of JDPs, especially in the initial stage, can be so large that they often exceed what has been foreseen in contracts. As a result, the arrival rates – i.e., the ratio between the pledged and actually utilized amount of investment – for JDPs are usually very high and can be more than 100% (see the last column of Table IV-1). Indeed, this is the very reason that China opened up its sovereign possession over its natural resources for joint Chinese-foreign development. The country was very shy about the huge capital commitment that such projects would require. For instance, in 1982-96, China was only able to make budgetary allocations totaling 1.45 billion RMB for the offshore oil industry. By contrast, for the 126 off-shore JDPs China had signed with 67 foreign countries by the end of 1996, the initial foreign investment during the exploration stage alone reached US$3.1 billion, with an additional US$2.28 billion used during the second stage of extraction (Wang Luolin 1997:67).

Table IV-1: Foreign Capital in China, 1979-98 (US$ billion)

Foreign capital	Actual	Contractual	Project #	Average size	Arrival rate
FDI	265.6	571.7	324,195	0.00176	46%
EJVs	128.6 (48%)	255.4 (45%)	191,122 (58%)	0.00134	50%
CJVs	54.9 (21%)	133.2 (23%)	45,861 (14%)	0.00290	41%
WFOEs	75.2 (28%)	177.3 (31%)	86.952 (27%)	0.00204	42%
JDPs	5.56 (2%)	5.28 (<1%)	158 (<1%)	0.03342	106%
Foreign loans	117.7	--	--	--	--
Other *	24.1	--	--	--	--
Total	407.4	--	--	--	--

Note: * The "other" category includes portfolio investment, compensation trade, processing and assembly, and international leasing. Shares of different modes of FDI as a percentage of the total are in parentheses.

Sources: *Zhongguo duiwai jingji nianjian* [China Foreign Economic Statistical Yearbook] (various years); *Zhongguo duiwai maoyi nianjian* [Almanac of China's Foreign Trade and Economic Relations] (various years).

Second, the relatively larger size of CJVs, as compared to EJVs or WFOEs, may reflect the fact that, as discussed in Chapter 3, a wider range of investable assets are allowed under CJVs, and evaluations of equity contributions may be less exact than that of EJVs. This is so because profit sharing under the CJV mode does not have to be carried out exactly according to the equity ratios between Chinese and foreign partners. There is thus no incentive, either for the Chinese or the foreign party, to bargain against inflated estimates of equity value under the CJV mode of investment. This line of reasoning, in turn, is consistent with the relatively low arrival rate of this particular mode of FDI. As Table IV-1 shows, the arrival rate of CJVs is the lowest among all modes of FDI. It is 41% against 42% for WFOEs and 50% for EJVs. We thus have reason to suspect that the real value of an average CJV may not be necessarily larger than that of an average EJV or WFOE in China.

The total amount of FDI that actually arrived in China for the period from 1979 through 1998 is US$265.6 billion. This is about 46% of the total contractual amount, and represents more than 65% of all foreign capital (US$407.4 billion), including foreign loans and portfolio investment, etc. that China utilized during the same period. Of the US$265.6 billion FDI, some US$128.6 billion (or 48%) came in the form of EJVs, US$75.2 billion (or 28%) in the form of WFOEs, US$54.9 billion (or 21%) in the form of CJVs, and US$5.56 billion (or 2%) in the form of JDPs. To put these figures in perspective, US$265.6 billion is about the same size as China's total GDP in 1987, which was about US$268 billion. In 1998 China's GDP stood at some US$960 billion.

Figure IV-1: Major Source Countries/Regions of FDI Stock, 1979-96

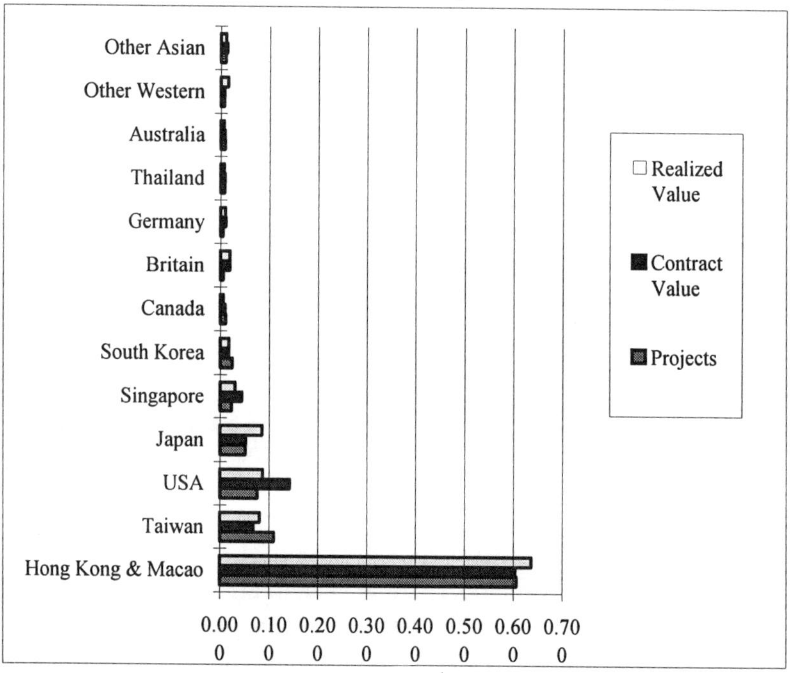

Sources: *Zhongguo duiwai jingji nianjian* [China Foreign Economic Statistical Yearbook] (various years); *Zhongguo duiwai maoyi nianjian* [Almanac of China's Foreign Trade and Economic Relations] (various years).

Source countries/regions of FDI in China are very diverse but rather skewed, as is illustrated by Figure IV-1. So far more than 150 countries/regions have made direct investment in China (Li Lanqing 1995:59). But a dominant share has come from a few countries/regions. As of 1996, Hong Kong, including Macao, represented more than 60% of all FDI, measured by project number, contractual value and actual amount. Specifically, as of 1996, Hong Kong's share is 60% in project number. It was followed by Taiwan (11%), the US (8%), Japan (5%), South Korea (2.4%), Singapore (2.3%), and Canada (1%). On a contractual basis, the order of ranking is Hong Kong (60%), the US (14%), Taiwan (7%), Japan (5%), Singapore (4%), Britain (1.9%), and South Korea (1.7%). In actual amounts, Hong Kong, whose share was 63%, once again dominated the scene by a wide margin. It was followed by the US (8.7%), Japan (8.6%), Taiwan (8.1%), Singapore (3%), Britain (1.9%), and Germany (1%).

The geographical distribution of FDI in China is shown in Table IV-2. While FDI has penetrated all provinces, autonomous regions, and central municipalities, an overwhelming share has so far concentrated in China's coastal areas. Specifically, from 1979 to 1995, the combined share of the coastal areas was 87% in contractual value, 84% in actual amounts and 83% in project number. A breakdown of these figures by provinces/central municipalities shows that Guangdong led the way. Specifically, Guangdong's share was 31% in contractual value, 29% in actual amountd, and 25% in project number. This is not very surprising, given that Guangdong, where 3 of China's first 4 SEZs are located, is the closest geographically, culturally and linguistically to Hong Kong, and Hong Kong, in turn, was responsible for 60% of all FDI stock in China. Beyond the Chinese context, an ample literature exists confirming that bilateral affinities between supplier and host countries of FDI are a positive predictor of investment flows, because such affinities minimize information and transaction costs or risks associated with firms making investment in a foreign environment.[2]

---

2. Davidson (1980: 9-22) showed that low transaction and information cost countries such as Canada, Britain, and Mexico figure prominently as destinations for US FDI. Studies on other source countries have come up with similar findings. Italian FDI starts with neighboring southern European

Table IV-2: Geographical Distribution of FDI in China, 1979-95 (US$10,000)

	Contract Amount		Actual Amount		Project Number	
Total	39530500		13315300		258788	
Coastal	34526949	(87%)	11231650	(84%)	213748	(83%)
Interior	5003551	(13%)	2083650	(16%)	45040	(17%)
Beijing*	1706289	(4.3%)	530246	(4%)	11734	(4.5%)
Tianjin*	1157628	(2.9%)	375359	(2.8%)	9417	(3.6%)
Hebei*	973824	(2.5%)	19555	(0.1%)	8021	(3.1%)
Liaoning*	1609956	(4.1%)	537583	(4%)	12971	(5%)
Shanghai*	3421018	(8.7%)	1161340	(8.7%)	13582	(5.2%)
Jiangsu*	4128059	(10.4%)	1401397	(10.5%)	29570	(11.4%)
Zhejiang*	1067640	(2.7%)	401174	(3%)	12559	(4.9%)
Fujian*	3859477	(9.8%)	1372860	(10.3%)	18552	(7.2%)
Shandong*	2243676	(5.7%)	850942	(6.4%)	19446	(7.5%)
Guangdong*	12321531	(31%)	3902357	(29%)	63809	(25%)
Guangxi*	849421	(2.1%)	278545	(2.1%)	6118	(2.4%)
Hainan*	1188430	(3%)	400292	(3%)	7969	(3.1%)
Shanxi	24343	(0.1%)	24343	(0.2%)	1588	(0.6%)
Inner Mongolia	10095	(n)	6555	(n)	111	(n)
Jilin	298537	(0.8%)	106617	(0.8%)	4199	(1.6%)
Heilongjiang	347223	(0.9%)	125800	(0.9%)	4711	(1.8%)
Anhui	240555	(0.6%)	120228	(0.9%)	3403	(1.3%)
Jiangxi	144567	(0.4%)	90625	(0.7%)	3602	(1.4%)
Henan	381672	(0.1%)	152536	(1.1%)	4958	(1.9%)
Hubei	–	–	209503	(1.6%)	–	–
Hunan	3812	(n)+	145552	(1.1%)	3812	(1.5%)
Sichuan	6198	(n)+	235253	(1.8%)	6198	(2.4%)
Guizhou	111238	(0.3%)	21051	(0.2%)	1119	(0.4%)
Yunnan	138887	(0.4%)	57411	(0.4%)	1122	(0.4%)
Shaanxi	343922	(0.9%)	124842	(0.9%)	2099	(0.8%)
Gansu	767229	(1%)	21507	(0.2%)	1144	(0.4%)
Qinghai	6628	(n)	1877	(n)	118	(n)
Ningxia	20252	(0.1%)	9986	(0.1%)	391	(0.2%)
Xinjiang	62545	(0.2%)	23033	(0.2%)	846	(0.3%)

Note: * denotes coastal regions. Beijing, strictly speaking, is not coastal. But it is listed here as coastal, following the convention of Chinese publications on FDI. "–" means no data available. "+" indicates probable data entry mistake. Shares of country total are in parentheses. "n" means negligible. Individual percentages may not add up to 100 percent because of rounding.

Sources: *Zhongguo duiwai jingji nianjian* [China Foreign Economic Statistical Yearbook] (various years); *Zhongguo duiwai maoyi nianjian* [Almanac of China's Foreign Trade and Economic Relations] (various years).

---

countries (Onida and Viesti 1988); Japanese FDI goes to Southeast Asia (Yoshihara 1978); Australian investment to New Zealand (Deane 1970); Sweden to neighboring European countries and the US (Swedenborg 1979); France to French-speaking lands and adjacent European countries (Michalet and Delapierre 1976). The positive effects of common language and neighbor status are confirmed by a statistical study by Veugelers (1991).

Following Guangdong was Jiangsu with 10% on the basis of contractual amount, followed extremely closely by Fujian with 9.8%. Shanghai was in the forth place with 8.7%. Other major FDI destinations in China included Shandong (5.7%), Beijing (4.3%), Liaoning (4.1%), Hainan (3%), and Tianjin (2.9%), all of which are located in coastal areas. As of 1996, none of the interior provinces had a share larger than 1%.

In addition to the Hong Kong factor, that FDI is largely concentrated in coastal areas can perhaps be explained on two accounts: economic and institutional. With respect to the economy, at the very outset of China's open-door policy, the coastal provinces and cities were economically more developed than the interior, such that they were in a better position to provide infrastructure, transportation, communications, and other facilities to foreign investors. With respect to institutions, as documented at length in Chapter 1, China's FDI regulatory framework has evolved in such a way that the coastal areas were many years ahead of the interior in conferring a wide range of privileges and incentives to foreign investors. Indeed, it was not until the 1990s that China's finally decided to open up its interior regions to foreign investment with similar, albeit in many cases still less, preferential policies to those available in the coastal areas.

The sectoral composition of FDI in China is presented in a highly aggregated fashion in Figure IV-2. Agriculture, or primary industry which includes forestry, animal husbandry, fishery and water conservancy, constitutes about 1% of all FDI stock in China. Industry, which is broadly defined in China to include extraction of natural resources, processing of food products, manufacturing of industrial goods, and generation of electricity, clearly has the lion's share, with 58%. Construction takes another 3%. The combined share of the service sectors is 34%. The bulk of it, in turn, is composed of real estate and land development (26%). The rest is taken up by commerce and food services (5%), posts and telecommunications (2%), and banking and insurance (1%). The fairly large share of FDI stock in the service sectors is largely a reflection of the institutional liberalization in recent years, as evidenced by the gradual relaxation in the early 1990s of sectoral restrictions in tertiary industries, especially in real estate and land development, and financial institutions.

Xin Ming (1995:8-26) reports that the share of FDI in real estate and land development occupied more than 30% of all FDI inflows two years in a row, in 1992 and 1993. Banking and insurance, as discussed in Chapter 1, is another fast growing in the latter parts of the 1990s. Of late, a new and rapidly growing area of foreign investment is the Internet.[3]

Figure IV-2: Industrial Composition of FDI Stock, 1982-97

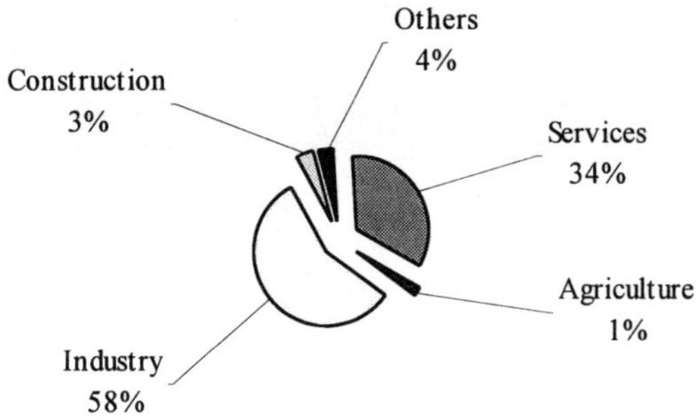

Note: Service sectors include real estate and land development (26%), commerce and food services 5%, post and telecom 2%, and banking and insurance (1%).
Sources: *Zhongguo duiwai jingji nianjian* [China Foreign Economic Statistical Yearbook] (various years); *Zhongguo duiwai maoyi nianjian* [Almanac of China's Foreign Trade and Economic Relations] (various years).

Finally, if we shift our focus away from FDI stock and instead proceed on a flow basis, we will see a very impressive overall upward trend of FDI flows into China for the entire reform period. Specifically, as Table IV-3 shows, the average yearly growth rate of FDI flows reached a high of 37% in contract value, 33% in actual amount, and 48% in project number. A closer look at the growth trends, especially in the contractual amount, reveals that FDI inflows into China began to show signs of an extraordinary upward surge at two points, i.e., in and around 1985 and 1991, so that the whole 1979-98 period cuts itself into three sub-periods in which the volumes of FDI flows assumed quite different and overall increased magnitudes.

3. "Chinese Web Opens Portals to New Way of Life," *Washington Post Foreign Service*, 13 February 2000, A1

Perhaps not coincidentally, these three sub-periods, i.e., 1979-84, 1985-90, and the 1990s, correlate closely with the three phases of improvement and liberalization of China's FDI regulatory framework. As we documented in Chapter 1, each phase, especially at its outset, is marked by major institutional innovations or policy changes to improve, clarify, and/or liberalize the regulatory environment for FDI. While more systematic analysis will be done through regression analyses to establish the causal effects of China's FDI regulatory framework on investment behavior, with other economic and cultural variables controlled for, in what follows we first turn to conduct a close investigation of the trends and patterns of FDI inflows in the three sub-periods.

Table IV-3: FDI Inflows in China, 1979-98 (US$ billion)

Year	Contractual	Growth	Actual	Growth	Projects	Growth
1979-82	4.962	--	1.167	--	922	--
1983	1.732	4%*	0.636	38%*	470	52%*
1984	2.651	53%	1.258	98%	1856	295%
1985	5.932	124%	1.659	32%	3073	66%
1986	3.332	-44%	1.874	13%	1498	-51%
1987	3.709	11%	2.314	23%	2233	49%
1988	5.298	43%	3.193	38%	5945	166%
1989	5.599	6%	3.392	6%	5779	-3%
1990	6.596	18%	3.487	3%	7273	26%
1991	11.976	82%	4.366	25%	12978	78%
1992	58.123	385%	11.007	152%	48764	276%
1993	111.435	92%	27.514	150%	83437	71%
1994	82.679	-26%	33.766	23%	47549	-43%
1995	91.281	10%	37.52	11%	37011	-22%
1996	73.280	-20%	41.73	11%	24556	-34%
1997	51.000	-30%	45.26	8%	21001	-14%
1998	52.100	2%	45.46	0%	19850	-5%
Overall	571.685	37%	265.603	33%	324195	48%

Note: * Year-by-year data are not available for the period prior to 1982. These are growth rates estimated under the assumption that the 1982 figure is a yearly average for 1979-82, i.e. sum for 1979-82 divided by 3 years. I use 3 years instead of 4, assuming there was very little investment in 1979, since the EJV Law was published late that year.

Sources: *Zhongguo duiwai jingji nianjian* [China Foreign Economic Statistical Yearbook] (various years); *Zhongguo duiwai maoyi nianjian* [Almanac of China's Foreign Trade and Economic Relations] (various years).

Initial Moderate Inflows (1979-84)

China's efforts to encourage FDI began in 1979, but large FDI inflows did not take place until 1984. During the initial period, although the EJV Law was promulgated in July 1979, the law was still cursory, leaving many critical issues about JV operations unanswered. It was not until 4 years later that the Detailed Implementation Act of the EJV Law was enacted. Further, even though the first EJV Law was meant to be applicable nationwide, many preferential terms to foreign investment – most noticeably fiscal incentives and streamlined regulatory controls – were, however, announced separately and were largely confined to the SEZs.

As a reflection of these institutional impediments, FDI inflows during the early period were rather moderate, averaging US$1.5 billion in contractual value per annum. This is only about one-third of the comparable figure for the 1985-90 period. The arrival rate was also low, averaging 30%, which is about 11% points lower than the average rate (41%) for the period 1979-98. One possible reason for the low arrival rate could be that for large, long-term projects, investment capital normally comes in installments to be paid over quite a number of years, a factor early statistics might have not captured in time. However, since very few large, long-term investment projects,[4] except JDPs,[5] were signed at the time, the low arrival rate seems to indicate a high degree of hesitation on the part of foreign investors. This is not surprising, given the incipient nature of China's FDI regulatory framework. Chinese officials interviewed almost uniformly used the word *guanwang,* or "wait and see," to describe the uncertain behavior of foreign investors at the time, especially before the Detailed Implementation Act of the EJV Law was enacted. Indeed, the mood of uncertainty during the initial years is well reflected by statistical evidence.

As Table IV-4 shows, at the end of 1984, only 3218 FDI projects were signed, which is less than one year's figure in the late 1980s. And more than half of these investment contracts, or 1856 projects, were concluded in 1984, i.e., one year *after* the EJV Implementation

4. Pearson (1991:119) reports that even in 1984, more than 82% of the joint venture contracts were for a duration of less than 15 years.

5. As is normally the case, the arrival rate for JDPs for 1979-84 is 95%.

Act was published. The timing suggests that improvements in China's FDI regulatory framework had a strong bearing on investment behavior. After all, the EJV Implementing Act gave greater clarification to many issues left ambiguous or undefined by previous legislative work, even though the regulations did not aim at expanding the geographical dimension of the preferential policies available only in the SEZs at the time. In this context it is also relevant to note that prior to 1983, an overwhelming share (more than 80%) of FDI came in the form of CJVs. By contrast, WFOEs in the 1979-84 period remained very insignificant – only 2% of total FDI in project number and 5% in pledged and 3% in utilized amount.

Such patterns of initial FDI inflows apparently add credence to our hypothesis about institutional development as a positive predictor of investment flows, even though further validation calls for controls of economic factors over a greater time span. For the moment, the rudimentary and restrictive nature of China's FDI regulatory framework is obvious. For one thing, WFOEs as an alternative investment mode, were not allowed beyond the geographical confines of the SEZs. For another, with a mere 15 brief articles, the 1979 joint venture law apparently fell short of guiding both Chinese and foreign partners in many crucial operational issues of JV projects. Under these circumstances, almost by default CJVs became a relatively safe mode of investment. As they are very flexible in organization (e.g., the venture does not have to form a distinct legal person), capitalization (e.g., the venture does not have to observe the minimal 25% foreign equity requirement), and profit-sharing (e.g., the venture does have to share profits by reference to equity ratios), they therefore best facilitated the short-term behavior of foreign investors, relative to other modes of investment.[6]

During this early period, also worth an elaboration is the amount of FDI in the JDP mode. As Table IV-4 shows, although the number of JDPs was small, they were very significant as a share of total FDI inflows at the time. This is especially true in 1983, when JDPs amounted to a huge 58% of all FDI in contractual value. By the end of 1983, China National Offshore Oil Corporation had signed a total of 31 contracts with a number of well-known foreign oil companies. Most noteworthy among them were Mobil, Chevron/Texaco, Amoco,

6. See previous discussion of CJVs as a mode of FDI in Chapter 3.

JNOC (Japan National Oil Corporation), Phillips, BP (British Petroleum), ELF (Societe Nationale Elf Aquitaine), Arco (Atlantic Richfield), – with a total foreign investment of more than US$1 billion. Note also that 18 of these natural resource projects (or a huge 72%) were signed in the year of 1983 alone, also one year *after* China had published its first set of rules governing JDPs in 1982.[7]

Table IV-4: FDI by Different Modes, 1979-84 (US$ billion)

Project #	*Total*	*EJV*		*CJV*		*WFOE*		*JDP*	
1979-82	922	83	(9%)	793	(86%)	33	(4%)	13	(1%)
1983	440	107	(24%)	300	(68%)	15	(3%)	18	(4%)
1984	1,856	741	(40%)	1,089	(59%)	26	(1%)	0	(0%)
Cumulative	3,218	931	(29%)	2,182	(68%)	74	(2%)	31	(1%)
Average	536	155	(29%)	363	(68%)	12	(2%)	5	(1%)
Contractual									
1979-82	4.962	0.140	(3%)	4.083	(82%)	0.366	(7%)	0.373	(8%)
1983	1.732	0.188	(11%)	0.503	(29%)	0.040	(2%)	1.001	(58%)
1984	2.651	1.067	(40%)	1.484	(56%)	0.100	(4%)	0	(0%)
Cumulative	9.345	1.395	(15%)	6.070	(65%)	0.506	(5%)	1.374	(15%)
Average	1.557	0.232	(15%)	1.011	(65%)	0.084	(5%)	0.229	(15%)
Actual									
1979-82	1.167	0.099	(8%)	0.531	(46%)	0.040	(3%)	0.497	(43%)
1983	0.636	0.074	(12%)	0.227	(36%)	0.043	(7%)	0.292	(46%)
1984	1.258	0.255	(20%)	0.465	(37%)	0.015	(1%)	0.523	(42%)
Cumulative	3.061	0.428	(14%)	1.223	(40%)	0.098	(3%)	1.312	(43%)
Average	0.510	0.071	(14%)	0.204	(40%)	0.016	(3%)	0.218	(43%)

Note: Shares of total by different modes of FDI are in parentheses.
Sources: *Zhongguo duiwai jingji nianjian* [China Foreign Economic Statistical Yearbook] (various years); *Zhongguo duiwai maoyi nianjian* [Almanac of China's Foreign Trade and Economic Relations] (various years).

Toward the end of the 1970s offshore oil exploration was considered very promising and potentially profitable as China opened

7. The Regulations of the PRC on the Exploitation of Offshore Petroleum Resources in Cooperation with Foreign Enterprises were promulgated on January 30, 1982 by the State Council; Also passed were General Customs Administration, Ministry of Finance Rules on Reduction and Exemption of Customs Duties and Consolidated Industrial and Commercial Tax for Import and Export Goods and Equipment occasioned at the China-Foreign Joint Exploitation of Offshore Oil (promulgated in April 1982).

its hitherto largely unexplored continental shelf, specifically in the Bohai Gulf, the South Yellow Sea, the Pearl River Estuary Basin, and the Yinggehai and Beibu Gulfs of the South China Sea.[8] The initial high expectations were tempered somewhat in subsequent years when world petroleum prices dropped significantly after 1983.

JDPs aside, the size of FDI projects during the early period appeared small, averaging less than US$1 million in 1981 (see Table IV-5). Except for a few high profile cases – such as Bejing Jeep Corporation (US), Shanghai Volkswagen Automotive Company (Germany), and China Schindler Elevator Company (Switzerland), all of which were established in and after 1983 – an overwhelming share of FDI inflows, as Table IV-5 indicates, were small-scale labor-intensive projects, such as textiles, food processing, electronic assembling, and hotel services, none of which required a large capital commitment and sophisticated technology.

Table IV-5: Sectoral Distribution of FDI in China, 1981 (US$ million)

Industrial Sector	# of EJVs	Foreign Capital	Average Size
Light industry	4	3.465	0.866
Food processing	3	5.293	1.764
Electronics	3	4.930	1.643
Machinery	3	2.353	0.784
Textile	2	2.462	1.231
Tourism	2	0.128	0.064
Petroleum	1	1.000	1.000
Commerce	1	0.200	0.200
Communications	1	0.150	0.150
Total	20	19.981	0.999

Note: Data contained here are for equity joint ventures approved in 1981 only.
Source: *Zhongguo jingji nianjian* [Almanac of China's Economy] (1982).

8. An extensive seismic survey under the auspices of the UN Economic Commission for Asia and the Far East concluded that "the continental shelf between Taiwan and Japan may be one of the most prolific oil reservoirs in the world." See Harrison (1977:46). Early discovery of a large gas field in the Yinggehai Gulf of the South China Sea by Arco presumably heightened high expectations. In that case, two highly productive gas wells were drilled, which tested at 1.2 million and 1.8 million cubic meters per day, respectively, with gas pay being more than 100 meters. See Sun Shujun and Shi Hongxi (1987:58) and Woodard (1980:153).

Perhaps not atypical of the JVs formed at the time was the Quanzhou Manmade Flower Factory located in Fujian. With a small investment of US$266,000 and a 60:40 equity ratio between Chinese and Hong Kong partners, the JV involved little technology but primarily took advantage of the low labor costs in China to produce artificial flowers, roughly 80% of which were sold abroad (Robinson 1987:37). This apparently was a project involving little foreign commitment of the kind of lumpy specific capital which is irreversible without incurring huge costs.

Most FDI during the initial period came just across the border from Hong Kong and Macao to nearby Guangdong and, to a much lesser degree, Fujian, and Hainan in south China. For the 1979-84 period, Guangdong, Fujian and Hainan, taken together, accounted for 88% of all FDI inflows in China. By contrast, the rest of the country attracted only 12%, of which 5% went to Shanghai, 2% to Beijing, and 1% each to Tianjin, Zhejiang, and Shandong respectively (see Table IV-6). Such an over-concentration of FDI in a few areas is a good indication of the effects of the very limited geographical scope of China's FDI preferential policies during the initial period. As is clear, before the 14 coastal cities were declared open to foreign investment in 1984 with similar (albeit still in many cases less preferential) policies, even Shanghai, for all its superior human capital and industrial infrastructure, was perhaps an under-achiever as a host of FDI.

Table IV-6: Geographical Distribution of FDI, 1979-84 (cumulative contract value)

Provinces/municipalities	As % of country total
Guangdong	82%
Shanghai	5%
Fujian	4%
Hainan	2%
Beijing	2%
Tianjin	1%
Zhejiang	1%
Shandong	1%
Rest of China	2%

Sources: *Zhongguo duiwai jingji nianjian* [China Foreign Economic Statistical Yearbook] (various years); *Zhongguo duiwai maoyi nianjian* [Almanac of China's Foreign Trade and Economic Relations] (various years).

Sources of FDI during the early period are illustrated in Table IV-7, which lists the 6 largest suppliers of FDI to China in contract value in 1984. Hong Kong and Macao clearly dominated the scene with 76%. Japan was a distant second with 7%, followed very closely by the US with 6%. West Germany was in the fourth place with 4%. The fifth and sixth places were held by Singapore and Thailand, with 2% and 1% respectively. If we add the figures for Hong Kong, Macao, Singapore, and Thailand together, i.e., all those countries/regions with large overseas Chinese populations, their combined share amounted to a huge 79%.

Table IV-7: FDI Source Country/Region Distribution, 1984 (contract value)

Country/region	As % of total FDI inflows
Hong Kong and Macao	76%
Japan	7%
United States	6%
West Germany	4%
Singapore	2%
Thailand	1%
Other	1%

Source: *Zhongguo duiwai maoyi nianjian, 1985* [Almanac of China's Foreign Trade and Economic Relations, 1985].

The overwhelming share of FDI from countries/regions with large overseas Chinese populations during the initial period further supports our contention about the development, or the lack thereof, of China's FDI regulatory framework as a predictor of FDI. Since China's FDI regulatory framework was in crude shape in the initial years, it is only natural that foreign investment, if it came at all, was more likely to be made by investors who were better equipped to overcome formal institutional uncertainty by relying on informal institutional mechanisms (such as cultural affinities and ethnic connections). To validate our claims still further, additional evidence is needed to support the other side of the story. That is, as the formal institutions of China's FDI regulatory framework became more mature, thus making the game of investment in China more accessible to those without informal institutional means, the share of FDI by those with cultural affinities and/or ethnic connections is expected to decrease, relative to the amount of FDI by investors who look more to the formal institutions to reduce information and transaction costs. As we shall see shortly, this is exactly what happened in the subsequent years.

A Significant Second Surge (1985-90)

During the 1985-90 period, China's FDI regulatory framework was augmented by, among other things, the promulgation of two landmark legislative works. In 1986 the WFOE Law was published, which legalized WFOEs as an alternative mode of FDI beyond the geographical confines of the SEZs. In 1988 another separate law was enacted which further clarified the legal status of CJVs which had until then been governed by the EJV Law and its Detailed Implementation Act applied "through analogies." Moreover, as documented in Chapter 1, not only was the geographic scope of many of China's preferential policies to FDI expanded during this period to cover all the major cities in the coastal areas, China also made an important institutional innovation – that of the swap centers – to ameliorate the problems caused by its hitherto very rigid system of foreign exchange controls.

As a reflection of the improvement and liberalization of China's FDI regulatory framework, FDI inflows during this period increased significantly. This was so in spite of the 1986 foreign exchange crisis, which apparently depressed FDI inflows temporarily, and the 1989 Tiananmen events, which caused many industrial democracies to impose economic sanctions on China. As Table IV-8 shows, FDI inflows during the 1985-90 period assumed greater magnitude, averaging US$4.99 billion in contract value per annum, of which more than 50% was actually realized, averaging US$2.6 billion per annum. This is more than 5 times the comparable average figure (US$0.5 billion) for the initial 1979-84 period.

For the whole 1985-90 period, a total of 25,801 FDI contracts were signed, of which 60% were EJVs, 28% were CJVs, and 13% were WFOEs. While all modes of FDI, except JDPs, had a significant increase over the previous period in absolute number, it is interesting to note that during this period the relative share of CJVs plunged to 28% from the previous 68%. By contrast, EJVs rose rapidly from 29% to 60%. Of particular significance was the steady increase of WFOEs, which involved more foreign commitment of the kind of investment which was reversible only at great cost. In terms of contract number, the relative share of WFOEs rose to 13%, as against 2% in the previous period.

Table IV-8: FDI by Different Modes, 1985-90 (US$ billion)

Project #	*Total*	*EJV*	*CJV*	*WFOE*	*JDP*
1985	3,073	1,412 (46%)	1,611 (52%)	46 (1%)	4 (0%)
1986	1,498	892 (60%)	582 (39%)	18 (1%)	6 (0%)
1987	2,233	1,395 (62%)	789 (35%)	46 (2%)	3 (0%)
1988	5,945	3,909 (66%)	1,621 (27%)	410 (7%)	5 (0%)
1989	5,779	3,659 (63%)	1,179 (20%)	931 (16%)	10 (0%)
1990	7,273	4,091 (56%)	1,317 (18%)	1,860 (26%)	5 (0%)
Cumulative	25,801	15,358 (60%)	7,099 (28%)	3,311 (13%)	33 (0%)
Average	4,300	2,560 (60%)	1,183 (28%)	552 (13%)	6 (0%)
Contractual					
1985	5.906	2.020 (34%)	3.490 (59%)	0.046 (1%)	0.350 (6%)
1986	2.834	1.375 (49%)	1.358 (48%)	0.020 (1%)	0.081 (3%)
1987	3.709	1.950 (53%)	1.283 (35%)	0.471 (13%)	0.005 (0%)
1988	5.297	3.133 (59%)	1.624 (31%)	0.481 (9%)	0.059 (1%)
1989	5.599	2.659 (47%)	1.083 (19%)	1.653 (30%)	0.203 (4%)
1990	6.596	2.703 (41%)	1.254 (19%)	2.445 (37%)	0.194 (3%)
Cumulative	29.940	13.840 (46%)	10.090 (34%)	5.116 (17%)	0.892 (3%)
Average	4.990	2.307 (46%)	1.682 (34%)	0.853 (17%)	0.149 (3%)
Actual					
1985	1.658	0.579 (35%)	0.585 (35%)	0.013 (1%)	0.481 (29%)
1986	1.874	0.804 (43%)	0.794 (42%)	0.016 (1%)	0.260 (14%)
1987	2.314	1.486 (64%)	0.619 (27%)	0.026 (1%)	0.183 (8%)
1988	3.193	1.975 (62%)	0.779 (24%)	0.227 (7%)	0.212 (7%)
1989	3.392	2.037 (60%)	0.751 (22%)	0.372 (11%)	0.232 (7%)
1990	3.487	1.886 (54%)	0.674 (19%)	0.683 (20%)	0.244 (7%)
Cumulative	15.920	8.767 (55%)	4.202 (26%)	1.337 (8%)	1.612 (10%)
Average	2.6530	1.461 (55%)	0.700 (26%)	0.223 (8%)	0.269 (10%)

Note: Shares of total by different modes of FDI are in parentheses.

Sources: *Zhongguo duiwai jingji nianjian* [China Foreign Economic Statistical Yearbook] (various years); *Zhongguo duiwai maoyi nianjian* [Almanac of China's Foreign Trade and Economic Relations] (various years).

Similarly, measured in dollar amount, the relative share of CJVs plummeted from 65% to 34% on a contractual basis, while those of

EJVs and WFOEs rose from 15% and 5% to 46% and 17% respectively. Similar changes also occurred on the basis of utilized amount. Specifically, the relative share of CJVs dropped from 40% to 26%, while EJVs rose from 14% to 55%, and WFOEs from 3% to 8%.

These dramatic shifts in the growth patterns of different modes of FDI strongly suggest that foreign investors during this period began increasingly to make longer-term commitments. This, in turn, reflected the improvement in China's FDI regulatory framework. For one thing, a separate law was promulgated in 1986 which legalized the establishment of WFOEs in China on a nationwide basis. In the same year, China also formally allowed FDI projects to be extended from the previous norm of 10-30 years to a maximum duration of 50 years. Second, in 1985 and again in 1988, more decision-making powers, in the form of a higher project approval limit, were delegated to local governments.[9] The end results were reduced red-tape and expedited approval procedures, as evidenced by the emergence in 1988 in many coastal cities of the so-called "one window" service, whereby one government office was authorized to handle all necessary government business and services on behalf of FDI firms.[10]

Third, there clearly was an increasing level of specification and sophistication of laws regarding FIEs during the second period. In addition to the increased specification of preferential tax treatment which we discussed in previous chapters, another example is the 1986 Provisions Concerning Autonomous Rights of Personnel Employment, and Salary, Insurance and Welfare Expenses in Foreign-Invested Enterprises.[11] The provisions set, *inter alia*, a reference minimal wage range for Chinese workers employed in FDI firms to the equivalent of 120-150% of the going local real wage[12] in

9. Coastal provinces and cities could now approve FDI projects of up to US$30 million each, and the approval power of the interior provinces and cities was increased to US$10 million for each project.

10. The "window" service did not eliminate the authority of the various government agencies, but did provide a government agency to coordinate the review and approval process. Luo Gengmo (1994:3).

11. This was adopted on November 12, 1996 by the Ministry of Labor and Personnel.

12. The concept of real wage in China consists of two parts: the direct wage and the indirect wage. The direct wage is the wage paid directly to the

the same line of business in state-owned enterprises.[13] These welfare-related provisions, presumably, could temper, if not stop, labor disputes which were reportedly on the rise (Du Xianzhong 1994:257), with the overall effect of reducing the *ex ante* costs of contracting and *ex post* costs of haggling, from the perspectives of foreign investors.

Table IV-9: Scales of Land-Use Fees in Shanghai* (RMB/m^2/year)

	A	B	C	D	E	F	G	H	I	J
a	130	110	90	70	40	24	18	12	8	
b	90	80	70	50	30	14	10	8	6	
c	100	90	70	30	20	12	9	6	3	
d	80	65	40	20	5	4	3	2	1	
e	75	65	50	35	20	12	8	5	2	
f	40	30	25	20	12	7	5	3	1	
g		12	10	5	4	2	2	1	0.5	
h			6	5	2.5	2	1	1	0.5	0.5

Note: * Excluding Pudong New Area. Upper-case letters stand for different grades of land. While the system of categorization is too complicated to be made clear without the aid of a city map, roughly grade A is in the commercial center of the city; grade J is in the suburban areas farthest away from the center. Lower-case letters stand for different purposes of land use, where:
a= commerce, finance, hotel
b= residence
c= industry, storage, transportation
d= TAEs and EOEs in industry, storage, and/or transportation
e= culture and recreation
f= education, science, health care, sports
g= farming, poultry
h= EOEs in farming and/or poultry
Source: Shanghai Municipal Land Bureau.

---

worker in cash and the indirect wage is the remuneration paid to the worker not directly but in the form of different social and state subsidies. The subsidies include labor insurance, medical expenses, housing and food price subsidies, transportation subsidies, and other subsidies. In general, the indirect wage is about 13% of the direct wage, varying in different localities and industries. According to Gao Chang (1995), of the indirect wage, labor insurance accounts for about 11%, medical care about 6%, housing 65%, food price subsidies 16%, and others 2%. Generally, a joint venture is required not only to pay direct wages to its workers, but also indirect wages to the relevant authorities. But as an incentive to encourage exports and transfers of high-technology, TAEs and EOEs are relieved from paying a range of government subsidies, according to the "22 Article."

13. If the firm is doing well, no upper cap is imposed.

Still another example has to do with land-use fees. At the national level, the EJV Implementation Act provided that while the provincial level governments have the power to determine the scales for land-use fees, once fixed, the fees cannot be adjusted in the first 5 years of business operations and thereafter no more frequently than every three years. At the local levels, regulations promulgated to supplement the national legislation were even more specific, as evidenced, for instance, by the land-use fees published by the Shanghai municipal government. In Shanghai, land is divided into 8 categories and 10 grades, depending on different geographical locations and the purposes of land use. The scale ranges from RMB130 per square meter per year at the maximum to RMB0.5 at the minimum, with each adjustment not exceeding 30% of the preceding standard (see Table IV-9). Similarly, Guangzhou has divided the scale of land-use fees into 6 categories and 4 grades (Du Xianzhong 1994:133).

A further example is the efforts made by China to provide a degree of consistency and stability amidst the rapidly evolving process of China's FDI regulatory framework. Specifically, a "grandfather" clause was written into the country's Foreign Economic Contract Law (Article 40) in 1988. What this means is that contracts involving FIEs are not adversely affected by any changes in law promulgated and implemented subsequent to the entering into the FIEs and they would continue to be governed by the law prevailing at the time they were entered into. In addition, the Foreign Economic Contract Law (Article 5) also provides that in the case that the provisions of the domestic laws do not cover a particular contractual issue, international practice applies.

Finally, China also promulgated the Provisions for the Encouragement of Foreign Investment, or the "22 Article," which went beyond legal clarification to liberalize substantially the general investment environment. In addition to making the institutional innovation specifically to address foreign exchange problems, the "22 Articles" contained more generous incentives explicitly designed to encourage FDI packaged with advanced technology and/or export capability, or the so-called technologically advanced enterprises and export-oriented enterprises.[14] Perhaps even more importantly, the "22 Articles" also attempted to further guarantee the autonomy of FIEs from bureaucratic interference, and to eliminate arbitrary local charges about which foreign investors had complained vociferously.[15]

While there is no easy way directly to assess the effectiveness of these provisions, especially regarding external interference and arbitrary local charges, indirect evidence suggests that they made a positive difference. According to a study on manufacturing FDI firms conducted by A.T. Kearney, a US consulting firm, in 1986, 60% of the 70 FIEs included in the study reported they were satisfied with their business operations in China; 25% had operational problems; and 15% gave no response. By contrast, in 1988 when the same

---

14. In an effort to encourage technology transfer and earn foreign exchange, the provisions attempted to attract hi-tech foreign companies and encourage export industries by providing additional incentives for technologically-advanced and export-oriented foreign-invested enterprises. FIEs that fulfill the criteria as TAEs or EOEs are eligible for a 50% reduction in the income tax rate. This reduction, however, is only available after the completion of the initial five-year statutory exemption and reduction period and is subject to a minimum tax rate of 10%, if an FIE is located in the SEZs. In addition, more incentives are offered by the local governments in the form of reduced land use fees. In the case of Shanghai, for instance, according to the Shanghai Joint Venture Land Procedures published in 1986, TAEs and EOEs are exempted from payment of land-use fees for the first 3 years of operation and will enjoy a 50% reduction in land-use fees from the 4th year onward.

15. On September 2, 1986, Deng Xiaoping was interviewed by Mike Wallace of CBS. A short excerpt from their conversation illustrates the loud complaints by foreign investors and awareness thereof by Chinese leaders.

Wallace: To modernize the Chinese economy and develop your country, Chairman Deng, you said China needs Western investment. But Western investors complained that China is making it difficult to do business here: exorbitant rents for offices, too much bickering about contracts, too many special taxes, labor that is too expensive, plus corruption, kickbacks, and the Chinese bureaucrats. Are you aware of these complaints?

Deng: Yes, I am aware of these things. Such phenomena do exist. As it is something new to us, some mistakes are unavoidable. We are working to change the present state of affairs. I do understand those complaints of foreign investors. No one would come here and invest without getting returns on their investment. We are taking effective measures to solve these problems. *People's Daily*, 15 September 1996.

survey was repeated with these firms, the satisfaction category went up to 91%; and only 9% continued to have operational problems (cited in Liu Yiming 1989:47).

There is other evidence, both statistical and anecdotal, pointing to heightened confidence by foreign investors in the investment environment in China thanks to Chinese efforts to improve the country's FDI regulatory framework during the second period. The Research Institute of MOFERT (cited in Zhang Ren 1993:7) reports that, 60% of the 48 FIEs sampled in 1986 said that they were making long-term strategic investment in China. Consistent with the findings of the report, there were quite a number of huge investment projects going on during this period. In 1985 the US Portman Companies began a massive construction project to build the Shanghai Exhibition Center in the heart of the city. The total investment of the project was estimated at US$200 million, about US$150 million more than the 1983 high profile case of Beijing Jeep Corporation whose total investment was US$51.03 million. Peugeot, a Chinese-French joint venture automobile company in Guangdong province, also commenced operations in 1985 with a total investment of 2.08 billion RMB. So too did the Panda Vehicle project in Huizhou, Guangdong province, a 100% foreign-owned subsidiary (of the US-based Panda Motor Corporation), capitalized at US$ 1 billion.[16]

There were many other high-profile cases in quite an array of different industrial sectors. Coca-Cola Company, which now occupies over 15% of China's soft drink market, also began to make long-term investment in China during this period. In October 1986 Coca-Cola signed a contract with the Shanghai Investment and Trust Company and the Food Development Center of Shanghai Light Industry to begin joint venture operations capitalized at US$14 million.[17] In Beijing, construction of the Lufthansa Center, one of the largest shopping centers in the capital, broke ground in 1987, with foreign investment totaling US$125 million (Wang Zhile 1996:116). For its part, DuPont Corporation set up a WFOE in Shenzhen in 1988. Other examples include General Electric, Motorola, and NEC, all of which

---

16. *China Trade Report*, April 1991, p. 1.

17. It was expected to increase to $500 million by 1996, according to one report. "Coca Cola Sells 2.4 Billion Cans to Chinese," America Online, 15 September 1994, Reuters News Service.

began serious negotiations to build plant cites in China as of 1988 (Liu Yiming 1989:47).

Beyond anecdotal cases, the increasing level of confidence of foreign investors was also reflected in systematic statistical evidence showing a dramatic shift of FDI from tourism-related services to manufacturing and infrastructure projects during this period. Manufacturing and infrastructure projects normally involve a great deal of immobile site-specific investments and are therefore more exposed to risks associated with institutional uncertainty. The rise of foreign investment in these kinds of projects can therefore be generally interpreted as a positive sign of the increased confidence of foreign investors in the institutional guarantees of property rights in the host country.[18] According to Crosby Securities, a Hong Kong stock brokerage firm, foreign investment as a share of China's expenditures on infrastructure development rose from 2% in 1982 to 13% in 1990. Separately, another study shows that while tourism-related industry was about 33% of all FDI in contractual amount in 1985, it dropped precipitously to 7% in 1988. By contrast, the share of manufacturing projects went up dramatically, reaching 90% in 1988 (Liu Yiming 1989:47).

More specifically, the rise of FDI in manufacturing toward the end of the 1980s also suggests that the situation regarding the foreign exchange problems that many FDI firms had suffered from in the mid-1980s was improving, thanks to the institutional innovation of the swap centers that were spreading in major cities across the

---

18. A possible objection to this line of reasoning is that tourism-related industries can also involve lumpy and fixed investments such as hotels. A note of clarification is thus in order. First, Chinese statistics on tourism-related industries also include catering services whose risks are relatively low. Second, during the initial years of the open door, while there were a few high profile cases where FDI was involved in constructing luxury hotels in China from scratch, such as the Jiangguo Hotel and the Great Wall Hotel in Beijing, and the Garden Hotel and White Swan Hotel in Guangzhou, much foreign investment was, however, involved in renovating existing hotel premises, and equipping them with superior services such as advanced booking system. Even though precise statistics are lacking, as any frequent traveler can attest, large-scale construction of luxury hotels, and office buildings for that matter, was largely a phenomenon in the late 1980s and especially in the early 1990s.

country. For, unlike non-manufacturing industries such as hotels which were able to balance foreign exchange relatively easily, unless FDI manufacturing projects could either export their products sufficiently, or find reliable local supplies of raw materials and/or quality intermediate parts, they were most prone to foreign exchange headaches.

Lending further support to our proposition about the rise of confidence on the part of foreign investors during this period is the increasing diversification of source countries/regions of FDI in China. Whereas in 1983, only 21 countries/regions made direct investment in China, in 1988 the number was more than doubled at 47.[19] Among the 47 countries/regions, Hong Kong, including Macao, continued to be the most active player in the investment scene, taking up 60% of all FDI in contract value for the 1985-90 period. The US during this period surpassed Japan to become the second largest source country with 11%. Japan was third with 7%, followed by Singapore with 2% (see Figure IV-3).

Figure IV-3: Leading FDI Suppliers in China, 1985-90 (contract value)

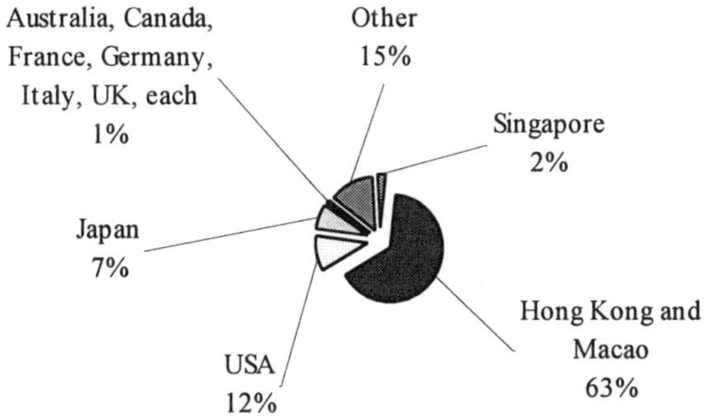

Note: "Other" includes all countries whose share is less than 1% of the total.
Sources: *Zhongguo duiwai jingji nianjian* [China Foreign Economic Statistical Yearbook] (various years); *Zhongguo duiwai maoyi nianjian* [Almanac of China's Foreign Trade and Economic Relations] (various years).

19. *Zhongguo duiwai maoyi nianjian* [China Foreign Economic Statistical Yearbook], 1984, p. IV-187, 1984; 1989/90, p. 46.

It is important to note that although Hong Kong continued to dominate the investment landscape in absolute terms in and beyond this period, as a relative share it was declining. Measured in contractual value, Hong Kong slipped to 60% in this period from a previous 76%, making a very significant 16% point drop. Measured by contract number, the downward trend of Hong Kong's share was also clear, consistent, and of similar velocity, as is illustrated by Figure IV-4,[20] from an average of 85% for the previous period to 75% in this period, and further down to 50% subsequently.

Figure IV-4: FDI Projects from Hong Kong and Macao as a Share of Total, 1983-98

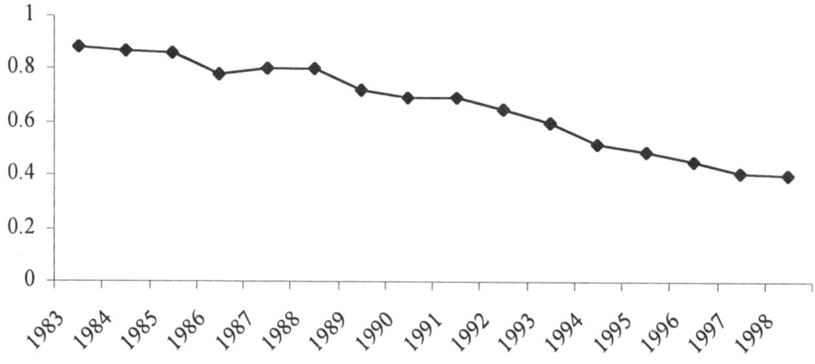

Sources: *Zhongguo duiwai jingji nianjian* [China Foreign Economic Statistical Yearbook] (various years); *Zhongguo duiwai maoyi nianjian* [Almanac of China's Foreign Trade and Economic Relations] (various years).

20. In reality, the real share attributable to Hong Kong is likely to be even smaller. Evidence suggests an increasing number of Western MNCs were making investment in China through their subsidiaries in Hong Kong. According to Weindenbaum and Hughes (1996:166-7), about 200 US companies have established regional headquarters in Hong Kong. About 70% of all US firms with headquarters in the Far East are in Hong Kong, noteworthy among which are Bank of America, Dun and Bradstreet, Exxon, Hyatt, May Department Stores, Motorola, PepsiCo, Polaroid, Time-Warner, Walt Disney, and Xerox.

Note also (Figure IV-3) that starting from this period more Western than Asian countries emerged as leading suppliers (defined as having a share of at least 1% of the total) of FDI to China. This seemed especially true in capital- and/or technology-intensive industries. In auto-related projects, for instance, Wang Loulin (1997:182) reports that by 1995, whereas Hong Kong had invested a total of US$272 million; German investment had reached US$215 million; US investment US$129 million; Japanese investment US$107 million; and French investment US$62 million. Since cultural and ethnic affinities are a well-established positive predictor of FDI flows because they serve to reduce information and transaction costs, the rise of FDI in China from countries whose cultures are distant belies the strengthening of the formal institution of China's FDI regulatory framework.

Finally, as documented in great length in Chapter 1, a salient feature of the development of China's FDI regulatory framework during this period was the dramatic geographic expansion of preferential policies into all major cities along the coast line. What this means is that many more local governments were now authorized to offer similar preferential terms to foreign investment hitherto available only in the SEZs, and that their power to review and approve FDI projects independently was also enlarged.

Very indicative of the effect of such institutional liberalization is the changed pattern of geographical distribution of FDI during this period. As Table IV-10 shows, although there was little sign that FDI was now moving inland in any significant way, it was undoubtedly meandering northward along the coastal provinces. This is evidenced by a sharp drop in the relative share of Guangdong – from the previous 82% to the current 43% – and the rise in Zhejiang (2%), Shanghai (9%), Jiangsu (5%), Shandong (3%), Hebei (2%), Tianjin (2%), Beijing (6%), Liaoning (5%), and Heilongjiang (1%). For further illustration of the changed pattern of geographical distribution of FDI in this period, I added the figures for Guangdong, Fujian, and Hainan (where all of China's five SEZs are located), and compared them to that of the rest of China's coastal provinces. The ratio was 88:10 for the 1979-84 period; it was 58:36 during this period. This suggests that the effects of the special policies previously offered only in the SEZs were gradually equalized.

Table IV-10: Geographical Distribution of FDI, 1985-90 (contract value)

Provinces/Municipalities	As % of country total
Guangdong	43%
Fujiang	12%
Shanghai	9%
Beijing	6%
Jiangsu	5%
Liaoning	5%
Hainan	3%
Shangdong	3%
Tianjin	2%
Hebei	2%
Zhejiang	2%
Guangxi	2%
Heilongjiang	1%
Rest of China	5%

Sources: *Zhongguo duiwai jingji nianjian* [China Foreign Economic Statistical Yearbook] (various years); *Zhongguo duiwai maoyi nianjian* [Almanac of China's Foreign Trade and Economic Relations] (various years).

On the basis of evidence reviewed thus far, it seems clear then that as China's FDI regulatory framework continued to improve and liberalize during the second period, the Hong Kong factor – a good proxy of the informal institutional effect on investment behavior, with all its salient features of geographical proximity, cultural affinities, and ethnic connections – became relatively less important in driving FDI in China.

A Phenomenal Third Growth (1991-96)

Although it looked as though China would reverse its open-door policy in the wake of the Tiananmen incident of 1989, that prospect did not materialize. Instead, China's open-door policy not only survived the political maelstrom but also intensified. Specific to the foreign investment, China's FDI regulatory framework continued with little delay to undergo further liberalization. Among the major developments in the early 1990s were the 1990 amendments to the 1979 EJV Law. Until then, foreign investors, regardless of the size of their equity stake, were not allowed to hold the position of chairman of the board of directors, and the duration of JVs, albeit already having undergone a round of relaxation in 1986, was nonetheless still limited to a maximum of 50 years. With the amendments to the 1979 EJV Law in April 1990, these restrictions were effectively removed.

There was more encouraging news for foreign investors. A year later, in addition to the promulgation of the Detailed Implementation Act of the 1986 WFOE Law in December 1990, China also published in April 1991 a unified tax code. The new tax code eliminated yet another discriminatory element in China's FDI regulatory framework by treating WFOEs equally as other modes of FDI for tax purposes. Accompanying all these dramatic developments were, as documented at great length in Part I, a series of steps taken by China to align itself with international practices in the protection of intellectual property rights.

In addition, many "inside documents" which might affect FDI firms were opened to the public to increase the transparency of China's FDI regulatory framework. According to one source, since 1991, MOFTEC has, on the one hand, nullified a total of 744 such documents, and, on the other, made available to the public a total of 93 documents previously reserved for internal circulation only (Chen Wenjin 1996:30). These moves were apparently part and parcel of China's efforts to join the World Trade Organization, the successor of the General Agreement on Tariffs and Trade. WTO membership entitles a contracting party most-favored-nation status on a non-discriminatory basis,[21] but also requires, *inter alia,* market-opening measures, transparency of a trade-related regulatory framework, and national treatment standards for contracting parties.

These continued improvements and liberalization of China's FDI regulatory framework seem to have worked effectively in mitigating the negative impact of the Tiananmen events of 1989. This was in part evidenced in part by the improved rating of the country's

21. China already enjoys permanent MFN treatment from every major country in the world. Only the US grants this status on a year-by-year basis. Under conditions imposed by the Jackson-Vanik amendment to the Trade Act of 1974, the US is precluded from extending permanent MFN status to China. Unless this amendment is suspended with respect to China, the US will have to invoke the nonapplication provision of the Uruguay Round Treaty establishing the WTO. In that case, China will be under no legal obligations to deliver to the US all the market opening concessions it has made to the US in the WTO trade agreement reached between the two countries on November 15, 1999.

political environment by risk assessment organizations such as the Economist Intelligence Unit. On a scale in which 100 is the riskiest rating, China was rated 15 in 1988, one of the EIU's lowest risk ratings. This jumped to 35 in 1989, but by 1992 had fallen back to 25 (*The Economist*, 21 May 1994:120). In the real world, FDI continued to grow rapidly even in 1990, although the growth potentials might have been stunted a bit by the political shock waves in the immediate aftermath of the Tiananmen events (see figures for 1989 in Table IV-8). In 1990, a total of 7,273 new FDI projects were signed, with a contract value amounting to US$6.596 billion (see Table IV-8). These represented a rapid rise of 26% and 17% respectively over the comparable figures for 1989.

More importantly, for the first time, the number of newly concluded projects in the mode of WFOE surpassed those in the CJV mode in 1990. That year, a total of 1,860 WFOE projects were signed with a combined contract value of US$2.445 billion. By comparison, the number of CJV projects was 1,317, with a contract value totaling US$1.254 billion.[22] This new development was a good indication of the growing confidence of foreign investors in the investment environment in China, and was, in retrospect, a harbinger of the phenomenal growth of FDI in China in subsequent years.

Table IV-11 contains data which reveal the growth patterns of FDI flows for the period from 1991 through 1996. On a yearly average, China attracted 42,383 FDI projects with a contract value of US$71.462 billion during these 6 years, representing a 9.8 times and 14.3 times increase over the comparable figures for the previous 6 years. Initial signs of the phenomenal growth had already become clear by 1991. That year, FDI stock was 1.78 times greater than that of the previous year, as measured by project number; 1.82 times greater as measured by contract value; and 1.25 times greater as measured by realized amount. FDI inflows of even greater magnitudes were to occur in 1992 and beyond.

---

22. *Zhongguo duiwai maoyi nianjian* [Almanac of China's Foreign Trade and Economic Relations], 1991, p. 580.

Table IV-11: FDI by Different Modes, 1991-96 (US$ billion)

Project #	*Total*	*EJV*	*CJV*	*WFOE*	*JDP*
1991	12,978	8,395 (65%)	1,778 (14%)	2,795 (22%)	10 (0%)
1992	48,764	34,354 (70%)	5,711 (12%)	8,699 (18%)	0 (0%)
1993	83,437	54,003 (65%)	10,445 (13%)	18,975 (23%)	14 (0%)
1994	47,549	27,890 (59%)	6,634 (14%)	13,007 (27%)	18 (0%)
1995	37,011	20,455 (55%)	4,787 (13%)	11,761 (32%)	8 (0%)
1996	24,556	12,628 (51%)	2,849 (12%)	9,062 (37%)	17 (0%)
Cumulative	254,295	157,725 (62%)	32,204 (13%)	64,299 (25%)	67 (0%)
Average	42,383	26,288 (62%)	5,367 (13%)	10,717 (25%)	11 (0%)
Contractual					
1991	11.976	6.08 (51%)	2.137 (18%)	3.668 (31%)	0.091 (1%)
1992	58.123	29.128 (50%)	13.255 (23%)	15.696 (27%)	0 (0%)
1993	111.435	55.174 (50%)	25.499 (23%)	30.456 (27%)	0.304 (0%)
1994	82.679	40.193 (49%)	20.300 (25%)	21.948 (27%)	0.236 (0%)
1995	91.281	39.320 (43%)	17.730 (19%)	33.657 (37%)	0.570 (1%)
1996	73.280	31.880 (44%)	14.300 (20%)	26.810 (37%)	0.290 (0%)
Cumulative	428.774	201.775 (47%)	93.221 (22%)	132.235 (31%)	1.491 (0%)
Average	71.462	33.629 (47%)	15.537 (22%)	22.039 (31%)	0.249 (0%)
Actual					
1991	4.366	2.298 (53%)	0.763 (17%)	1.134 (26%)	0.169 (4%)
1992	11.007	6.114 (56%)	2.122 (19%)	2.770 (25%)	0 (0%)
1993	27.514	15.347 (56%)	5.237 (19%)	6.505 (24%)	0.424 (2%)
1994	33.766	17.932 (53%)	7.120 (21%)	8.035 (24%)	0.678 (2%)
1995	37.520	19.077 (51%)	7.535 (20%)	10.316 (27%)	0.590 (2%)
1996	41.730	20.750 (49%)	8.110 (19%)	12.610 (30%)	0.260 (1%)
Cumulative	155.903	63.518 (52%)	30.887 (20%)	41.370 (27%)	2.121 (1%)
Average	25.984	10.586 (52%)	5.148 (20%)	6.895 (27%)	0.354 (1%)

Note: Shares of total by different modes of FDI are in parentheses.
Sources: *Zhongguo duiwai jingji nianjian* [China Foreign Economic Statistical Yearbook] (various years); *Zhongguo duiwai maoyi nianjian* [Almanac of China's Foreign Trade and Economic Relations] (various years).

Indeed, take Shanghai for instance. In 1992 alone, Shanghai's recently opened Pudong New Area attracted a total of 2,012 FDI projects, with a contract value of US$3,357 million. This exceeded the combined figures of the previous dozen years, both in number and value. Across the nation in 1993, China was, to borrow the words of

Nicholas Lardy (1995:1065), "the site of more FDI than any other country." In 1994 the realized amount of FDI in China continued to bulge to reach US$33.766 billion, making China the largest FDI recipient among all developing countries, second only to the US in the whole world (World Bank 1994a:16).

Beyond aggregate statistical data, particularly worth mentioning is the fact that, perhaps as a reflection of the improving investment environment, especially with respect to the protection of intellectual property rights and domestic market access in the 1990s, a growing number of large multinational corporations began to invest heavily in China during this period. There were reports that major computer manufacturers all moved rapidly to set up both manufacturing and software development ventures in China after the promulgation of the Copyright Law in 1990.[23] According to a Chinese study (Wang Luolin 1997:122), in 1991-95 FDI in the computer industry in China reached US$1.3 billion and output value generated by FDI firms accounted for 60% of the country's total. Leading the field in terms of investment were IBM, AST, Compaq, Siemens, Conner, Seagate, Phillips (Taiwan), Intel, and Hewlett Packard.

According to another study conducted more recently, of the 231 investment projects by 30 leading Japanese and German MNCs surveyed, only 10.8%, or 25 investment projects, occurred prior to 1990. The rest all took place in the 1990s, and especially after 1992, the year in which China moved aggressively to open itself up further, both regionally and sectorally, for FDI in the wake of Deng Xiaoping's southern inspection tour (see Table IV-12).

The industrial composition of these MNC investment projects constituted a sharp contrast to many of the earlier investments made by overseas Chinese, which, as shown earlier, were mostly small-scale and labor-intensive projects involving little sophisticated technology. Of the 231 projects by the 30 leading Japanese and German MNCs, as Table IV-13 shows, a large majority of them were in capital- and/or technology-intensive sectors such as electronic equipment, automobiles, telecommunications, electricity, chemical engineering, and pharmaceutical products.

---

23. "Software Hard Drive," *China Trade Report*, May 1991, p. 8

Table IV-12: Temporal Distribution of FDI by 30 Leading Japanese and German MNCs,* 1980-95

Year	Number of Projects	Year	Number of Projects
1980	0	1988	2
1981	1	1989	7
1982	0	1990	5
1983	1	1991	5
1984	5	1992	16
1985	4	1993	37
1986	1	1994	69
1987	4	1995	74
		Total	*231*

Note: * Defined as having a yearly sales value among the top 500 firms in the world according to *Fortune Magazine*. Examples include Toyota, Hitachi, Sony, Nissan, Toshiba, NEC, Canon, Mazda, Mercedes-Benz, Siemens, Volkswagen, and Bosch, etc.
Source: Wang Zhile (1996) *Zhuming kuaguo gongsi zhongguo de touzi* [Investment of Transnational Corporations in China], p. 13.

Table IV-13: Industrial Composition of FDI by 30 Leading Japanese and German MNCs, 1980-95

Industrial Sector	Number of Projects	Industrial Sector	Number of Projects
Electronics	48	Light industry	15
Automobiles	28	Investment management	11
Household electric appliances	23	Trade and commerce	7
Chemical engineering	18	Resources	5
Telecommunications	17	Pharmaceutical products	4
Machinery	17	Food & tobacco	3
Research & design	17	Textiles & garments	2
Electricity and gas	16	*Total*	*231*

Source: Wang Zhile (1996) *Zhuming kuaguo gongsi zhongguo de touzi* [Investment of Transnational Corporations in China], p. 18.

At a sub-national level, available information on investment activities by MNCs was consistent with the picture painted above. In Shanghai, for instance, by the end of 1994 there were a total of 281 projects by 142 world-class MNCs – such as AT&T, Northern Telecom, DuPont, Johnson & Johnson, Dunlop, Hitachi, Mitsubishi, Fuji, Sony, Sharp, Omron, BASF, Henkel, Siemens, Bell, Pilkington, Volkswagen, and Phillips – with a total investment of US$4,800 million, representing more than 20% of the total FDI in the city on a contractual basis. The average scale of these projects was large, demonstrating clear signs of expansion. Specifically, it was US$11 million up to 1992, US$14 million in 1993 and US$20 million 1994 (Tian Gang 1996:174). By comparison, the average size of FDI projects in China as a whole was only about US$1.5 million.

Shanghai was, of course, not alone in attracting big MNC investment projects, even though there is little doubt that it was the most popular site for such investments.[24] Across the nation, Beijing was also a popular site, and in fact it was the second largest region hosting huge investment projects. The Zhongguancun district in Beijing, for instance, or the so-called Silicon Valley in China, where the country's best research institutes and universities are located,[25] has now become host to an impressive array of world-class high-tech firms such as HP, IBM, AT&T, INTEL, GE, NEC, and Microsoft. By contrast, Guangdong province, even though it remained a favorable location for many Hong Kong investors, only ranked third in attracting large MNC investment. Following Guangdong, and in order, were Liaoning, Zhejiang, Shandong, and Fujian provinces, as is shown in Table IV-14.

Evidence also suggests that, due to the steady liberalization of China's FDI regulatory framework, FIEs were increasingly able to capture a large share of China's domestic markets in the 1990s. Motorola subsidiaries, for instance, manufactured about 50,000 cellular phones and 1,000,000 beepers each year, accounting for 50% and 70% respectively of the total output of China. Mobile telecom products manufactured by FIEs exceeded 90% of the domestic market share (Wang Loulin 1997:119). In pharmaceuticals, although the number of FIEs increased rapidly from less than 200 in 1991 to close to 800 in 1995, the number of EOEs, as a share of all FIEs approved

---

24. The trend of increasing investment by MNCs was also apparent in other cities. Motorola in Tianjin, for instance, started in 1990 with an initial investment of US$300,000; in 1992, it increased its investment to US$ 120 million, which again was expanded by adding US$160 million in 1994 and US$720 million in 1995. See Li Yong (1997:161).

25. The Zhongguanchun district in Beijing is arguably the most human capital intensive place in China. Within an area of 100 square kilometers, it boasts of a total of 138 research institutions, including Peking and Tsinghua Universities, with a labor force, 70% of which hold college degrees or higher (Li Lanqing 1995:310). Also see Kennedy (1997).

each year in the 1990s, displayed a general downward trend, very much a reflection of increased access to the domestic market (Figure IV-5).

Table IV-14: Geographical Distribution of Top Manufacturing FDI Projects by 1995 (US$ million)

	Project > $100 M		*Project >$50 M*		*Project >$20 M*	
Shanghai	563	(81.2%)	662	(56%)	839	(37%)
Beijing	130	(18.8%)	248	(21%)	309	(14%)
Guangdong	0	(0%)	60	(5.1%)	181	(8%)
Liaoning	0	(0%)	52	(4%)	163	(7%)
Zhejiang	0	(0%)	0	(0%)	128	(6%)
Shandong	0	(0%)	108	(9%)	108	(5%)
Fujian	0	(0%)	0	(0%)	91	(4%)
Others	0	(0%)	50	(4%)	377	(15%)
Total	693	(100%)	1180	(100%)	2196	(100%)

Note: Figures in parentheses are percentage of the country's total.
Source: Tian Gang (1996) *Shanghai's Role in the Economic Development of China*, which is based on *Asian Wall Street Journal*, 22 November 1994.

Figure IV-5: Number of Export-oriented Pharmaceutical FIE Firms as a Share of Total, 1991-95

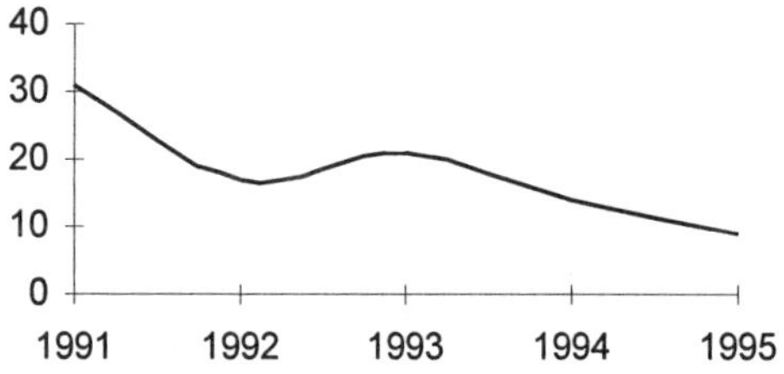

Note: The absolute number of all FDI projects in 1995 was 796; that of export-oriented enterprises (i.e., exports 70% or more of output ad valorem) was 98.
Source: Wang Luolin (1997), *Zhongguo waishang touzi baogao* [Report on Foreign Investment in China], pp. 205, 208.

Consistent with the above evidence, in Tianjin, another central autonomous municipality along with Beijing, Shanghai, and now Chongqing, about half of all the big MNCs operating as of 1992, or 7 out of 15 to be exact, were allowed by the local government to target their products entirely at the domestic market. Measured by the total value of their sales, from 1992 through the first half of 1995, MNCs in Tianjin were consistently able to sell as much as about 76% of their products on domestic markets (see Table IV-15).

Table IV-15: Domestic Sales by MNCs in Tianjin, 1992-95 (billion RMB)

	1992	1993	1994	1995 (Jan-July)
Number of MNCs in operation	15	24	46	46
Firms with products on domestic markets	7	9	19	16
As share of total	46.7%	37.5%	41.3%	34.8%
Total sales	0.823	3.048	9.218	10.083
Domestic sales	0.620	2.288	7.000	7.621
As share of total	75.3%	75.1%	75.9%	75.6%

Source: Tianjin kaifaqu waiguo gongsi touzi xiangmu tongji ziliao (1996) [Statistics on FDI Projects in Tianjin Development Zone].

Table IV-16: Yearly Average FDI in Interior Regions, 1985-90 and 1991-95 (US$10,000)

	(I) Yearly Average 1985-90	(II)Yearly Average 1991-95	Increase (II)/(I)
Contract Amount	32862	327635	10
Realized Amount	18043	272188	15
Number of projects	328	7468	23

Sources: *Zhongguo duiwai jingji nianjian* [China Foreign Economic Statistical Yearbook] (various years); *Zhongguo duiwai maoyi nianjian* [Almanac of China's Foreign Trade and Economic Relations] (various years).

A further reflection of the improving investment environment in China in the 1990s was the continued diversification of both the geographical distribution of FDI and the investment source countries/regions. In terms of geographical distribution, there was evidence that FDI began to meander increasingly into the interior regions of the country, especially after 1992 when China decided to expand into its inland cities many of its preferential FDI terms hitherto only available in coastal regions.

The inward movement of FDI was clear in both absolute and relative terms. In absolute terms, as Table IV-16 shows, on a yearly average, the average yearly figures for 1991-95, as measured by the contract amount, realized amount and number of projects were respectively 10, 15, and 23 times larger than the comparable figures for 1985-90. In relative terms (see Figure IV-6), FDI in the interior regions as a share of the country's total, measured either by project number or by dollar amount, demonstrated a general upward trend –

which is particularly striking in and after 1992 in realized amount as well as in the number of contracts newly concluded in this period.

Figure IV-6: FDI in the Interior Regions of China as a Share of Total, 1989-95

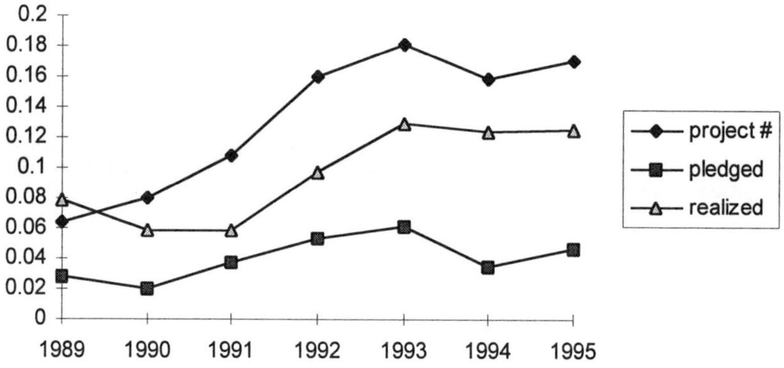

Sources: *Zhongguo duiwai jingji nianjian* [China Foreign Economic Statistical Yearbook] (various years); *Zhongguo duiwai maoyi nianjian* [Almanac of China's Foreign Trade and Economic Relations] (various years).

The diversification of the geographical distribution of FDI in China during this period was accompanied by a rapid multiplication of investment source countries/regions. Recall that the number of FDI source countries/regions was 21 in 1983 and 47 in 1988. It jumped to 80 in 1991, 122 in 1992, and 146 in 1993,[26] and as of 1995, it was over 150 (Li Lanqing 1995:59). As Table IV-17 shows, Hong Kong, including Macao, continued to be the leading supplier of FDI in the 1990s, with its relative share stabilized around 60%, measured by project number, contract value, and realized amount. While this may be true statistically, in reality, however, there is reason to believe that the investment that could really be attributed to Hong Kong is smaller. As Chen Jinghan (1993:180) has observed, a growing number of Western MNCs choose to make investment in China through their subsidiaries in Hong Kong, a factor not readily reflected by the statistics.

26. *People's Daily*, Overseas edition, 7 April 1995, p. 1.

Table IV-17: Leading FDI Suppliers in China, 1990-95 (US$ billion)

Country/region	Project Number		Contract Amount		Actual Amount	
HK & Macao	139880	(59%)	221.600	(61%)	71.396	(60%)
Taiwan	28472	(12%)	26.761	(7%)	10.745	(9%)
US	18763	(8%)	22.685	(6%)	8.952	(8%)
Japan	12197	(5%)	18.591	(5%)	8.423	(7%)
Singapore	5456	(2%)	16.664	(5%)	3.760	(3%)
South Korea	6222	(3%)	6.781	(2%)	2.267	(2%)
Britain	1380	(1%)	6.944	(2%)	1.919	(2%)
Canada	2650	(1%)	3.418	(1%)	0.689	(1%)
Australia	2228	(1%)	3.084	(1%)	0.606	(1%)
Thailand	1996	(1%)	3.329	(1%)	0.869	(1%)
Germany	1156	(0%)	3.892	(1%)	1.030	(1%)
Malaysia	1208	(1%)	2.689	(1%)	0.578	(0%)
Other	15404	(6%)	27.242	(7%)	7.537	(6%)
Total	237012	(100%)	363.680	(100%)	118.770	(100%)

Note: Leading suppliers of FDI are defined here as having at least a 1 percent share of the country's total, measured either by project number, or by dollar amount. Shares of national total are in parentheses.

Sources: *Zhongguo duiwai jingji nianjian* [China Foreign Economic Statistical Yearbook] (various years); *Zhongguo duiwai maoyi nianjian* [Almanac of China's Foreign Trade and Economic Relations] (various years).

Although the precise number of de facto Western firms which use Hong Kong as a gateway to mainland China eludes investigation, it is by no means a small number. Weidenbaum and Hughes (1996:166-67) report that about 200 US multinationals established regional headquarters in Hong Kong, and about 70% of all US firms with headquarters in the Far East are in Hong Kong – notable among them are Bank of America, Dun and Bradstreet, Exxon, Hyatt, May Department Stores, Motorola, PepsiCo, Polaroid, Time-Warner, Walt Disney, and Xerox. While the country origin of these big-name companies can be readily recognized, the home countries of lesser names are not immediately apparent.

The Cases of South Korea and Taiwan

It is also worth noting that South Korea and Taiwan emerged as leading investors. As Table IV-17 shows, Taiwan surpassed the US to become the second largest supplier of FDI and South Korea held the 6th place. These developments highlight our proposition that flows of

FDI are not shaped by economic factors alone. In fact, they seem to be better explained as a function of the development of non-market institutions – formal institutions in particular.

In the case of South Korea, because of the lack of diplomatic relations with China until very recently, South Korean FDI in China has a very short history. Although South Korea's first investment in China, camouflaged as a Hong Kong firm, was realized as early as 1985, as Table IV-18 indicates, South Korean FDI flows of substantial magnitude did not occur until after 1990. That is, after China and South Korea decided in 1990 to establish semi-official trade representatives with consular functions, in the name of KOTRA (Korea Trade Promotion Corp.) and CCOIC (China Chamber of International Commerce), to facilitate commercial transactions in the absence of formal diplomatic ties. Note the dramatic rise of FDI in the wake of this event. There was roughly a threefold increase in 1990 over the previous year, measured in project number, and again there was another extraordinary increase of 195% in 1991.

That investment growth took place in tandem with the development of the formal institutional infrastructure was even more salient in 1992, during which time China signed a bilateral investment protection agreement with South Korea in May, as it did with some 50 other countries around the world. Moreover, in August 1992 the formal diplomatic relations were established between the two countries. Accordingly, FDI registered a 480% increase in project number in 1992 over the previous year; 396% in contract value, and 183% in realized amount. As Table IV-18 further reveals, the phenomenal surge of FDI from South Korea continued in subsequent years, even though the growth rate tapered off significantly in recent years in the aftermath of the Asian financial crisis.

In the case of Taiwan, in spite of the fact that it shares the same customs, dialects and consanguinity with Fujian province in south China, Taiwan FDI of considerable magnitude in mainland China was largely a phenomenon after 1988, when mainland China promulgated the Regulations on Encouraging the Investment of Taiwan Compatriots (REITC).[27] Prior to that year, only a small flow of

27. Coincidentally, with martial law in Taiwan repealed in July 1987, Taiwan lifted its ban on civilian visits to the mainland and relaxed its control over foreign currencies around 1988.

clandestine investment trickled from Taiwan to mainland China through third countries/regions.[28] In 1983, Xiaxing Jewelry Co., an affiliate of a Taiwan firm registered in Singapore, made the first Taiwan investment in the Xiamen SEZ where much of Taiwan investment is now located,[29] and by 1987 there were only 19 projects by Taiwan investors in Xiamen, with a total investment of US$19.35 million in realized value,[30] a minuscule amount, as we shall see, compared to subsequent years.

Table IV-18: South Korean FDI to China, 1988-97 (US$ million)

Year	Project Number		Contract Amount		Actual Amount	
1988	2	--	3.400	--	N/A	--
1989	12	(500%)	9.770	(187%)	6.350	--
1990	38	(217%)	54.493	(458%)	15.974	(152%)
1991	112	(195%)	84.721	(55%)	42.468	(166%)
1992	650	(480%)	420.540	(396%)	120.250	(183%)
1993	1748	(169%)	1556.690	(270%)	381.490	(217%)
1994	1849	(6%)	1806.260	(16%)	722.830	(89%)
1995	1975	(7%)	2998.390	(66%)	1042.890	(44%)
1996	1896	(-4%)	4240.000	(41%)	1360.000	(30%)
1997	1753	(-8%)	2180.980	(-49%)	2142.380	(58%)

Note: Annual growth rates are parentheses.
Sources: *Zhongguo duiwai jingji nianjian* [China Foreign Economic Statistical Yearbook] (various years); *Zhongguo duiwai maoyi nianjian* [Almanac of China's Foreign Trade and Economic Relations] (various years).

Taiwan investment posed special problems, the solution to which required special institutional arrangements. Given that Taiwan is

28. While the precise size of that investment remains unclear, it was perforce extremely limited, as reflected by the volume of indirect trade (through an intermediate location such as Hong Kong) between the two sides of the Taiwan straits. For years, Taiwan customers clandestinely purchased mainland Chinese medicinal herbs, tea, and other native products, the total value of which never exceeded the dismal level of US$50 million per year. On the other hand, mainland China also imported limited quantities of goods from Taiwan, the value of which never exceeded US$50,000 per year. See *Beijing Review*, 3-9 April 1989, p. 24.

29. In 1989 as much as 40% of Taiwan's FDI in mainland China was concentrated in the Xiamen SEZ. See Hu Peizhao, et al. (1991).

30. Interview. Statistics Bureau, Xiamen City Government.

officially accepted by the authorities on either side of the Taiwan straits as an integral part of China, Taiwan investment is, *de jure*, domestic instead of foreign, and as such it does not enjoy the preferential treatment given to foreign firms.

The significance of the 1988 REITC is that it represented a compromise by mainland China by viewing Taiwan investment as domestic,[31] but granting it the same preferential treatment as foreign investment. Further, to allay Taiwan investors' fears of expropriation, it explicitly prohibited nationalization of Taiwan investment without compensation (REITC, 8th and 9th sections). These provisions were again reaffirmed in the Law Regarding the Protection of the Investment by Taiwan Compatriots promulgated by the NPC in 1994. Further still, in the absence of formal intergovernmental contacts, two civilian, yet officially authorized organizations, the Straits Exchange Foundation in Taipei and the Association for Relations Across the Straits in Beijing, were established 1990 and 1991, respectively, to deal with issues ranging from civil affairs to prevention of crime and protection of the rights of Taiwan investors in mainland China (Zhang Guilong and Liu Shuqiang 1994:10-11).

The effects of these institutional arrangements are reflected in the enormous surge of Taiwan investment in mainland China in the immediate wake of the institutional developments. As Table IV-19 shows, the number of investment projects in 1988 alone was 435, representing a 444% increase over the total number for the previous years. Growth of similar magnitudes was also registered in contract amount. It amounted to US$520 million, representing a 420% increase over the combined figure of the previous years. Following the establishment of the semi-official bodies – the Straits Exchange Foundation and the Association for Relations across the Straits in 1991, growth again underwent a sharp increase in following years (see Table IV-19).

---

31. As such the duration of Taiwan-invested firms had no limits and, moreover, Taiwan investors were permitted to hold the position of chairman of the board of directors of JVs. By comparison, foreign nationals were not allowed to do so until 1990 when the 1979 EJV Law was amended.

Table IV-19: Taiwan FDI to Mainland China, 1987-97 (US$ million)

Year	Project Number	Contract Amount	Actual Amount
1987	80 *	100.000 *	N/A
1988	435 (444%)	520.000 (420%)	N/A
1989	552 (27%)	437.000 (-16%)	N/A
1990	1103 (100%)	892.000 (104%)	N/A
1991	1700 (54%)	1451.000 (63%)	2100.000 *
1992	6430 (278%)	5547.900 (282%)	1053.350 (-50%)
1993	10948 (70%)	9970.040 (80%)	3139.130 (198%)
1994	6247 (-43%)	5394.880 (-46%)	3391.040 (8%)
1995	4847 (-22%)	5849.070 (8%)	3161.550 (-7%)
1996	3184 (-34%)	5140.000 (-12%)	3480.000 (10%)
1997	3014 (-5%)	2814.490 (-45%)	3289.390 (-6%)

Note: * This number is cumulative investment up to that year. Annual growth rates are presented in percentage points.
Sources: Data before 1992 are from Lee-in Chen Chiu, "The Pattern and Impact of Taiwan's Investment in Mainland China," in Sumner La Croix, et al ed. (1997), *Emerging Patterns of East Asian Investment in China*, p. 149. Data for subsequent years are from *Zhongguo duiwai jingji nianjian* [China Foreign Economic Statistical Yearbook] (various years); *Zhongguo duiwai maoyi nianjian* [Almanac of China's Foreign Trade and Economic Relations] (various years).

Taiwan and Hong Kong Compared

Further reflecting the improvement in the late 1980s of China's FDI regulatory framework in general and the institutional arrangements across the Taiwan straits in particular was the micro-investment behavior of Taiwan investors. Although in many ways Taiwan entrepreneurs resembled early Hong Kong investors by moving small-scale labor-intensive firms to mainland China to take advantage of the relatively low labor costs,[32] their investment behavior differed from their Hong Kong counterparts in at least two aspects, both of which indicated confidence in mainland China as an investment outlet. First, in comparable early stages of investment, Taiwan investment demonstrated an exceedingly low ratio of CJVs and a very high ratio

32. For instance, of the total of 169 Taiwan investment projects in Xiamen in 1988-89, 124 projects, or 73%, were in light and textile industries such as food processing, garments, footwear, umbrellas, toys, suitcases, and bags. Interview, Statistics Bureau, Xiamen City Government.

of WFOEs, which was especially true after 1988, as Table IV-20 shows. This stood in sharp contrast to Hong Kong investment in the early years, the bulk of which, as we discussed earlier, came in the form of CJVs, the investment modality best suited to accommodate short-term investment behavior.

Table IV-20: Different Modes of Taiwan Investment in Xiamen, 1983-90

Mode	1987		1988		1989		1990		Total	
WFOE	3	(16%)	53	(66%)	109	(85%)	144	(85%)	309	(78%)
EJV	13	(68%)	23	(29%)	17	(13%)	15	(9%)	68	(17%)
CJV	3	(16%)	4	(5%)	2	(2%)	10	(6%)	19	(5%)
Total	19	(100%)	80	(100)	128	(100)	169	(100)	396	(100)

Note: Shares of total are in parentheses.
Source: Interview, Statistics Bureau, Xiamen City Government.

Table IV-21: Project Duration of Taiwan Investment in Xiamen, 1988-89

Project Duration	1988		1989		Cumulative	
Over 30 years	11	(14%)	45	(35%)	56	(27%)
20-30 years	19	(24%)	36	(28%)	55	(26%)
10-19 years	46	(58%)	46	(36%)	92	(44%)
Below 10 years	4	(5%)	1	(1%)	5	(2%)
Cumulative	80	(100%)	128	(100%)	208	(100%)

Note: Shares of total are in parentheses.
Source: Interview. Statistics Bureau, Xiamen City Government.

Second, when Taiwan investors began to make investments of considerable magnitudes in and after 1988, they showed little hesitation to opt for long-term investment projects. In fact, as Table IV-21 shows, more than half of the 208 investment projects in Xiamen for the 1988-89 period had a duration well beyond 15-20 years. In contrast, the average duration for most Hong Kong FDI projects during the initial years of China's open door was less than 15 years. Indeed, beginning in 1990, Taiwan-owned firms routinely re-invest, expand enterprise scale, purchase factories and buildings, or otherwise shift from labor-intensive manufacturing to more diversified projects, including property construction, service industries, high-tech industries, and even railway and infrastructure projects.[33] A few have even formed large consortia to develop entire industrial zones in mainland China (Wu Jianghu 1994: 2-3).

Concluding Remarks

In this chapter, we have examined the variant patterns of FDI in China in the reform years using quantitative data. Our examination first proceeded on a stock basis, which gave us an overall sense of the magnitude of FDI that China has received thus far. We then put FDI under scrutiny in a flow fashion, and found that, *prima facie* at least, the growth patterns of FDI in China follow closely the institutional development of China's FDI regulatory framework that we documented in Part I of this study.

To highlight the formal institutional effect on investment behavior, we pointed to the extraordinary surges around 1990 of FDI flows from South Korea and Taiwan, both in the wake of the solidification of bilateral institutional arrangements to facilitate trade and commerce. In addition, we also briefly contrasted the investment behavior of Taiwan and Hong Kong investors, both being relatively equal in terms of cultural advantages. But the fact that Taiwan investors showed a propensity to make investments that were of a longer duration, and with more sunk capital, than Hong Kong investors in comparable stages belies the underlying institutional improvement of China's FDI regulatory framework: After all, in the late 1980s when the first wave of Taiwan investment arrived in mainland China, China had already had about a decade's time to develop and improve its FDI regulatory framework.

Finally, to conclude this chapter, let us turn to a set of statistics whose implications I have deliberately avoided exploring thus far. If we take a close look at the statistics showing the growth trend of Taiwan investment in mainland China (see Table IV-19), there are tell-tale signs that Taiwan investment began to slow down dramatically in 1994. In fact, this slowdown was not exclusive to the case of Taiwan FDI. It also happened in the case of the growth trend of South Korean FDI (see Table IV-18), and indeed it was true at the aggregate level of FDI inflows to China as a whole (see Table IV-11,

33. *Lianhebao*, [United Daily News], 7 August 1992.

especially numbers of newly concluded projects).[34] The question then is: Does this contradict our contention that FDI flows are systematically related to improvements in China's FDI regulatory framework? My answer is no. Instead, I argue that the slowdown in fact further supports our institutional explanation of investment behavior, for it provides concrete evidence showing that as China finally decided in 1994 to narrow the gap of special treatment between FIEs and their domestic counterparts, it removed an institutional source of what may be called an "abnormally high demand" for FDI in China, a topic to be further explored in the next chapter.

---

34. The drop of FDI inflows in 1997 in terms of contract value and project number is understandable. To a great extent it reflected the Asian financial crisis that hit many of China's neighboring countries/regions.

Part III:

Evidence

CHAPTER 5

Politics of Taxation and High Demand for FDI

Part I of the study traced the evolution of China's FDI regulatory framework in the reform era and highlighted the relatively liberal nature of that framework in international perspective. Part II juxtaposed the evolutionary dynamics with the patterns of FDI flows in China. In doing so, our aim was to build up a *prima facie* case showing how institutional changes affect investment behavior. Methodologically, while the simple juxtaposition is helpful as a first step in establishing a causal link between institutions and investments, understandably it *ipso facto* is by no means free from *post hoc* fallacy.[1] Could not the same pattern of FDI flows, the suspicious may wonder, be caused by economic factors such as market size, labor costs and infrastructure? Or, for the same matter, could they not be simply caused by the effects of culture – after all Hong Kong has been the largest investor? Given these concerns, the central task of Part III of the study is to go beyond a *prima facie* case to validate our institutional claims. Accordingly, our analytical effort in this part is to zero in on those effects that are attributable only to the formal institutions of China's FDI regulatory framework to the exclusion of cultural and economic conditions.

To accomplish this task, in the present chapter we focus on China's disparate treatment in terms of taxation in particular, between FIEs and their domestic counterparts, a topic briefly broached but left largely unexplored previously. Our principal hypothesis is that different tax

---

1. A common fallacy which often arises in interpreting cause-and-effect relationships. For illustration, it occurred in ancient times when the medicine man believed that both witchcraft and a little arsenic were necessary to kill his enemy. In logic, this fallacy is known as the *post hoc, ergo propter hoc* fallacy (translated from the Latin as "after this, therefore necessary because of this").

treatments between FIEs and domestic firms, when coupled with the effects of fiscal decentralization in the reform era, gave rise to what I call an "abnormally high demand" for FDI in China. That is, the aggregate demand for FDI in China is greater than would normally be the case if the different treatments between FIEs and domestic firms did not exist in the first place. This is a unique aspect of China's transitional economy that was in part responsible for the seemingly massive inflows of FDI in China, especially in the early 1990s. To unravel the intricacies of this story, we begin by providing a contextual background of fiscal decentralization in China during the reform era.

Fiscal Decentralization: A Brief Overview

Central to China's market-oriented economic reform, as many studies have pointed out (Li 1998; Breslin 1996; Wang and Hu 1993), is economic decentralization in an incremental yet steady way, as contrasted with the shock therapy administered in Russia.[2] The most critical element of that decentralization is arguably the various new fiscal arrangements installed between the central and local governments on the one hand and between the state and the enterprises on the other. On either hand, new fiscal arrangements attempted to tackle the problems of inefficiency associated with soft budget constraints embedded in a planned economy.[3] To understand what specific measures are entailed in these attempts, in the sections that follow we look first at the new fiscal arrangements between the state and the enterprises on the one hand, and between the central and local governments on the other. We then discuss the implications of the new

---

2. There is a vast literature on gradualism vis-à-vis shock therapy. See, for example, Qian and Weingast (1995); Solnick (1996); Burawoy (1996); Woo (1994); Nolan (1995); and Naughton (1996).

3. Soft budget constraints, a term coined by Kornai (1980), refer to the capacity of state-owned enterprises to continue to operate in spite of chronic financial losses. According to Kornai, two principal reasons account for soft budget constraints in a planned economy. The first has to do with the heavily bureaucratic role in the running of SOEs, including managerial appointments and promotions, and decisions over credit allocations and project financing. The second, and related to the first, are the implicit or explicit guarantees that the state will not let SOEs go bankrupt for ideological, political, and social reasons.

fiscal arrangements for the economic behavior of local governments, and, in particular, how they affected the demand side of FDI in China.

The State vis-à-vis Enterprises

In the reform era, institutional innovations in the fiscal relationship between the state and the enterprise are perhaps best epitomized by what is known in Chinese as "*li gai shui*," or "tax-for-profit" reform.[4] The reform began in the early 1980s as an experiment to increase the efficiency of state-owned enterprises by linking financial rewards with performance. The incentives contained in the new system are readily appreciable in comparison with the old system. Under the old system, nominally at least, SOEs did not pay taxes. But they had to hand over all profits to the state and in return received budgetary allocations along with production quotas (Song 1998:157). There was thus little incentive for the enterprises to strive for better performance, since there was no automatic link between rewards and profits. With the reform, that situation changed considerably. Now, instead of turning all profits over to the state, SOEs could retain profits after paying an enterprise income tax to the state.

By replacing the obligation of profit remittance with that of tax payments, reforms attempted to reach two goals at once, i.e., to provide the state with a steady stream of revenue and at the same time to increase the incentives for enterprises to be more efficient and profitable. In operational terms, a graduated tax system, ranging from a low of 10% for profits under 1,000 RMB to a high of 55% for profits over 200,000 yuan, was employed. Applied first to SOEs in the early 1980s, the graduated tax system was subsequently expanded, in 1985 and again in 1988, to cover both collectively-owned enterprises and privately-owned enterprises (Wang 1996:29). Thus, by the end of the 1980s, all domestic enterprises had fallen within the purview of this progressive tax system. Then in 1994, in an effort to create a level playing field, China introduced yet another new tax system. This time, it was a flat enterprise income tax of 33%. This substantially narrowed, if not completely filled, the gap in taxation between FIEs and domestic

4. The earliest experiments of such reforms were reportedly conducted in 1979 in some selected enterprises in Shanghai, Hubei, Guangxi, and Sichuan. See Wang (1996:25).

firms. Recall that 33% is the maximum enterprise income tax rate for FIEs not located in special investment areas.[5]

The Center vis-à-vis Localities

Fiscal decentralization between the central and local governments boils down to what is popularly known as "fenzao chifan," or dividing the kitchen and eating separately (Shirk 1993:149). Specifically, it involves various revenue-sharing schemes between the central and local governments, which began in a few selected provinces in the early 1980s and continued into the 1990s. For example, during the initial period, Guangdong was allowed to keep all revenues after remitting a pre-fixed lump-sum to central coffers. Jiangsu, for its part, operated with a fixed revenue-sharing contract with the central government (Zhou 1994). In all, a World Bank study identifies six basic types of revenue-sharing schemes, which began to be implemented in 1988 and continued into the 1990s to cover all provinces. The principal features of the various revenue-sharing schemes are summarized in Table V-1.

To better appreciate the incentives contained in the revenue-sharing schemes from the perspective of local governments, several points need to be highlighted. First, who gets what type of revenue-sharing scheme was largely a matter of negotiation between the central and provincial governments in light of local economic conditions.[6] But once a particular scheme was agreed upon, it was solidified in a contract that remained valid for five years. As such, the new fiscal system, while tightening local budget constraints, also signified a *credible* commitment by the central government to allow local governments to become *stable* residual claimants on revenues generated in their jurisdictions.[7] This is in marked contrast to the *ad hoc* approach in the

5. For tax incentives available in China's special investment areas, see Table I-4 in Chapter 1.

6. Huo Shitao (1994:181-206) argues that variations in revenue-sharing schemes are largely a reflection of the central government's concerns to redistribute resources between rich and poor regions.

7. Property rights can be conceptualized as a bundle of rights over property, including the right to sell the property, the right to the income from the property, and the right to manage or use the property. However, here I use the term primarily to refer to the right to possess and use the income. For a

pre-reform years. Previously, even though revenue-sharing schemes had existed sporadically, they were *unstable* because they changed yearly.[8]

Table V-1: Revenue-sharing Schemes between Central and Local Governments

Scheme Types	Features
Fixed subsidies	Localities (usually very poor ones) receive fixed subsidies from the center and retain whatever revenues they can generate in their jurisdictions
Fixed quota delivery	Localities remit a specified, nominal amount to the center and retain whatever revenues beyond that nominal amount
Fixed sharing	Localities remit a fixed proportion of revenues to the center and retain the rest
Incremental sharing	Localities retain a certain proportion of revenues up to a quota and then keep a higher proportion in excess of that quota
Sharing up to a limit with growth adjustment	Localities retain a specified proportion that is within a specific percentage of revenue from the previous year and retain all revenue above that quota
Fixed quota with growth adjustment	Localities remit to the center a fixed amount of revenue which increases at a contracted rate

Source: Richard Bahl and Christine Wallich (1992), "Intergovernmental Fiscal Relations in China." World Bank, WPS 863.

Second, a crucial feature common to all revenue-sharing schemes is that the central government's share of revenues at the margin is decreasing, so that the provincial governments, now as residual claimants, have more to gain if they increase their revenue base. The same principle also applies to similar revenue-sharing schemes with

theoretical treatment of this aspect of property rights as an incentive, see Barzel (1989) and also Demsetz (1983).

8. An exception was the revenue-sharing experiment with Jiangsu province between 1977-80. For the pre-reform fiscal arrangement between central and local governments, see Donnithorne (1967); Oksenberg and Tong (1991); and Wu (1987).

lower strata of governments all the way down to the township level.[9] This, again, is quite different from pre-reform years. Prior to the reform, local governments had to remit all revenues to the center, and in return received their revenue shares in the form of budgetary allocations, the size of which in principle were determined by central planners.[10] As such, there was less incentive for local governments to nurture and increase their revenue base, if only because increased revenues did not automatically result in increased allocations. Perhaps worse yet, local governments were not free to use their budgetary allocations the way they saw fit. Local expenditures were contingent upon upper level approvals.

Finally, all revenue-sharing schemes, it must be emphasized, were applicable only within the formal budgetary system, i.e., on the basis of revenues collected and channeled, by way of national statutory taxation, to the Ministry of Finance in Beijing through local governments. In China, this formal system is called "*yusuannei*," or the within- or intra-budgetary system. But the intra-budgetary system is only one dimension of fiscal decentralization during the reform years. The other aspect, perhaps more important but certainly less studied, is what is known as "*yusuanwai*," or extra-budgetary revenues. Although both the intra- and extra-budgetary funds draw ultimately from the same tax base, unlike the intra-budgetary funds which are subject to revenue-sharing schemes, the extra-budgetary funds remain entirely at the local levels.[11] As such, these are funds,[12] from which local

9. Oi (1992:103) reports that beginning in 1985, similar revenue-sharing schemes, albeit with some variations, were also implemented at each level below the province: between provinces and prefectures, prefectures and counties, and counties and townships.

10. In practice, according to Lampton (1987a:3-24), extensive bargaining was involved between upper and lower levels of government.

11. Another area which is not subject to sharing is the tax base designated exclusively as "central tax." This include taxes on centrally-owned enterprises, such as government commercial agencies like banks and post offices, custom duties, taxes on rail, tobacco, liquor, and oil-related activities such as offshore drilling. See Agarwala (1992:67).

12. The extra-budgetary revenues, as defined by official statistical sources until 1993, have three components: (1) tax supplements collected by local tax departments, (2) receipts by other government units, and (3) retained earnings of state-owned enterprises and receipts by their supervisory bureaus.

governments can ultimately profit by charging various *ad hoc* fees on the enterprises within their jurisdictions.[13] For illustration, in the mid-1980s, according to one estimate (Zhao 1986:118), about 5% of enterprise profits were collected as fees by local governments.

Implications

What implications does fiscal decentralization have for the economic behavior of local governments? For one thing, if local governments can increase the total revenue base in their jurisdictions there is now more for them to gain, since the marginal rate of taxation by the central government is decreasing in all cases of revenue-sharing schemes. Thus, all else being equal, one would expect that local governments are more likely now to push for local economic growth. For another, given that intra-budgetary revenues are subject to sharing with the central government, while extra-budgetary funds are not, it would also make sense for them to minimize the intra-budgetary revenues, so as to maximize the extra-budgetary funds.

Given the implications outlined above, it is not surprising then, whereas economic growth spearheaded by local governments in the reform years is now a well-documented fact (Oi 1995), extra-budgetary funds also expanded at the same time, with signs of outstripping the growth trend of intra-budgetary revenues.[14] As Figure V-1 illustrates, after a relatively slow rise in the early 1980s, extra-budgetary revenues grew rapidly, approaching the size of the entire intra-budgetary revenues in the late 1980s and finally overtaking them in 1992. Then, in 1993, the government decided that it would no longer include the funds from SOEs and their supervisory bureaus as extra-budgetary

13. As part of the decentralization process, in the early 1980s more SOEs were delegated to local governments at the provincial, municipal, and county levels. As a result, by 1985 SOEs controlled by the central government accounted for only 20% of the total industrial output at or above the township level, while provincial and municipal governments controlled 45%, and county governments controlled 9%. See Qian and Xu (1993).

14. To be sure, the extra-budgetary funds also existed prior to the reform. But they never approached the size during the reform era. For instance, as a proportion of GNP, in 1978 the extra-budgetary revenue was 9%, whereas the within-budgetary revenue was 35%. Besides, localities were not entitled to use these funds before gaining approval from upper levels. See Sicular (1992).

revenues, presumably as a signal to make SOEs more autonomous as business entities. But even with this modification, signs were clear that the extra-budgetary revenues of local governments continued to grow, accounting for as much as about 40% of the entire intra-budgetary revenues in 1995.

Figure V-1: Intra- and Extra-Budgetary Government Revenues, 1983-95 (billion RMB)

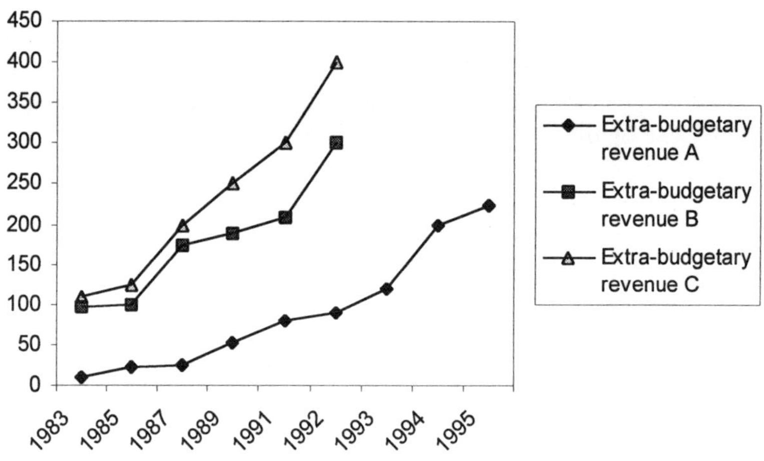

Notes: Extra-budgetary revenue A = extra-budgetary revenue of local governments, non-business and administrative.
Extra-budgetary revenue B = extra-budgetary revenue of SOEs and their supervisory bureaus. Beginning in 1993, this category of revenue was no longer included in the statistics for extra-budgetary revenue.
Extra-budgetary revenue C = sum of extra-budgetary revenue A and extra-budgetary revenue B.
Sources: *Zhongguo tongji nianjian* 1993 [Yearbook of Chinese Statistics 1993]; *Zhongguo tongji nianjian* 1997 [Yearbook of Chinese Statistics 1997].

In view of the new fiscal arrangements sketched above, the reason for the expansion of extra-budgetary funds in the reform years may no longer seem so puzzling. But what remains unclear, however, is exactly how local governments were able to increase their share of extra-budgetary funds without at the same time burdening local enterprises and thus stunting economic growth? After all, empirically, the growth of extra-budgetary revenue does not seem to have hindered economic development at the local levels in China. On the contrary, Wong reports (1997:299) that local governments in fast-growing provinces all seem to have collected more extra-budgetary revenue than local governments in slow-growing provinces, and the pattern is especially evident between the coastal and interior regions. Theoretically, this suggests that what is at work here between local governments and enterprises must be some sort of Pareto-improvement,[15] even though that may be achieved at the cost of the central government.

Along that vein, it has been argued that local governments, taking advantage of information asymmetry,[16] could in effect withhold revenues from the central government through illegal practices such as winking at tax evasions by local enterprises or, more blatant still, granting them unwarranted tax holidays (Wang Shaoguang 1994:94). The idea is to keep as much money as possible at the local levels, so that a greater reservoir of funds becomes available for local governments to tap into. While it is by no means easy to ascertain the extent of these illegal practices, there apparently is much to this line of inquiry. Indeed, according to Wang Bingqian (1988), the Finance Minister of China, in 1987 revenue losses attributable to tax fraud or evasion were estimated at 7 billion RMB, even though it is not at all clear how much of that amount was due to the complicity of local governments.

However, to pursue this line of inquiry, albeit tempting, is beyond the scope of the current study. What we will do, instead, is to take on a somewhat similar line of investigation, except that the proposed

---

15. This refers to a scenario of resource allocation that makes someone better off without making another person worse off. A related concept is Pareto optimal, which refers to an efficient allocation of resources such that there is no other available allocation that makes someone better off without making another person worse off. Vilfredo Pareto was an Italian economist and sociologist who is credited with developing this criterion for problems with multiple objectives.

16. In economic theory, this refers to situations where one economic agent knows something that another economic agent does not. For example, a worker might have a better idea of how much he can produce than his employer does, or a producer might have a better idea of the quality of a good he produces than a potential consumer has. Theoretical implications arising from asymmetric information are covered by an extensive principal-agent literature which addresses the moral hazard problem. See, e.g., Pauly (1968), Akerlof (1970), Spence and Zeckhauser (1971), Ross (1973), Jensen and Meckling (1976), Grossman (1981), Hart and Holmstrom (1987). For various reasons for the existence of information asymmetry, see Hayek (1974).

investigation will deal with the subject of FDI. In particular, in light of the fiscal arrangements as outlined above, we hypothesize that because China's tax system treated FIEs more favorably than domestic firms, an effective way for local governments to maximize extra-budgetary funds without putting an undue burden on local enterprises was by forming joint ventures with foreign capital. As we will show shortly, a mere JV status could make Pareto-improvement possible between local governments and enterprises in terms of revenues, even if we assume, for the sake of analytical clarity, that no foreign capital, technology, and know-how were actually brought to the deal. This in time brings us to what I call an "abnormally high demand" for FDI in China, a subject to which we now turn.

Abnormally High Demand for FDI

In today's world, in developing and transitional economies in particular, where FDI is being hotly pursued as a catalyst for economic growth – in large ventures it can often provide the critical ingredients of capital, technology, and management, and even in small, labor-intensive ventures, it is often relied upon for new designs, quality control, and export marketing – the notion of "abnormally high demand" for FDI may sound anachronistic. That may indeed be the case, inasmuch as FDI is genuinely sought for its intrinsic values of capital contributions, advanced technology, and sophisticated managerial skills broadly construed.

But in China, because FIEs are granted a wide range of benefits that are off-limits to domestic firms, there is an institutional cause for Chinese local officials and managers to seek FDI not simply for the sake of capital, technology, and/or know-how, but also for policy-conveyed benefits, including tax holidays, duty-free inputs, and import and export rights that are not readily available to domestic firms.[17] The disparate treatment between FIEs and domestic firms – in tax payments in particular – I argue, gave rise to what may be conceptualized as

17. Foreign trade also underwent decentralization in the reform years. However, the decentralization of trade authority was mainly from MOFTEC in Beijing to provinces and other ministries, and not directly to firms. It was until the 1990s that a small number of large enterprises were granted the right to trade directly, a valuable status conferred usually by the provincial trade departments. On trade decentralization, see Lardy (1992a:691-720; 1994).

"abnormally high demand" for FDI, i.e., the aggregate demand for FDI in China is greater than would normally be the case if these institutional conditions did not exist in the first place.

In what follows, we advance the argument in two steps. First, for analytical clarity, we appeal to a stylized case to illuminate the institutional logic of "abnormally high demand" for FDI, focusing on the effects of China's differentiated tax regimes. Second, we document empirical evidence to validate the various aspects of our hypothetical example.

The Logic of Abnormally High Demand for FDI

"Abnormally high demand" for FDI in China has its source in the country's institutional design that until the mid-1990s treated FIEs and domestic firms very differently. Recall that the enterprise income tax rate for a Chinese domestic firm was 55% if its yearly profits reached 200,000 RMB, or roughly US$24,000. In contrast, as detailed in Part I of this study, FIEs were taxed at 15-24% in special investment areas and 30% generally in the rest of China. Besides the great disparity in tax rates, FIEs also enjoyed a long list of other operational and fiscal privileges such as duty-free imports.[18]

To illustrate the magnitude of tariff-related benefits to FIEs, one recent study shows that of the US$80 billion in customs duties that ought to be have been collected in 1994 for 25 goods under examination, only US$27 billion was actually collected (cited in Rosen 1998:63). In short, policy-conveyed advantages to FIEs are substantial – relative to domestic firms – so that local governments and enterprises gain considerably if they can manage to change the status of a domestic

---

18. At the same time as China moved to substantially lower tariff rates across the board in 1996, it also decided to rescind import tax exemptions for FIEs as of April 1, 1996. The policy change, however, was made with the cushion of a phase-in period. In addition, for FIEs established prior to April 1, 1996, actual implementation was to go into effect as of the end of 1997. But, in the wake of the Asian financial crisis, competitive pressure from neighboring countries from devaluating their currencies forced China to further delay the rescinding of tariff exemptions for FIEs. In fact, at the beginning of 1998, China announced wide-ranging duty exemptions for high-tech capital goods in a bid to prevent FDI from falling (Rosen, Liu, and Dwight 1998).

firm into that of an FIE. To crystallize the logic here, we appeal to a stylized case below.

Scenario I: Revenue Distribution among E, L, and C, without FDI

- E: $22,500 = $50,000 (total profit) minus $27,500 (intra-budgetary revenue collected at 55% tax rate)
- L: $8,250 = intra-budgetary revenue ($27,500) shared with C at a 30:70 ratio
- C: $19,250 = intra-budgetary revenue ($27,500) shared with L at a 30:70 ratio
- E+L: $30,750 = total revenue that remains locally

Suppose that we have a locality, named L, whose revenue-sharing scheme with the central government, C, is defined by a simple formula of 30:70, whereby whatever amount of intra-budgetary revenue L collects, L retains 30%, and 70% goes to C. Suppose again that L has just one state-owned enterprise, named E, which is capitalized at US$2 million and is able to earn US$50,000 profits yearly. Since E's annual profit level exceeds 200,000 RMB (or roughly US$24,000), E is subject to an income tax of 55%, at which rate L is legally obligated to collect revenues from E, which in turn must be shared with C at the 30:70 ratio set in its revenue-sharing scheme. Now before FDI enters the picture, revenue distributions among E, L, and C in our hypothetical case are presented in Scenario I.

Now consider two other scenarios, but this time including FDI. First, suppose further that L is a coastal city authorized by C to have an ETDZ, where, under China's FDI regulatory framework, a 15% national tax, plus a 3% local tax, are chargeable on FIEs.[19] By contrast, the tax is 55% for purely domestic firms. Given the huge tax differentials, E clearly has a strong incentive to become a joint venture. This is the same for L, to the extent that L wants to maximize locally retained funds, from which it can benefit ultimately by charging *ad hoc* fees on E without simultaneously burdening it too much.

19. For simplicity, we do not include the additional tax exemptions and reductions which, as discussed earlier, were available to FIEs during their initial years of operation. Suffice it here to say that if the additional preferential treatment were to be included in our calculation, it would make our case all the more compelling.

Theorctically, there are two ways to turn E into a joint venture. One is to round-trip capital. This method, essentially, is to move the assets of E, say half of them, i.e., US$1 million, offshore first, register as a foreign company, and then return as FDI, such that E becomes, *de jure*, if not *de facto*, an FIE, named EE. Under such a scenario, designated here as Scenario II, revenue distributions among EE, L, and C are as follows:

Scenario II: Revenue Distribution among EE, L, and C, with Round-tripping FDI

- EE: $41,000 = $50,000 (total profit) minus $7,500 (intra-budgetary revenue at 15% tax rate) and $1,500 (local tax at 3%)
- L: $3,750 = $1,500 (local tax) plus $2,250 (intra-budgetary revenue of $7,500 shared with C at a 30:70 ratio)
- C: $5,250 = intra-budgetary revenue of $7,500 shared with L at a 30:70 ratio
- EE+L: $44,750 = total revenue that remains locally

Scenario III: Revenue Distribution among EF, L, and C, with Round-tripping FDI

- EF: $42,500 = $50,000 (total profit) minus $7,500 (intra-budgetary revenue at 15% tax rate). Specifically, E has $31,875, F has $10,625, per an equity ratio of 75:25.
- L: $2,250 = intra-budgetary revenue of $7,500 shared with C at a 30:70 ratio
- C: $5,250 = intra-budgetary revenue of $7,500 shared with L at a 30:70 ratio
- E+L: $34,125 = total revenue that remains locally, assuming F repatriates all of its profits

In reality, however, L cannot move capital offshore freely, because all investment projects abroad, big or small, by Chinese SOEs have to be approved by the State Council, even though approval conditions have been relaxed in recent years.[20] Thus, should Scenario II fail to materialize, Scenario III becomes necessary.

20. As of 1993, the State Council delegated its approval power to MOFTEC. A summary of current policies, according to the Approval Procedure and Management Method of Chinese Enterprises with Investments

Under Scenario III, both L and E have to try hard to attract FDI, in order to turn E into a joint venture, EF, where F stands for a foreign equity contribution, worth, say, US$0.5 million. But, under the conditions of competitive bidding from other regions of the country, in order to increase the chance that F chooses L as the investment location, L has to waive the 3% local tax – an option open to L under China's FDI regulatory framework. In addition, E, with the cooperation of L, underestimates its assets, say, by 25%, thus making the deal even more attractive to F.[21] For, holding the real sizes of equity of both E and F constant, a nominally underestimated equity share by E means an increase in the equity share by F, which in turn means a proportionally increased share of profits for F.

Attracted by such generous concessions, F joins hands with E, resulting in an equity joint venture capitalized at US$2 million, with a Chinese-foreign equity ratio at 75:25 (E = $1.5 million [i.e., $ 2 million underestimated by 25%] and F = $0.5 million). Under this scenario, Scenario III, revenue distributions among EF, L, and C, even assuming F creates zero positive, if not negative, externalities (e.g., managerial skills and profits) and leads to zero increase in total profits, are as follows.

Now let us compare the results of the three scenarios with special attention to the size of locally retained revenues (see Table V-2). With FDI in the picture, even if we assume that F brings no positive externalities but simply becomes an additional claimant of profits, E still comes out a clear winner, with its revenue share going up from $22,500 in Scenario I to $41,000 and $31,875 in Scenarios II and III. By contrast, C is a net loser, as its share goes down from $19,250 in Scenario I to $5,250 in both Scenarios II and III. What about L? L may,

---

Aboard issued by MOFTEC, includes: (1) projects between US$1-3 million in value, which incur government loans, or require domestic collateral in the case of foreign loans, or whose products target domestic markets, must be reviewed and approved by both MOFTEC and the State Planning Commission; (2) projects above US$3 million must first be reviewed by MOFTEC and then approved by the State Council; (3) projects below US$1million can be approved by local supervisory agencies, but are subject to review by MOFTEC. Guojia guoyou zichan guanliju (1995a:61).

21. E needs the cooperation of L in this respect, because, officially, asset valuations must be reviewed and approved by a specialized government office called the State Assets Appraisal Office.

at first sight, appear to be a loser in the first round of revenue distribution, since its share drops from $8,250 in Scenario I to $3,750 and $2,250 in Scenario II and III. But in the real world, as the upward movements of extra-budgetary revenue contained in Figure V-1 indicate, L will eventually be a winner eventually.

Table V-2: Revenue Distribution and Redistribution among the Center, Local Government and Enterprise (a hypothetical example)

	Claimants	Scenario I	Scenario II	Scenario III
1st round of distribution	F=foreign investor	n/a	n/a	$10,625
	C=central government	$19,250	$5,250	$5,250
	L=local government	$8,250	$3,750	$2,250
	E=enterprise	$22,500	$41,000	$31,875
	L+E =local total	$30,750	$44,750	$34,125
2nd round of distribution*	F	n/a	n/a	$10,625
	C	$19,250	$5,250	$2,250
	L	$8,250	$14,000	$9.938
	E	$22,500	$30,750	$24,187
	L+E	$30,750	$44,750	$34,125

* Assuming 25% of funds retained in L in the first round of distribution ends up as extra-budgetary funds of L.

The trick here is that, with FDI in the picture, i.e., in Scenarios II and III, the size of locally retained revenue increases significantly – from $30,750 in Scenario I to $44,750 and $34,125 in Scenarios II and III respectively – and that as long as the total amount of locally retained revenue grows, a Pareto-improvement between local governments and enterprises becomes possible, even though it comes at the expense of the central government.

Now that more funds are kept at the local levels, local governments can compensate for their first-round shortfalls by charging a variety of *ad hoc* fees on local enterprises, a practice known in China as "*tanpai*."[22] *Tanpai*, in effect, is a second round of revenue distribution

---

22. Originally, *tanpai* was an innovation of rural cadres in China. After de-collectivization, accumulation funds of teams, brigades, and communes were no longer available to them. *Tanpai* was thus used by local officials to secure a new source of funds to support the operations of government and to feed grass-roots cadres. In the early 1980s, with fiscal decentralization, *tanpai* made its way into the cities, as a way, at least in name, for local governments to augment their financial resources to perform public services, such as roads, public schools, and sanitation, etc.

between local governments and enterprises. Indeed, as several reports (Zhao 1986; Liang 1989; Zhu 1990; Li 1991; Wang 1992) showed, anywhere from 5% to 50% of funds originally retained in the name of enterprises could end up as extra-budgetary funds of local governments. In our case, suppose that as much as 25% of E's share in the first round of revenue distribution eventually ended up with L in the second round of revenue distribution, both E and L would still be better off than their original positions in Scenario I.

Now a final comment. Note that none of the scenarios presented has considered the additional fiscal benefits offered exclusively to FIEs, including, but not limited to, two-year tax holidays, three-year 50% tax reductions, and extensive duty-free imports, which can be critical for production operations based heavily on foreign inputs.[23] Besides fiscal and monetary benefits, FIEs also enjoy extra advantages over SOEs in terms of operational autonomy, which provide an additional motivation for SOE managers to change their corporate status to FIEs. Although several rounds of SOE reforms in the 1980s and 1990s were designed to decrease discretionary bureaucratic interference and increase the operational autonomy of SOE managers, the results remained questionable. A World Bank report (1997a) shows that a majority of the SOEs surveyed indicated that they continued to lack autonomy in several key operational areas, such as trade, investment, personnel appointments, and wages. Had all these fiscal and non-fiscal factors been included in our calculations, there would have been no question that a more compelling case could be made to illuminate the institutional logic of "abnormally high demand" for FDI in China.

Evidence for Abnormally High Demand for FDI

Fiscal Concessions

Initial evidence, circumstantial to be sure, of "abnormally high demand" for FDI in China is the observation that local governments

23. A case in point is China's tire industry which imports 45% of the rubber from foreign countries. Until 1996, while FDI firms could import rubber duty- free, domestic firms were subject to as high as 37% tariff rates (Wang 1997:261).

have a strong propensity to offer fiscal concessions to FIEs beyond the limits allowed by the central government. It is well known that Chinese localities compete with one another to attract FDI by reducing taxes, land-use fees, and by providing infrastructure. To a certain extent, this is similar to the expensive bidding war among Ohio, Pennsylvania, and Ontario for a Honda plant in 1987 (Graham and Krugman 1991). But a deeper reason, as our stylized case illustrated above, is that by giving concessions to FIEs, local governments also confer fiscal advantages to local enterprises that are partners to joint ventures, and as long as funds are kept at the local levels, they are within the reach of local governments.

A careful reading of the investment guidelines of 1991 and 1992 for 60 localities, ranging from provincial to county level governments, reveals that 33 localities, or 55%, explicitly offered concessions that exceeded, in one way or another, the limits allowed by the central government.[24] One example is Yongji, a county in Shanxi province. Although the central government only allowed a maximum of 2 years of tax exemptions for FIEs, Yongji offered tax holidays for as long as 5 years.[25] As a further illustration, recall that when the central government decided to expand preferential FDI policies into the inland areas in the early 1990s, the preferential treatment never really matched that available in China's Special Economic Zones. But, Haila'er, a city in Inner Mongolia, according to its investment guideline, was ready to beat the price, so to speak, around the country in terms of preferential treatment to JVs.[26]

A mirror image of the propensity of local governments to give more concessions than are authorized by the central government is their tendency to relax conditions in approving FDI projects. For example, as mentioned in Chapter 1, projects valued over US$30 million need to be approved by the central government. To circumvent the gate-keeping intention by the central government to avoid over-capacity, local governments often resorted to the practice of project miniaturization. That is, to "slice" a big project into several smaller ones so as not to trigger the approval limits. Further, while the central

---

24. *Zhongguo gedi touzi youhui zhengce* [Preferential Policies Up and Down China], 2 vols. vol. Beijing: Renmin zhongguo chubanshe, 1993.

25. Ibid., vol. 2, p. 83.

26. Ibid., vol. 1, p. 53.

government has legislated explicitly against introducing pollution-intensive FDI projects, a study by China's State Planning Commission (1994) estimates that in 1991 about 22% of FDI projects funded by Hong Kong, Macao, and Taiwan investors were pollution-intensive. A separate study (cited in Feng Yushu 1997) shows, out of a total of some 11,000 FDI projects that went into operation in 1991, 29% were in pollution-intensive industries. Apparently, in a rush to attract FDI, extra-legal practices at the local levels contributed to China's problems associated with industrial over-capacity and environmental degradation. In 1998 China's Environmental Protection Agency was elevated to ministerial status, indicating that stronger environmental protection measures may be forthcoming.

Finally, to the extent that the creation of various "development zones" was equivalent to a low enterprise income tax rate of 15% for FIEs, a similar pattern can be found in the behavior of local governments, i.e., a strong urge to erect development zones to host JVs within their jurisdictions. In 1990, for instance, as far as the central government was concerned, only one development zone was approved, i.e., the Pudong Development Zone in Shanghai, where FDI enjoyed largely the same preferential policies as those available in the SEZs. However, Jiangsu, Zhejiang, Shandong, Anhui, and even Xinjiang and Inner Mongolia, all attempted to develop Pudong-type development zones without the approval of the central government.[27] Indeed, in the early 1990s, the spread of unauthorized development zones was so rampant at the local levels,[28] that in 1993 the central government had to re-institute strict requirements for central approval of all development zones,[29] and that Jiang Zemin, the Party General Secretary, had to be

27. *Zhongguo jingji yuebao* [Chinese Economic Monthly], no. 20, (December 1990), p. 32.

28. According to one press report, the State Planning Commission estimates 1,700 zones, the State Council SEZ Office estimates 1,800, the State Land Administration estimates 2,700, and the Ministry of Agriculture estimates 9,000. See Yin Xin, "Government to Tighten Restrictions on Zones," *China Daily Business Weekly*, 7 February 1993, p. 1, in FBIS, China, February 9, 1993, p. 33. For numbers of various kinds of officially authorized zones, see Table I-7 in Part I.

29. Governments below the provincial level were stripped of their power to approve development zones, and all approvals at the provincial level had to be ratified by the State Council. "State Council Issues Development Zone

personally involved in issuing instructions to clamp down on many unauthorized zones.[30]

Fire Sales of State Assets

Additional evidence is the tell-tale sign that many SOEs, in order to qualify for the preferential treatment accorded FIEs, do not seem hesitant, and indeed are very ready, to under-value their equity positions in JVs, resulting in what may be construed as "fire sales" of state assets. As discussed in Chapter 3, when forming a JV, equity contributions by both the Chinese and foreign sides can be made in the form of cash, as well as non-cash components including goods, industrial rights, factory buildings, and land-use rights. But while cash components are relatively easy to calculate, the non-cash parts are not.[31] This is especially true in the case of SOEs whose property rights are still ill-defined in China. Not inconceivably, then, managers of SOEs, when left on their own and tempted by the prospect of windfalls for themselves,[32] will likely sell state assets at bargain prices.

As a reflection of these concerns, theoretically SOEs are not given a free hand to value their own assets. Instead, they are required, according to an injunction by the State Council,[33] to subject all non-cash components to independent appraisals by specialized accountants licensed by the State Bureau of State Asset Management (SBSAM) – itself a specialized government agency formed in 1988 to exercise oversight over state-owned properties.[34] But, in practice, many SOEs

---

Circular," Xinhua News Agency, 15 May 1993, in FBIS, China, 18 May 1993, p. 43.

30. Lu Ren, "Jiang Zemin Issues Order to Rectifying Development Zones," *Ching Pao* (Hong Kong), 5 June 1993, pp. 34-35, in FBIS, China, 7 June 1993, p. 35.

31. The US and China have chosen contrasting solutions to this problem. In the US, a corporation's board of directors assigns values to assets, subject to judicial review only in the case of fraud. China has opted for greater regulation.

32. Interviewees reported that such gains include higher salaries, better cars, and even chances to travel overseas.

33. See "Guoyou zichan pinggu guanli banfa" [Methods of Management of State-owned assets], in Guojia guoyou zichan guanliju (1995b:3)

34. It was approved by the First Session of the 7th NPC in April 1988. See *Zhongguo guoyou zichan nianjian* (1994:preface).

seem to have managed, in one way or another, to side-step independent appraisals especially during the early years of the 1990s. According to one SBSAM report, of some 10,000 SOEs approved by MOFTEC to form JVs in 1992, only 2,900, or less than 30%, went through asset valuations by independent agents.[35]

Although no one knows exactly how much equity has been undervalued in the process, figures that are available give a rough sense of the magnitude of the problem. In 1989-92, nationwide a total of 16,800 projects, including JVs, underwent independent appraisals. The results were striking. Whereas the total value of all assets involved in these projects prior to independent appraisals had been estimated (by SOEs themselves) at only 142.67 billion RMB; after the independent appraisal they were estimated at 222.24 billion RMB.[36] This suggests that there is a strong propensity for SOEs to under-estimate assets, and that on average the under-valuation rate for projects without independent appraisals may be as high as 55%.[37]

Anecdotally, Liu Yuesheng (1999:157) reports that in a hotel project, the Chinese partner was willing to offer a low figure of only 18.8 million RMB for what was worth 38.4 million RMB according to an independent appraisal. In another case, for a piece of land valued independently at 34.9 million RMB, the Chinese partner asked for only 6.6 million RMB to form a JV. Not surprisingly, the government estimated an annual loss of US$3.4 billion due to under-valuation of state assets to JVs with foreign firms.[38] Even if we do not take the face value of these figures seriously, there seems little question that losses due to "fire sales" were real and substantial.

---

35. Guojia guoyou zichan guanliju (1995b:62).

36. SBSAM, *Zhichan pinggu gongzuo fagui zhidu huibian*, (Beijing, Jingji kexue chubanshe, 1995), p. 62.

37. A possible challenge to this line of reasoning is that there is no such thing as under-valuations, on the justification that a market clearing price, i.e., when demand and supply reach equilibrium, best represents true value. My answer is that such an argument is valid only to the extent that there are no market distortions, such as disparate tax treatment between FIEs and domestic counterparts. What we are dealing with here is "abnormally high demand." The abnormal part derives from calculations to take advantage of tax benefits offered exclusively to FIEs in China.

38. "China limits Sale of Assets Held by State Companies," *Wall Street Journal,* 17 May 1994, A15.

Indeed, for a time, SBSAM became so concerned that it issued two "urgent notices," one in 1992 and another again in 1993, asking local governments to take asset valuations seriously.[39] Nationwide, other Chinese estimates suggest that asset stripping, including the formation of JVs, was a serious problem. For the years 1987 through 1992, the state lost 230 billion RMB in assets drained away from SOEs, or about 33 billion RMB annually (Yu 1996). An estimate by a researcher in the Policy Research Office of the State Council placed cumulative losses between 1990 and 1995 at more than 300 billion RMB or more than 50 billion RMB annually.[40] Concern over this problem became so severe that in early 1997 the State Council established a leading group under Zhu Rongji to investigate the extent of asset stripping and to try to put an end to this problem (Jen 1997).

Round-tripping FDI

Direct, and therefore more persuasive evidence, comes from what is known as round-tripping FDI, a phenomenon that began to emerge on the investment scene in the late 1980s. Round-tripping FDI refers to capital of Chinese origin that moves offshore first and then returns as FDI. Its existence is direct evidence of abnormally high demand for FDI, since such investments embody little advanced technology and critical managerial know-how, and are made *solely* to capture policy-conveyed benefits available to FIEs. The reason is obvious: All else being equal, firms that move and operate overseas – even in the form of shell companies – would incur more costs than those operating domestically, and, therefore, round-tripping capital would not make sense unless policy-conveyed benefits available exclusively to FIEs could *at least* cancel out the additional costs associated with cross-border operations.

Over the reform years, while China has received a huge volume of FDI inflows, the government has also approved a significant number of Chinese FDI projects going overseas. MOFTEC reports that at the end of 1998 the number of Chinese firms investing overseas reached 5,666, of which 3,288 were trade companies, and another 2,378 were non-

---

39. See SBSAM documents no. 88, 1992 and no. 66, 1993, in Guojia guoyou zichan guanliju (1995b:61-64).

40. Interview.

trade firms. They represent a total value of Chinese FDI outflows of US$6.33 billion (Ma and Wang 1999: 181). Although their exact geographical distribution is not made clear by the report, other relevant evidence suggests that many of them are located in Hong Kong and Macao. According to one estimate, the number of Chinese firms investing in Hong Kong was 400 in 1991; it rose quickly to 2,000 by 1994 (Chan 1995). Consistent with the rapid growth of Chinese firms operating overseas in the early 1990s, official statistics also have at the same time registered very dramatic increases in Chinese FDI outflows. Whereas the outflows averaged $835.8 million yearly for the 1985-90 period, they jumped to an average yearly amount of $3.085 billion for the 1991-96 period.[41]

There is plenty of evidence, however, that a significant portion of China's outward FDI has been channeled back into the country to take advantage of the generous policy benefits available to FIEs. According to one source, about 90% of Chinese firms operating overseas have plowed capital back into the country, even though the precise dollar amount remains unknown.[42] The large negative errors and omissions in China's balance of payment statistics give a hint of its magnitude. These unaccounted sums stood at $3.1 billion (1990), $6.8 billion (1991), $6.8 billion (1992), $9.8 billon (1993), $7.8 billion (1994), and $17.8 billion (1995). How much of that money was plowed back into China or simply disappeared into the private foreign accounts of corrupt officials or SOE managers remains elusive. Researchers at the World Bank guessed that in 1992 round-tripping capital may have comprised as much as 25% of China's total FDI inflows (Harrold and Lall 1993:24). In another study, Huang (1998:63), using regression analysis, estimated the size of round-tripping capital in 1992 to be at some $2.5 billion, which was about 22.5% of China's total FDI inflows that year.

According to the Statistical Bureau of Guangdong, the only province in China that actually publishes investment figures by Chinese firms operating overseas (see Table V-3), round-tripping capital began to emerge in 1987 and grew rapidly in the early 1990s;

---

41. Calculated on the basis of figures from *Zhongguo tongji nianjian* [China Statistical Yearbook] (various years).

42. *Jingji yanjiu cankao* [References on Ecnomic Research], no. 80, issue 280, Q-7, 1993, p.11.

but as a share of the yearly total FDI inflows into the province, it fluctuated around 2%. For China as a whole, if we assume that other coastal provinces received the same amount of round-tripping FDI as Guangdong did in 1992 and all of the interior provinces each received half of that amount – admittedly, a unrealistic assumption with a bias of overestimation in view of Guangdong's geographic proximity to Hong Kong plus its three SEZs – we would arrive at $1.5 billion. This is about 13% of China's total FDI intake in 1992. Given the above estimates, it seems plausible that "fake" FDI may have been anywhere between 10% and 25% of China's total yearly FDI intake until 1994 when China decided to close the gap between FIEs and domestic firms in terms of tax treatment, thus removing one critical incentive for round-tripping FDI.

Table V-3: FDI and FDI of PRC Origins in Guangdong, 1986-93 (US$ million)

Year	1986	1987	1988	1989	1990	1991	1992	1993
Total FDI	1428.29	593.96	919.08	1156.44	1459.84	1822.86	3551.50	7498.05
PRC origin	0	34.66	21.63	36.78	48.98	48.66	76.55	83.58

Source: *Guangdong tongji nianjian* [Statistical Yearbook of Guangdong] (various years).

Critical Evidence

Lest our analytical focus become blurred after the lengthy discussion above, let us once again return to the original hypothesis laid out at the start of this chapter. That is, abnormally high demand for FDI in China is a function of the country's unique institutional arrangements, notable among which is the disparate tax treatment between FIEs and domestic firms. To be sure, the evidence marshaled thus far all lends support, more or less, to such institutional claims. But, ultimately, for our institutional hypothesis to be validated, we must present evidence showing signs of decline in the demand for FDI in China once such institutional conditions as are postulated to have led to abnormally high demand are removed. Do we have such evidence? A quick answer is yes; specifics follow next.

Figure V-2: Trends of Chinese FX Reserves, Portfolio, and FDI Outflows, 1985-95

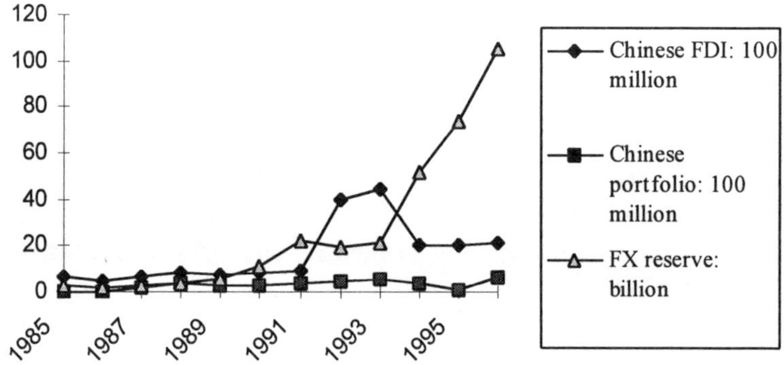

Source: *Zhongguo tongji nianjia* [China Statistical Yearbook] (various years).

As Figure V-2 demonstrates, when, in 1994, China decided to lower the enterprise income tax rate for domestic enterprises from 55% to 30%, and planned to gradually scale back on import privileges for FIEs in subsequent years, China's outward FDI tumbled immediately from a peak of $4.4 billion in 1993 to about $2 billion in 1994 and remained at that level thereafter through 1996. Consistent with this decline, the number of Chinese FDI projects going overseas that were reviewed and approved by MOFTEC also plummeted drastically, from close to 300 in 1993 to a little more than 100 in 1994 and thereafter (see Figure V-3). Such dramatic downward movements are strong evidence that institutional changes had a significant impact on investment behavior, as they effectively reduced, if not completely removed, the driving force for abnormally high demand for FDI, manifested most clearly by the phenomenon of round-tripping capital.

Figure V-3: Number of Chinese FDI Projects Overseas, 1979-96

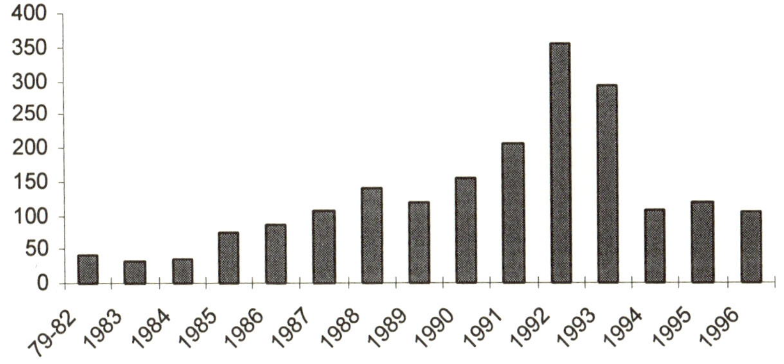

Source: *Zhongguo duiwai maoyi nianjian* [Almanac of China's Foreign Economic Relations and Trade] (various years).

Figure V-4: Growth Trends of Different Modes of FDI, 1991-96

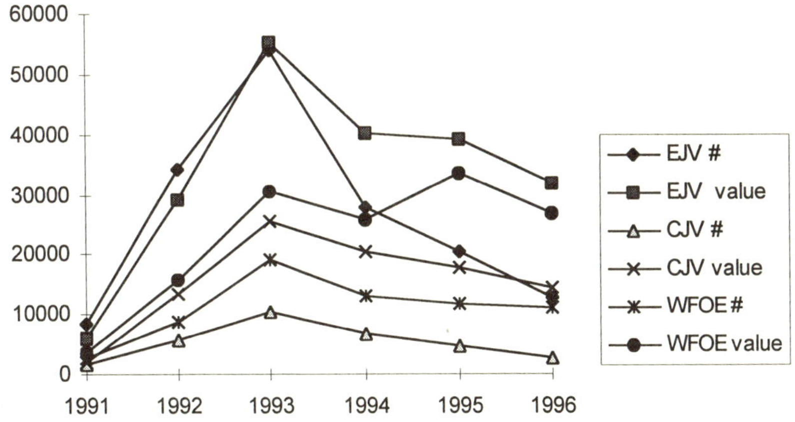

Note: Value is based on contract amount in US$ million. Contract amounts are used here because such figures reflect the immediacy of investors' response to policy changes better than realized amounts.

Sources: *Zhongguo duiwai jingji tongji nianjian* [China Foreign Economic Statistical Yearbook] (various years); *Zhongguo duiwai maoyi nianjian* [Almanac of China's Foreign Trade and Economic Relations] (various years).

The evidence here is all the more compelling in light of two further observations from Figure V-2. First, China's foreign exchange reserves skyrocketed beginning in 1994 to reach well over $100 billion by 1995. Second, China's overseas portfolio investments managed to maintain largely the same level at the time, except for a one-time drop in 1995. The implication of these observations is that, to the extent that China's capital outflows are ultimately a function of the availability of foreign exchange, the very dramatic decline in China's outward FDI since 1994 cannot be satisfactorily explained simply by a lack of funds – foreign exchange in particular. Otherwise, why did China's overseas portfolio investments not undergo a similar pattern of decline? Clearly, answers must be sought elsewhere, namely, the removal, or, rather, the reduction, of the very institutional sources that gave rise to the abnormally high demand for FDI in China.

Further validating our institutional hypothesis is the fact that the year 1994 also witnessed the beginning of an across-the-board decline of FDI in the form of newly contracted JVs. As Figure V-4 illustrates, the downward slope was very appreciable in the mode of CJVs but especially steep in the mode of EJVs, as measured by both project number and contractual dollar amount. By contrast, the comparable growth trends in the WFOE mode were largely stable, and at times even showed signs of further growth in contractual amount. This is not surprising, and indeed, can be predicted, since it was essentially through the vehicle of JVs, and the EJV mode in particular,[43] that Chinese domestic firms benefited from the generous policy advantages available to FIEs. Now that the institutional impetus that led to the abnormally high demand for FDI in China was reduced in 1994, it is only natural that the "abnormal" part in that demand began to deflate, as reflected by the immediate drop in FDI in the form of joint ventures, but, predictably, not in the mode of 100% foreign-owned subsidiaries.

Concluding Remarks

In this chapter, we have made an attempt to demonstrate the institutional effect on investment behavior. Our analysis began by

43. Less so in CJV, because profit distributions in CJVs, as discussed in Chapter 3, usually favor the foreign partners, especially during the initial years of operation.

highlighting the logic linking fiscal decentralization, disparate taxation between FIEs and domestic firms, and abnormally high demand for FDI in China. To validate our institutional claims, we showed, among others, critical evidence that the institutional rearrangements, i.e., the removal of disparate tax treatment between FIEs and domestic firms, were followed by an appreciable decline of new FDI contracts beginning in 1994. While this was the case, it does not follow that it should be taken as a sign that China's FDI regulatory framework has since deteriorated.

Indeed, if anything, the contrary seems to be true for at least two reasons. First, if our foregoing analysis is correct, the decline resulted from a correction of market distortions in China in the form of disparate taxation between FIEs and domestic firms. It is actually salutary in the sense that that the decline very likely represented a reduction only in those investments that would likely entail "fire sales" of state assets, and/or, in the case of round-tripping capital, involve few transfers to China of the intrinsic values of FDI, such as advanced technology and critical managerial expertise. In other words, available evidence suggests that the abnormal part of "abnormally high demand" for FDI in China was reduced after China narrowed the gap in tax treatment between FIEs and domestic firms.

Figure V-5: US FDI in China, 1990-98 (US$ million)

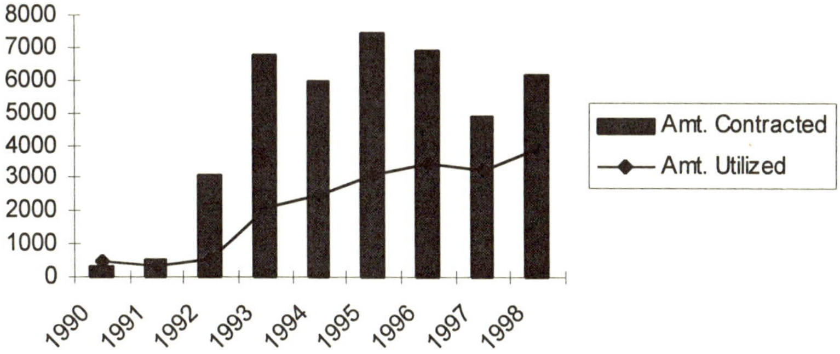

Source: <www.uschina.org/press/investmarch99.html>

Supporting this line of reasoning is the fact that, although total FDI inflows to China on a contractual basis declined dramatically subsequent to 1993, those from the US remained rather stable and indeed even surpassed the 1993 level, reaching more than $7 billion in 1995 (Figure V-5). In a way, this should be expected, because by virtue of the absence of a "tax-sparing" clause in the double tax treaty between China and the US, US FDI is at least in theory not sensitive to changes in tax treatment in China, unless the tax rates in China become higher than those in the US.[44]

Finally, notwithstanding the drop in the total contractual amount of FDI inflows after 1994, the actual realized amount of FDI continued to grow in China. Whereas it was $11 billion and $27.51 billion in 1992 and 1993, it was $33.76 billion, $37.52 billion, and $41.73 billion, in 1994, 1995, and 1996 respectively. Correspondingly, the FDI arrival rate – defined as the ratio between the pledged and realized amount of investment – improved significantly in and after 1994. Whereas the overall arrival rate for the whole period of 1979-96 was 37%, it was 40%, 41%, and 57% in 1994, 1995, and 1996 respectively. By contrast, the figures for 1992 and 1993 are only 19% and 25%, indicating a considerable amount of "fake" FDI in these years.

The increased FDI arrival rate suggests that foreign investors became more confident in China as an investment outlet in recent years, as they were more willing to translate their pledges into actual investments. According to a recent Chinese report (Ma and Wang 1999:180), in 1998 FDI inflows to China from advanced countries such as the US and the EU continued to rise. And so did the size and quality of new investment projects. Further, the FDI growth rate in the interior provinces was higher than that in the coastal areas. All this seems to fit well with the apparently improved institutional framework for FDI in China in the 1990s, a conclusion that the empirical results of our regression analysis, to be performed in the next chapter, support.

---

44. For further discussion, see "Tax Relief and Other Incentives" in Chapter 2 of this study.

CHAPTER 6

Institutions Matter

In Chapter 5, as part of our efforts to go beyond a *prima facie* case in linking institutions and investments, we focused on one unique aspect of China's FDI regulatory framework. That is, the disparate treatment, in terms of taxation in particular, between FIEs and domestic firms. We demonstrated how that particular institutional aspect affected investment behavior via the demand side of FDI. In this chapter, our task is to consolidate our institutional claims by examining the more general effect of China's FDI regulatory framework on investment behavior with the aid of multiple regression analysis, a technique widely used in social science research. A critical advantage of this method, as compared to a more qualitative approach, is its ability to deal with a large number of cases and to take into account the many factors that may be simultaneously responsible for an outcome under investigation. In our present case, to the extent that investment decisions are not based on a single factor, but rather on a complex amalgam of both economic and institutional considerations, multiple regression analysis comes in handy. It allows us to control for economic variables so that we are in a better position to judge if institutional factors indeed matter.

To further illustrate the point, let us use a concrete example. Over the reform years it is well known that coastal Guangdong province attracted far more FDI than, say, the interior province of Sichuan. Why? One hypothesis is that Guangdong attracted more FDI because its overall economic capacity, measured by market size, labor costs, and infrastructure provisions, is superior to that of Sichuan. A second hypothesis, which is apparently a cultural (or informal institutional) argument, is that Sichuan ranked behind Guangdong because the latter enjoys closer cultural ties with overseas Chinese business communities. A third hypothesis is that since Guangdong has been allowed to take one step ahead of others in making preferential policies available to foreign investors, it is only natural that Guangdong has been in the lead. This last hypothesis in effect is our formal institutional argument.

While all these hypotheses are not necessarily mutually exclusive and indeed can be complementary, for us to validate our formal institutional claims in this causal complexity, we need to control for the effects of economic and cultural variables. Indeed, it is precisely for this purpose that our investigation in this chapter will be carried out on the basis of multiple regression analysis using cross-sectional data on 29 Chinese provinces.[1] Before we proceed further, it is also helpful to be reminded here that since the development of China's FDI regulatory framework has been an evolutionary process, it is critical that our spatial modeling, which is static by itself, has a dynamic and temporal element as well. In operational terms, it means we will employ what I call periodized spatial models (or PS model in short).[2] Specifically, we will build three separate but identical spatial models to match the 1979-84, 1985-90, and 1991-96 periods, the three easily identified phases in the development of China's FDI regulatory framework, discussed at considerable length in Chapter I.

The rest of this chapter is organized as follows. We start with a brief theoretical review of the determinants of FDI. We then discuss the selection and operationalization of the variables used in our PS models. Finally, we present and examine the empirical results of our multiple regression analysis.

Determinants of FDI: A Brief Literature Review

There is a vast literature on determinants of FDI. An exhaustive survey is beyond the scope of the current study.[3] In this section we only review the most important works in the field so that our PS models, to be constructed next, do not become a blindfolded statistical exercise. Given the usual complexity of establishing causality in social science research, it behooves us to be on the alert that mere statistical

1. Tibet is omitted because no data on FDI are available.

2. Needless to say, the SP model constructed here is different, in meaning and content, from the spatial model by Anthony Downs (1957) which concerns political elections.

3: For a rather comprehensive review, consider Caves (1996).

associations are no guarantees for causal claims, if not accompanied by proper theoretical guidance.[4]

FDI traditionally was a concern of international economics, a branch of economics disposed to use general equilibrium tools to study the cross-national phenomena of trade, movements of factors of production, and the international distribution of income. As such, the Heckscher-Ohlin-Samuelson (HOS) model, a textbook staple in explaining international trade, was often employed in the study of FDI as well. Accordingly, FDI was viewed as a vehicle for arbitrage of equity capital from countries where its return is low to countries where it is high, with the empirical implication being that investment should move from capital-rich countries to capital-poor ones. Albeit elegant and parsimonious, this line of reasoning, however, was not borne out by empirical results. One needs only to be reminded here that in the world today FDI remains more a phenomenon amongst capital-rich countries than a phenomenon from capital-rich to capital-poor countries.[5]

Initial breakthrough in this seemingly tranquil but unsatisfactory situation came in 1959 with the doctoral thesis by Stephen Hymer (1976). It is Hymer who first articulated the now widely accepted notion that foreign firms incur costs that indigenous rivals do not. These costs range from those associated with cross-border management to the intrinsic difficulties of operating in linguistically and culturally unfamiliar environments with varying degrees of legal and political uncertainty. In order to offset the handicaps posed by these extra costs, foreign firms must possess some advantages over their domestic rivals. These advantages, known as "ownership-specific advantages," can take the form of advanced technology, product differentiation, financial strength, marketing expertise, and/or superior managerial skills. Clearly, to the extent that Hymer's thesis recognizes different, and therefore incomplete and imperfect, market conditions in cross-border operations, it is consistent with the transaction-cost approach which explicitly considers the role of non-market institutions in studying industrial organizations.

---

4. On risks of spurious correlation resulting from mere statistical co-variation, see Bohrnstedt and Knoke (1994:406-41).

5. See Table 2 in the introduction to this study.

A pioneer in the transaction-cost approach, Ronald Coase (1937; 1960) first proposed the notion of the firm as an organization whose existence can be understood as a way to overcome market imperfections. According to Coase, as well as Alchian and Demsetz (1972), Arrow (1970; 1974), and Williamson (1975;1985;1989) following him, in real competitive markets it is often costly to exchange services or products because of the presence of strategic or opportunistic behavior among transactors – a prospect made all the more real when products and services are ambiguously defined and where contractual obligations have to be enforced over time. In light of these concerns, the firm, as a non-market, hierarchical institution, can replace particularly complex, and potentially very costly arms-length market transactions with internal transactions a crucial concept known as "market internalization."[6]

Although Coase and Williamson did not address FDI specifically, the relevance of the transaction-cost approach to the subject was explored fruitfully by Peter Buckley and Mark Casson (1976; 1988). According to their analysis, since international production has to carry out a series of interrelated economic activities involving a complex chain of transactions across national borders, between the two modes of transactions – market and hierarchy[7] – the latter is often found to be superior to the former in organizing intermediate products and proprietary assets across long distances.[8] This is so if only because, unlike technologies in the form of hardware, many forms of proprietary assets such as marketing expertise and managerial skills which are all part and parcel of a firm's "ownership-specific advantages" are not amenable to commercialization through exporting or licensing. Viewed

---

6. For a good survey article on the theory of the firm, consider Holmstrom and Tirole (1989). For a fascinating account of the importance of the firm as a non-market organization in industrial development in the US, see Chandler (1962; 1977).

7. Beyond international production, Friedrick Hayek (1945) made early important contributions to the debate about the relative merits of market versus hierarchy in the wake of the establishment of central planning in the USSR.

8. This echoes Chandler (1977:1) who has made the following famous comment: "Modern business enterprise took the place of market mechanisms in coordinating the activities of the economy and allocating its resources. In many sectors of the economy, the visible hand of management replaced what Adam Smith referred to as the invisible hand of market forces."

in this light, FDI, made with an eye to acquiring managerial controls,[9] is but a conscious choice on the part of investors to *internalize* markets across national boundaries (Caves 1996; Hennart 1991).[10]

To be sure, while the above theoretical explanation has illuminated two key ingredients, i.e., "O" (ownership-specific) and "I" (market internalization) advantages, that are necessary for international production to take place, they are still insufficient to account for why foreign investors participate in international production in the first place. Equally unclear is why they choose one particular foreign country/region over another. To answer this part of the question, we need to draw upon John Dunning's "eclectic theory" of FDI (1979; 1980; 1988; 1993; 1995).

The basic premise of the eclectic paradigm of FDI is that the so-called "O" and "I" advantages, while necessary, are, *ipso facto,* insufficient conditions for FDI to take place. For FDI to occur, the "O" and "I" advantages must also interact with location-specific, or "L," advantages. The so-called "L" advantages, which were implied by Hymer[11] and are now made explicit by Dunning in his paradigm, may conceivably include a wide array of variables. They may include not only natural assets (e.g., land, labor, and market size) and infrastructure (e.g., transportation and telecommunications), but also institutional arrangements, both formal (e.g., legal framework and other policy-specific advantages) and informal (e.g., cultural and linguistic affinities). In short, a host country/region must, *ceteris paribus*, possess some desirable location-specific advantages relative to those of other countries in order to attract FDI.

As it is, the eclectic paradigm is particularly relevant to our analytical work to be carried out in this chapter because it has an explicit spatial dimension to explain FDI. So far, empirical studies on the spatial, or geographical, distribution of FDI tend to focus only on economic variables such as market size, labor costs, and the provision of physical infrastructure (Coughlin, Terza, and Arromdee 1991; Woodward 1992; and Schneider and Frey 1985). Within the category

---

9. See the definition of FDI in Chapter 3 of this study.

10. The effort to explore the advantages of internalization is ultimately part of the theory of why firms exist. It has generated a large literature. For a rather extensive survey, see Rugman (1985; 1986).

11. For instance, when he referred to costs associated with operating in a culturally and linguistically unfamiliar environment.

of the so-called "L" advantages as an important driver of FDI conceivably there is room for institutional variables as well. After all, if reducing costs is a mirror image of maximizing profits about which business is all,[12] different institutional arrangements can, as North (1995) has eloquently argued, increase or reduce transaction costs.

Armed with the theoretical guidance outlined above, we now turn to the overall structure and mechanics of our PS models.

Model Building

Model building is about the proper selection of dependent and independent variables and about the operationalization of such variables. The process is mainly dictated by the issues of interest for analysis, and can be constrained in some instances by the availability of data. Central also to model building is hypothesis generation, that is, to specify *ex ante* expectations as to what direction – positive or negative – the independent variables will affect the dependent variable. After the hypotheses are laid out, we then turn to assess their validity in light of *ex post* empirical results generated by regression analyses. The hypotheses will be accepted if the statistical analyses yield results that are consistent with our expectations. Otherwise they will be rejected.

There are two overarching analytical concerns that shape the overall structure of the models to be constructed here. First, since our aim is to go beyond a *prima facie* case in demonstrating the effect of the formal institution of China's FDI regulatory framework, we must give an equal chance for other important variables to show their effects at the same time. In other words, unless we control for the effect of other variables, our institutional argument would remain weak. Given

---

12. Profit "maximizing," is a standard assumption in economics theorizing efforts. In reality, however, it may not be accurate in all instances. Indeed, as Nobel Laureate Herbert Simon (1957) notes, real people are not omniscient and perfectly far-sighted, and they know they are not likely to find the mathematically best solution to all complex problems. Instead, they are *boundedly rational*. Simon (1982) further proposes that because human beings are so limited in their capacity to gather and process information that it is difficult to examine an exhaustive range of options and compare their costs and benefits, they thus engage in "satisficing" behavior. That is, they seek and adopt solutions that meet their minimum requirements for satisfaction.

this requirement, the multiple regression technique is appropriate. It allows us to perform "quasi experiments" in the sense that when the effect of one independent variable on the dependent variables is under scrutiny, the effect of all other independent variables is automatically held constant, thus satisfying what is known as the *ceteris paribus* condition, that is, holding other things equal.

Second, since we are interested in testing the effect of the formal institution of China's FDI regulatory framework on foreign investment over *both* space and time, the structure of our models must be such that there is not only a spatial dimension but also an element of time. Indeed, in a way, the temporal element is more important, because without it we would be ill-equipped to validate our central argument, that is, the formal institution of China's FDI regulatory framework has improved and strengthened over time, thus making a significant difference in attracting the huge inflows of FDI in the 1990s vis-à-vis the initial period. In order to meet the temporal requirement, our strategy is to periodize our spatial models in a way that reflects the evolutionary dynamics of China's FDI regulatory framework that we have detailed in previous chapters. Specifically, three separate, consecutive, and identical models will be built for the 1979-84, 1985-90, and 1991-96 periods.

A note about analytical units, as well as number of observations, employed in our PS model is in order. First, about analytical units: Given that many of China's preferential policies to FDI originate from specially designated cities such as the SEZs, ideally our analytical unit should be at the city level. However, because data at that level are too fragmented for us to systematically compare across all three periods, our analysis has to remain at the provincial level for the present study, where systematic and comparable data are available.[13] Accordingly, all

---

13. Head and Ries (1996) tried to analyze the effects of China's incentives areas at the city level. However, due to lack of systematic data, they had to rely on sample data. The patchy data cover only 143 equity JVs (no contractual JVs nor wholly foreign affiliates) that appeared in only 54 cities sometime between 1984 and 1991. And perhaps because of the difficulty of trackability, their measure of policy had to be crude even at the city level. They employed dummies. It is interesting to note, however, their findings are consistent with the results of my empirical analysis to be carried out at the provincial level in this chapter. That is, policy incentives, among others, become less important in attracting FDI over time.

the variables included in our PS models are broken down by 29 provinces,[14] as well as by periods I, II, and III (i.e., 1979-84, 1985-90, and 1991-96).

Now about the number of observations. For each period under analysis, our model covers 174 data points, that is, 29 (provinces) multiplied by 6 (years). It is important to note, however, that the real number of investment activities is much larger than 174. This is so because, in reality, behind one yearly aggregate figure of realized FDI in each province, there are hundreds, if not thousands, of investment activities, even though each investment comes in different sizes. To further illustrate the point here, for instance, the realized amounts of FDI in Shanghai and Beijing in 1998 were US$3.6 billion and US$2.2 billion respectively. But the number of FDI projects registered in Shanghai and Beijing for that year was 1,490 and 651 respectively (*Zhongguo tongji zaiyao* 1999: 136).

In the sections that follow, we discuss issues related to the selection of variables to be included in our model and their operationalization.

Dependent Variable

The dependent variable in our PS model is the cumulative amount of FDI inflows broken down by 29 provinces and by periods I, II, and III. I use the actually realized amount[15] of FDI flows in each of the 29 provinces broken down by three periods. Basic statistics of the dependent variable are summarized in Table VI-1. Note the means and the standard deviations of the dependent variable. There clearly is a great deal of variation in the dependent variable for all three periods. This gives us an initial indication that it is not futile to focus our

---

14. For semantic simplicity, I also use "province" to denote Beijing, Tianjin, and Shanghai, three autonomous municipalities that are empowered as a province and report directly to the central government. Chongqing, formerly the capital of Sichuan province, was elevated to the same status only in 1997. Thus it is not covered in our regression analysis whose time span runs only from 1979 through 1996 for data consistency.

15. As discussed in Chapter 3, Chinese statistics report both actual and contractual figures. I chose the actual realized amounts over the contractual figures, because contractual figures refer to the projected amount of investment when the contract is signed. Very conceivably, some of that may never be realized in reality.

analysis on the so-called "L" (location-specific) advantages of each province as the independent variables.

Table VI-1: Basic Statistics of the Dependent Variable (US$10,000)

	PERIOD I: 1979-84	PERIOD II : 1985-90	PERIOD III: 1991-96
Mean	5040	42721	533236
Std. dev.	23800	100007	899573
Min.	0*	0*	1977
Max.	128529	528851	4407339

Note: * Qinghai realized zero FDI

Sources: *Zhongguo duiwai jingji tongji nianjian* [China Foreign Economic Statistical Yearbook] (various years); *Zhongguo duiwai maoyi nianjian* [Almanac of China's Foreign Trade and Economic Relations] (various years).

Independent Variables

Now consider the independent variables. At a general level of conceptualization, I consider three categories of independent variables: economic, cultural (informal), and institutional (formal) advantages. Conceivably, each category can be broken down further to include variables of higher specificity. For instance, under the category of economic advantage, we can consider market size, labor costs, and infrastructure as location-specific advantages in attracting FDI. However, since my interest is primarily to isolate, as far as is methodologically feasible, the effect of the institutional variables, I include economic advantage variables mainly as "control" or "setting" variables. Below I elaborate on each of the categories of independent variables, outlining key testable hypotheses at the end of this section.

Economic Advantage

One can of course think of many factors that fall under the rubric of a location-specific economic advantage, but an exhaustive tabulation is neither fruitful nor necessary for our purposes. In light of our analytical interest and data availability, I include market size, labor costs/skills and infrastructure. These variables, taken together, represent the economic advantage of each province in terms of its propensity to attract FDI.

Market size

There seems little doubt that market size is a key locational determinant of FDI. Among industrialized economies, FDI from the US is found to have a statistically significant correlation with the market size, measured by GDP, of the EEC countries (Scaperlanda 1969). Similarly, FDI from developed to developing countries are also found to be sensitive to the market size of the host countries (OECD 1983). In our case, according to a 1992 survey of 60 FIEs in Beijing (Zhen 1992:29), market size (60%) surpassed labor costs (53%) as a locational consideration for investment, indicating that market size is a critical determinant of FDI.

The way that I delineate market, and, indeed, other economic variables, on a provincial basis, instead of treating China as an integrated market for FDI, needs some comment. My justification is straightforward. The Chinese market remains segmented, thanks in large part to Mao's developmental strategy that prodded the Chinese economy toward regional and local self-sufficiency from the 1950s onward (Naughton 1996:51,62). Wedeman (1995), in his *Bamboo Walls and Brick Ramparts,* shows that, in spite of central government efforts to fight local protectionism, local governments continued to protect their local resource bases by setting up interprovincial trade barriers in the reform era. Take the auto market for instance: autos produced in Tianjin, Wuhan, or elsewhere were essentially locked out of Shanghai by the anti-competitive practices of the Shanghai local government that favored the local JV product of Volkswagen,[16] although the recent entry of General Motors may soon end Volkswagen's dominance of the local market. GM rolled the first Buick off the line of its US$1.5 billion facility in Shanghai in December 1998.

The Harvard Business School case on Otis is a further illustration of the depth of local protectionism in China (cited in Huang 1998:28). In 1984 Otis formed a JV, China Tianjin Otis Elevator Company

16. One such practice, for example, concerns taxi fleets in Shanghai. The Shanghai local government requires that only cars with 1.6-liter (or above) engines may be used as taxis. This happens to fit the specification of Shanghai-built VW cars, and effectively bans smaller cars produced elsewhere such as, the Tianjin Xiali, or the Wuhan Citroen Fu Kang.

(CTOEC), with Tianjin Elevator Company (TEC), which had a 65% equity position in the venture. As the business grew, in 1988 Otis tried to set up another JV in Suzhou in Jiangsu province. But the plan was rejected by the Tianjin government, even though CTOEC would have held a 50% equity stake in the new venture. The Tianjin government viewed Otis' branching efforts as shifting rents to other regions of the country. In another move, Otis attempted to forge a JV in Guangzhou, but this time the Guangzhou government turned down the original proposal because it involved equity participation of TEC. As these stories show, there is a good reason for foreign investors to evaluate market potentials on a regional rather than national basis in China.

To operationalize market size on a provincial basis, I use both GDP and IOV (industrial output value) figures. The idea here is to take into consideration different strategies of FIEs. To the extent that foreign investors aim to sell their products domestically, GDP is a better measure because it represents the total purchasing power of a particular province. In this context, GDP figures proxy more closely for the goods market. On the other hand, if investors are interested in M&A (merger and acquisition) and are export-oriented, IOV is a better measure because it more closely represents the existing industrial capacity of a particular province. In this context, IOV figures proxy for the assets market.[17]

I use the initial levels of GDP and IOV of each province in each of the three periods. Specifically I use 1979, 1985, and 1991 GDP and IOV figures to represent the market size of each province for each of the three periods. The reason for doing so is both theoretical and technical. Theoretically, according to the Cobb-Douglas production function model, since output is a function of inputs, including capital broadly construed,[18] it may well be that the causal arrow between GDP

---

17. I am indebted to Yasheng Huang for calling my attention to the assets market. Empirically, there is evidence to suggest that domestic-market-oriented investment and export-oriented investment respond differently to different location-specific advantages (Santiago 1987).

18. Indeed, until more recently when Robert Lucas and Paul Romer of the University of Chicago shifted gears to pay more attention to human skills and knowledge, capital formation was generally agreed to hold the top priority role in economic development. Historically, technical progress was, according to Robert Solow of MIT, fairly steady and automatic, labor similarly grew

or IOV (output) and FDI (input) runs from the latter to the former. Take China's SEZs for instance. They all have risen from barren areas to dynamic industrial centers with a huge influx of FDI. To make our PS model structurally causal rather than merely covariational, technically a simple way is to impose a "time order" condition, which helps establish the essential asymmetry in a causal relationship (Bohrnstedt and Knoke 1994:407-9).

Labor costs

Labor costs as a location-specific economic advantage are easily understood in light of the overall cost significance of wages paid to workers as a production factor. In the US, where production tends to be highly technology- and capital-intensive, wages paid to workers as a share of production costs remain high, comprising about 25% of the value-added for all manufacturing industries, or about 45% if wages paid to non-production workers are included (Dicken and Lloyd 1990:151-60). In China, given that regional wage disparities have become more pronounced in the reform years,[19] and that many FDI projects are labor-intensive, labor costs as a production factor tend to be accentuated. Indeed, many FIE managers whom I interviewed reported that to simultaneously control wage bills and retain skilled workers has become a formidable challenge. They suggested that even in low-skill sectors such as garment manufacturing in southern China, staff turnover is high. Thus, all else being equal, a province that offers cheap labor is apparently better positioned to attract FDI.

Guided by similar considerations of causality regarding market size and FDI, I use the initial level of the average yearly wage for staff and workers in urban areas in each of the three periods as a first step to measure labor costs.[20] Labor costs, to be sure, are more complicated

---

steadily for demographic reasons, leaving capital accumulation as the key source of growth. See Minford (1993), and Rostow (1963).

19. For instance, in 1996 the average salary for an unskilled worker employed in an FIE in Shanghai was twice as high as that for a comparative worker in Hangzhou, Wuxi, or Nanjing. For a further discussion on income and inequality in China in the reform era, consider Khan and Riskin (1998).

20. I do not use average wage rates in a province because very few FDI projects are agriculture-related; wages for urban workers are thus a better measure.

than what can be measured by wage rates. The quality aspect of labor is also very important.[21] Given the vast regional disparities in education and industrial development in China, nominal wages can be misleading if labor skills are not taken seriously. Indeed, surveys of FIEs consistently identify "local management and skills shortage" as among the greatest impediments to productivity growth in FIE operations (EIU 1997: xv). Thus, to better reflect labor costs, I also include labor productivity. For this variable I use the total value of industrial output by industrial enterprises with independent accounting systems in each province divided by the total number of workers in these industrial enterprises.

Infrastructure

Infrastructure as a location-specific advantage, broadly construed, entails both a "soft" and a "hard" facet. The soft side can include such services as accounting, legal, and even recreational, which in a way can be regarded as part and parcel of institutional development. The hard side, often known as the physical infrastructure, is what I am looking at here as an economic advantage of a particular province in terms of its capacity to attract FDI.

Physical infrastructure itself also covers a wide range of dimensions: from power supplies to public transportation, from posts to telecommunications, from railroads to highways, from harbors to airports, and from residential housing to office buildings. Very conceivably, all these dimensions are relevant to the success of an FIE operation. For instance, as Rosen (1998:192-93) notes, currently, prompt delivery, which very much depends on reliable infrastructure, is critical to garment manufacturing. New designs prepared in New York

---

21. In addition, another factor that foreign investors have to consider is non-wage costs, including pensions, unemployment insurance, health insurance, enterprise-based welfare funds, housing subsidies. According to a US-China Business Council study (1996), the non-wage overhead costs were about 14% of wages in the 1980s; they increased to an average of 30% in the mid-1990s. Variations apparently exist in non-wage costs in different localities. But because they are often subject to negotiation between FIEs and local governments, it is difficult, if not impossible, to systematically tract the non-wage costs across regions, and thus they are not included in our regression analysis.

are transmitted instantly. Delivery of finished products from southern China to the New York market is now possible within 15-24 days, thanks to fast trucking, efficient port services, and frequent shipping routes. It is therefore appropriate that we include infrastructure as a location-specific economic advantage. However, since there is no easy way to capture all the dimensions of infrastructure, for this study I settle on a readily available figure as a proxy for physical infrastructure. The figure represents the output value of transportation, postal, and telecommunications services in each province.[22]

Cultural Advantage

As discussed earlier, the informal institution, or culture, as a location-specific advantage, refers to such conditions as cultural homogeneity, linguistic familiarity, and kinship ties. Theoretically, that culture facilitates investment can be explained from at least two angles. First, to the extent that culture is understood as a language-based framework for encoding and interpreting the information that our senses presents to our brain (Johansson 1988:172-88), culture can facilitate investment by reducing information costs. The use of quality interpreting services in China now, for instance, incurs considerable costs, over US$100 dollars per hour. Little wonder that language consultancy firms are booming in the major cities in China.

Second, to the extent that culture is viewed as a rich and tightly-knit social network, culture can promote investment by mitigating against opportunistic behavior, as an iterated game illustrates.[23] Here reputation is a critical asset (Kreps and Wilson 1982). Empirically, using extensive interview data, Wang Hongying (forthcoming) has documented how personal connections, or *guanxi* in Chinese, facilitated FDI flows in China. Sociologist Peter Berger (1994:72), who studies the relations between Chinese culture and economics, notes that Chinese firms are often family based because, within traditional Chinese culture, "you can only trust close relatives." Beyond China,

22. The economic advantage data used here are from *Gaige Kaifang shiqinian de Zhongguo diqu jingji* [China Regional Economy: A Profile of 17 Years of Reform and Opening Up] (1996).

23. For theoretical illumination on how repeated games can deter defection and foster cooperation, see Nash (1950; 1953); Kreps, et al. (1982); and Kreps and Wilson (1982). For theoretical application, see Axelrod (1984).

several studics on Japanese FDI suggest that cultural distance is a negative predictor of FDI (Yoshino 1976; Tsurumi 1976; Ozawa 1979).

Coding of cultural variable

The cultural variable as a location-specific advantage does not exist in standard format and it has to be created. My coding of the cultural variable is guided by three considerations. First, China is huge and is not culturally monolithic, and each of its provinces is individually more populous than most European nations. Given that overseas Chinese business communities are dominated by Guangdong, Shanghai, and Fujian natives whose dialects are so distinct as to be hardly comprehensible to one another, I take Guangdong, Shanghai, and Fujian as three cultural poles, from which I measure the "cultural distance" of each province vis-à-vis overseas Chinese investors. Specifically, cultural distance is measured in kilometers from each provincial capital to each of the three poles and the shortest of the three measurements is taken as the initial valid value.[24]

Second, in view of the fact that coastal provinces are in greater contact with the outside world than interior provinces, and that culture is often a function of the frequency of interactions between people, the coastal provinces, as a group, should be treated differently from the interior provinces. For that reason, the initial values of the cultural distance of all interior provinces are then weighted by a value of 2. In this way, all the coastal provinces are distinguished from the interior provinces.

Third, the variable thus created is only meant to be a rough proxy for the cultural homogeneity, linguistic familiarity, and kinship ties that each province enjoys vis-à-vis overseas Chinese business communities. But since these attributes are not likely to change appreciably in the short run, I use the same value of cultural distance for all the three periods that our PS model covers.[25]

24. The measurement is based on Hsieh and Hsieh (1995).

25. Admittedly, this is a very rough measure of cultural affinity. Conceptually, perhaps a better measure is the number of natives of Fujian, Guangdong, or Shanghai as a percentage of the total population of each province. Unfortunately, such data, which are even more difficult to collect due to China's growing migrant population during the reform era, are not available.

Institutional Advantage

China's FDI regulatory framework, or the formal institution, as documented extensively in Part I of this study, has both a policy and legislative dimension, which need to be treated differently, because the way they vary differs. The legislative dimension has only a temporal variation, without a spatial dimension. Investment laws, such as the EJV, CJV, WFOE laws and their auxiliary rules, developed over time and are meant to be applied evenly up and down the country. As such, they do not constitute a salient institutional advantage that is location-specific. This being the case, their effects are not amenable to spatial modeling directly. However, as I mentioned in the introduction to this study, because the relevance of the formal and informal types of institution to facilitate investments is inversely related, we can therefore infer the effect of the formal institutions from that of the informal institution. To the extent that we argue that the formal institution becomes stronger, we would expect the cultural effects to become weaker, and vice versa.

Unlike the legislative dimension, the policy dimension of China's FDI regulatory framework displays attributes that are spatial by policy designs and therefore constitutes location-specific advantage. Recall that many special policies, such as the preferential tax treatment and the high project approval power, are not applied evenly up and down China. They thus constitute a location-specific advantage, even though over time they became somewhat equalized, as more regions were authorized to offer similar preferential treatments to foreign investors. Since policy advantages cover a wide range of areas – from fiscal concessions and project approval limits to priority status to host FDI projects in sectors not open everywhere – it is reasonable to expect that they would increase a province's chance to attract FDI.

Coding of the policy variable

Like the cultural variable, the policy variable does not exist in standard format and it has to be created. As documented in Chapter 1, preferential policies exist in different degrees and are often isolated in the geographical confines of cities. But since our analytic unit has to remain at the provincial level given the data constraints, it is difficult to keep track of the policy advantages in ways that capture every nuance and shade. This being the case, for this study I settle for two important components of the policy advantage, i.e., the preferential tax rates and the FDI project approval limits, and construct a rough index, indicating the policy advantage across different provinces over time.

Recall that in terms of project approval power, there are three basic levels – US$100 million, US$30 million, or US$10 million, each of which the central government has allowed different localities the discretion to approve FDI projects. For projects over US$100 million, they have to obtain the approval of the central government. Recall further that over time, however, the central government has gradually allowed greater approval power to more local governments. This is consistent with the gradual decentralization of economic decision-making powers during the reform era as central planning has been increasingly replaced by the market. In terms of tax rates, on the other hand, there are also basically three levels, i.e., 15%, 24%, or 30%, at which the income of an FIE is taxed, depending on the locality of the particular FDI project. Recall that in the early years of reform, only SEZs were authorized to offer the very preferential tax rate of 15% to foreign investors. In the mid-1980s and again in the early 1990s, more localities were authorized to offer preferential tax rates.

Based on the above, our policy advantage index uses the following formula: (1 - tax rate) + project approval scale. As such, the larger the value of the index, the more advantageous a locality is in terms of policy. For instance, if a locality offers a tax rate of 24% and has the authority to approve an FDI project up to US$30 million (i.e., 0.3 of the highest level of 100 million), its policy advantage index is (1-0.24) + 0.3 = 1.06. A locality that offers a tax rate of 15% and can approve a project of up to US$100 million, policy advantage index has a 1.85. A locality that offers a tax rate of 30% and can only approve projects below US$10 million, policy advantage index has a 0.7. As can be seen, our policy advantage index ranges from a low of 0.7 to a high of 1.85.

Model Assembly and Testable Hypotheses

Having laid out all the key ingredients of our PS model, we proceed to assemble them in summary form here, and to outline the principal testable hypotheses. As mentioned earlier, our PS model covers both space and time. Expressed formally, it takes the following form:

$$\begin{aligned}FDI_{x(I,\,II,\,III)} = \alpha_{0\,(I,\,II,\,III)} + \alpha_{1\,(I,\,II,\,III)}\ POLICY_{x\,(I,\,II,\,III)} + \\ \alpha_{2\,(I,\,II,\,III)}\ CULTURE_{x\,(I,\,II,\,III)} + \\ \alpha_{3\,(I,\,II,\,III)}\ MARKET\ goods/assets_{x\,(I,\,II,\,III)} + \\ \alpha_{4\,(I,\,II,\,III)}\ WAGE_{x\,(I,\,II,\,III)} + \\ \alpha_{5\,(I,\,II,\,III)}\ PRODUCTIVITY_{x\,(I,\,II,\,III)} + \\ \alpha_{6\,(I,\,II,\,III)}\ INFRASTRUCTURE_{x\,(I,\,II,\,III)}\end{aligned}$$

where:

- *I* refers to the initial period (1979-84), *II* the second period (1985-90), and *III* the third period (1991-96).
- FDI $_{x\,(I,\,II,\,III)}$ is the logged value of the realized amount of FDI in province *x* in periods *I, II,* or *III.*
- POLICY$_{x\,(I,\,II,\,III)}$ is the value of the index, from 0.7 to 1.85, indicating the policy advantage enjoyed by province *x* in periods *I, II,* or *III.*
- CULTURE $_{x\,(I,\,II,\,III)}$ is the logged value of "cultural distance," as a proxy of the cultural (dis)advantage of province *x*, vis-à-vis the overseas Chinese business communities and in periods *I, II,* or *III.*
- MARKETgoods/assets $_{x\,(I,\,II,\,III)}$ is respectively the logged value of GDP and of IOV of province *x* in periods *I, II,* or *III.*
- WAGE $_{x\,(I,\,II,\,III)}$ is the logged value of the average yearly wage rate of urban workers in province *x* and in periods *I, II,* or *III.*
- PRODUCTIVITY $_{x\,(I,\,II,\,III)}$ is the logged value of the average labor productivity of urban enterprise workers in province *x* and in periods *I, II,* or *III.*
- INFRASTRUCTURE $_{x\,(I,\,II,\,III)}$ is the logged value of the output value of transportation, and posts and telecommunications, as a proxy for the physical infrastructure in province *x* and in periods *I, II,* or *III.*

The basic statistics of the variables included in our PS model are contained in Table VI-2. Key testable hypotheses are presented as follows:

Prediction 1:
$\alpha_{1\,(I)} > 0$; $\alpha_{2\,(I)} < 0$; $\alpha_{3\,(I)}$, $\alpha_{4\,(I)}$, $\alpha_{5\,(I)}$, or $\alpha_{6\,(I)}$ = (?)

Interpretation: During period I, a province's level of FDI is expected to be positively correlated with its policy advantage and negatively correlated with its cultural distance. However, given the highly restrictive and immature nature of China's FDI regulatory framework in this period, we would not expect that the level of FDI in a province to be all properly (i.e., with the "correct" signs) correlated with its economic advantage variables. The reason is that, even if the investors had gone to China looking for market size and cheap labor, etc., because the formal institutional framework was weak at this time, they would not have had the adequate freedom (i.e., from excessive red-tape, and/or from worries about the institutional protection of their investment) to scour the country to invest in ways that make most sense economically. Market size for foreign investors means market access, which in turn is a function of the institutional arrangements. Until China's command economy has sufficiently moved to a rule-based market system, we would not expect a close correlation between FDI and market size, and, for that matter, the other economic advantage variables.

Prediction 2:
$\alpha_{1\,(II)} > 0$; $\alpha_{2\,(II)} < 0$; $\alpha_{3\,(II)} > 0$(?); $\alpha_{4(II)} < 0$(?); $\alpha_{5(III)} > 0$(?); $\alpha_{6\,(II)} > 0$(?)

Interpretation: During period II, a province's level of FDI is expected to be positively correlated with its policy advantage and negatively related with the cultural distance variable. Further, it is expected, albeit without great confidence (thence question marks) that the level of FDI is also properly (i.e., with the "right signs") correlated with its economic advantage variables. The reason is that, if indeed as we have argued, China's FDI framework became better defined, thus more predictive and less arbitrary, we would expect that investors would have a higher degree of freedom, relative to period I, to go up and down China to invest in ways that make more sense economically. Statistically, this would mean a stronger association between FDI and the economic advantage variables.

Table VI-2: Basic Statistics of Dependent and Independent Variables

VARIABLE		PERIOD I	PERIOD II	PERIOD III
FDI	mean	1.382	3.845	5.221
	std.dev.	1.556	1.163	0.778
	min	0	0	3.296
	max	5.109	5.723	6.644
POLICY*	mean	0.786	0.855	1.794
	std.dev.	0.126	0.189	0.044
	min	0.7	0.7	1.76
	max	1.15	1.15	1.85
CULTURAL DISTANCE	mean	2.812	2.812	2.812
	std.dev.	1.028	1.028	1.028
	min	0	0	0
	max	3.716	3.716	3.716
MARKETgoods	mean	2.036	2.350	2.806
	std.dev	0.452	0.463	0.462
	min	0.845	1.204	1.748
	max	2.745	3.015	3.500
MARKETassets	mean	2.015	2.356	2.743
	std.dev.	0.367	0.363	0.365
	min	1.146	1.477	1.851
	max	2.474	2.832	3.257
WAGE	mean	2.832	3.061	3.367
	std.dev.	0.051	0.055	0.064
	min	2.757	2.977	3.265
	max	2.985	3.235	3.528
PRODUCTIVITY	mean	-.071	0.089	3.367
	std.dev.	0.145	0.104	0.064
	min	-.238	-.054	0.257
	max	0.336	0.394	0.691
INFRASTRUCTURE	mean	1.217	1.620	2.059
	std.dev.	0.304	0.255	0.246
	min	0.833	1.279	1.631
	max	2.074	2.325	2.792

Note: * The variable is an index, ranging from 0.7 to 1.85, that is not logged. Others are logged values.

Sources: FDI data are from Zhongguo duiwai jingji tongji nianjian [China Foreign Economic Statistical Yearbook] (various years); Zhongguo duiwai maoyi nianjian [Almanac of China's Foreign Trade and Economic Relations] (various years). Other economic data are from *Gaige Kaifang shiqinian Zhongguo jingji* [China Regional Economy: A Profile of 17 Years of Reform and Opening Up] (1996). Cultural distance is based on Hsieh and Hsieh (1995), *China: A Provincial Atlas.*

Prediction 3:
$\alpha_{1\,(III)} > 0$; $\alpha_{2\,(III)} < 0$; $\alpha_{3\,(III)} > 0$; $\alpha_{4\,(III)} < 0$; $\alpha_{5(III)} > 0$; $\alpha_{6\,(III)} > 0$

Interpretation: During period III, a province's level of FDI is expected to be positively correlated with its policy advantage and negatively related with the cultural distance variable. Further, it is predicted that the level of FDI would be properly correlated with all the economic advantage variables. The reason is that China's FDI framework has now undergone significant liberalization, and all the key investment laws, i.e., EJV, CJV, and WFOE laws, together with their detailed implementation acts, are now in place. In addition, China has entered into a rather sophisticated web of international guarantees, both bilateral and multilateral, regarding foreign investment. We would thus expect that investors now enjoy a still higher degree of freedom, relative to period II, to put their investment wherever it makes most sense economically.

Prediction 4:
$\alpha_{1\,(I)} > \alpha_{1\,(II)} > \alpha_{1\,(III)}$

Interpretation: It is predicted that *across the three periods* the effect of a province's policy advantage on the level of FDI should decrease over time. The reason is that, as we discussed in Chapter 1, over the reform years special policies, such as those originally available only in the SEZs, gradually expanded into the coastal areas in the latter part of the 1980s and then into the interior regions of the country in the 1990s. As the special policies became less special over time, their effect is expected to become equalized.

Prediction 5:
$\alpha_{2\,(I)} > \alpha_{2\,(II)} > \alpha_{2\,(III)}$

Interpretation: To the extent that we argue that China's FDI regulatory framework has improved significantly over the years, it is expected that the effect of the cultural variable would decrease *across the three periods*. The reason is that if we are correct in arguing that China's formal institutional framework has become more transparent, better defined, and less arbitrary, foreign investors should have less of a need to rely on informal means, such as personal friends and kinship ties, for information and/or to hedge against investment risks.

Prediction 6:

$\alpha_{3\,(I)} < \alpha_{3\,(II)} < \alpha_{3\,(III)}$

Interpretation: It is expected that *across the three periods* the effect of market size (both goods and assets markets), on a province's level of FDI should increase. This is because as an ever widening share of China's domestic markets has been gradually opened up to FDI, which is especially true in the 1990s, foreign investors, especially huge multinational corporations, are increasingly able to pursue their strategies of exploiting domestic markets in China. Consequently, we would expect a growing correlation between FDI level and market size.

Interpreting the Empirical Results

Table VI-3 reports the basic OLS multiple regression results of our PS model. Since a log-linear relationship is assumed between a province's level of FDI and its explanatory variables for each of the three periods that our PS model covers, all the α coefficient estimates reported here are thus elasticity measurements. Discussions of the regression results, at times supported by auxiliary models, follow and will proceed in the order of the 6 key predictions outlined above.

Prediction 1:

Look first at the boldfaced statistics[26] in Column One for Period I, in Table VI-3. As expected, the coefficient estimates of both the policy and culture variables bear the predicted signs. Moreover, they are statistically significant. By contrast, but by no means unexpected, the economic advantage variables yield mixed results. The signs of market, wage, and labor productivity are clearly "wrong." On the other hand, the coefficient estimate of the infrastructure, although carrying a "correct" sign, is statistically insignificant.

---

26. For clarity of discussion, I only focus on the boldfaced statistics. The non-boldfaced statistics basically show the same results, indicating the model is robust, whether we use the goods market or the assets market specification.

Table VI-3: Empirical Results of the Multiple Regression Analyses

	COLUMN ONE PERIOD I (79-84)		COLUMN TWO PERIOD II (85-90)		COLUMN THREE PERIOD III (91-96)	
POLICY	**3.19**** **(1.91)**	3.23** (1.90)	**1.58*** **(1.76)**	1.54 (1.32)	**1.34** **(0.67)**	0.97 (0.57)
CULTURAL DISTANCE	**-2.51**** **(-1.83)**	- 2.27** (-1.96)	**-0.98** **(-1.01)**	-0.86 (-1.17)	**-0.71** **(-0.97)**	-0.80 (-0.75)
MARKETgoods	**-0.13** **(-0.18)**	--	**0.86**** **(2.19)**	--	**0.92***** **(4.65)**	--
MARKETassets	--	-0.25 (-0.38)	--	0.85** (2.30)	--	0.76*** (5.14)
WAGE	**4.42** **(0.63)**	3.65 (0.53)	**-4.54*** **(-1.49)**	-4.68* (-1.61)	**-4.07**** **(-2.19)**	- 4.69*** (-2.71)
PRODUCTIVITY	**-1.09** **(-0.46)**	-1.09 (-0.45)	**3.99**** **(2.08)**	3.89** (2.08)	**2.53**** **(2.01)**	2.76** (2.32)
INFRASTRUCTURE	**0.37** **(0.94)**	1.55 (1.01)	**-0.05** **(-0.06)**	-0.22 (-0.26)	**0.75*** **(1.69)**	0.61 (1.37)
Constant	**-7.57** **(-0.38)**	-5.57 (-0.29)	**16.01*** **(1.65)**	17.28** (1.91)	**13.25*** **(1.66)**	16.45** (2.29)
R^2	0.59	0.59	0.70	0.71	0.85	0.87
Adjusted R^2	0.47	0.47	0.62	0.64	0.81	0.83

T-statistics are in parentheses. *** Statistically significant at 1% confidence level. ** Statistically significant at 5% confidence level. * Statistically significant at 10% confidence level.

These results show that in the initial period what really counted for a province's level of FDI was only its policy and cultural advantages. Economic advantage variables were poor, if not totally irrelevant, predictors. Indeed, when the same regression (for period I) is run without all the economic advantage variables, the model's explanatory power, as indicated by the adjusted R^2, actually increases from 0.47 to 0.52 (compare Tables VI-3 and VI-4). This further indicates that economic variables were not really relevant during the initial period.

These empirical results are not surprising, given that the Chinese economy at the time was still very much a command system; and its FDI regulatory framework was in rudimentary form. An economy heavily controlled by central planners meant that, as a practical matter, foreign investors, even when they so desired, were not allowed to search up and down the country in pursuit of cheap labor and a big market. This explains why the economic advantage variables are poor predictors of FDI during the initial period.

Table VI-4: Regression Results of Auxiliary Models without Economic Advantage Variables

	Period I	Period II	Period III
POLICY	5.42** (2.34)	2.77** (2.15)	1.18** (2.13)
CULTURE	-0.96* (-1.78)	-0.79 (-1.22)	-0.66 (-1.47)
CONSTANT	1.36 (0.93)	4.51 (1.44)	-6.64 (1.25)
R^2	0.54	0.43	0.61
Adjusted R^2	0.52	0.38	0.57

T-statistics are in parentheses. ** Statistically significant at the 5% level. * Statistically significant at the 10% level.

What is more, given the incipient nature of China's FDI regulatory framework, it is only "rational" that investors, many of them overseas Chinese, cluster in areas where they are culturally familiar, so that they can count on informal means, such as kinship ties, to reduce transaction costs. Little wonder that during the initial period, a very high portion of FDI headed for Guangdong, Shanghai, and Fujian, the three provinces that enjoy the closest cultural ties with overseas Chinese business communities.[27]

Prediction 2:

Turn next to the boldfaced statistics in Column Two for Period II. It is clear that Prediction 1.2 is largely borne out by the empirical results here. As expected, all variables, save infrastructure, show the "correct" signs. Note, in particular, the coefficient estimates of the economic advantage variables – market size (both goods and assets markets), wage rate, and labor productivity. Not only do they carry the "correct" signs, they are also statistically significant at high confidence levels. Substantively, these results indicate that China during this period indeed offered a better investment environment. Recall that not only were two additional landmark laws on alternative modes of investment

27. Their combined portion is about 32% of the country's total measured in realized amount of FDI. Individually, it is about 12%, 10%, and 10% for Guangdong, Fujian, and Shanghai respectively.

(i.e., WFOE and CJV) promulgated in 1986 and 1988, special policies that had existed only in the SEZs began to be available along much of China's coastal area after 1984.

Worth emphasizing in this context is the fact that restrictions on foreign access to the domestic market and labor began to be relaxed. Instead of "encouraging foreign investors to market their products outside of China," as the 1979 law stipulated (Article 9), China now allowed them to sell their products domestically if their products "are urgently needed or are import substitutes."[28] Efforts were also made to improve foreign access to domestic labor – witness the publication in 1986 of the Provisions Concerning Autonomous Rights of Personnel Employment, and Salary, Insurance, and Welfare Expenses in Foreign-Invested Enterprises.[29] Seen in this light, the statistical evidence reported here points to the efficacy of the efforts thus rendered.

Now that investors were given a better chance to pursue cheap labor and a big market in China, it is only logical that economic advantage variables became more critical in predicting FDI. Accordingly, when the same regression (for Period II) is run without all the economic variables, the model's explanatory power, as indicated by the adjusted R^2, decreases from 0.62 to 0.38 (compare Tables VI-3 and VI-4), indicating the effect of policy and cultural variables, while still relevant, became less so compared to Period I. By contrast, the economic advantage variables now began to be more important.

Prediction 3:

The boldfaced statistics contained in Column Three (Table VI-3) that cover Period III strongly support Prediction 1.3. Now all the variables bear "correct" signs. Note, in particular, when compared to Period II, the coefficients of the market (both goods and assets markets) and the wage variables for this period increase measurably in terms of statistical significance, with the t-statistics advancing from 2.19 to 4.65

---

28. According to the Detailed Implementation Act of the EJV Law. See Zheng Yan'er (1985:57-59)

29. Promulgated by the Ministry of Labor and Personnel in November 1986. Autonomy regarding employment for FIEs was also emphasized in many subsequent legislative works, e.g., the "22 Articles," and "Opinions on Further Insuring the Autonomy of Personnel Management in Foreign-Invested Enterprises," issued in 1988. See also Du Xianzhong (1994:251-52).

for the goods market, from 2.30 to 5.14 for the assets market, and from 1.49 to 2.19 for wage. These results are quite in keeping with my documentation in Part I of the study that China's FDI regulatory framework became further liberalized in the early 1990s, especially after Deng Xiaoping's famous southern tour in 1992.

Now with fewer bureaucratic impediments standing in the way of foreign access to China's domestic markets, the effect of the economic advantage variables – relative to those of the policy and cultural variables – become more pronounced. Accordingly, when the same regression (for Period III) is run without all the economic variables, the model's explanatory power, as indicated by the adjusted R^2, decreases very significantly from 0.81 to 0.57 (compare Tables VI-3 and VI-4). Note, also, the model for Period III has greater explanatory power, compared to that for Period II (0.81 as against 0.62, adjusted R^2). This suggests strongly that investors now enjoy a much higher degree of freedom to scour up and down China to invest in ways that make most sense economically.

Predictions 4, 5, and 6:

Now take a look at the boldfaced statistics contained in Table VI-3 again, but this time across the three consecutive periods. If we take Period I as a benchmark with which to compare later Periods II and III, the direction and size of the coefficient estimates of policy, culture, and market all progress in much the same way that is expected by Predictions 4, 5, and 6.

Specifically, the coefficients of the policy advantage variable decrease over time, from 3.19 to 1.58 to 1.34, and their statistical significance levels decrease as well, from 1.91 to 1.76 to 0.67. Substantively, these results lend support to the argument that while special policies make a difference in attracting FDI, over time they become less important. The reason is obvious. As the interior provinces also began to offer similar policies that were originally available only in the SEZs, the effect of the policy advantage across different regions in China becomes increasingly equalized. In the case of culture, not only does the coefficient shrink from -2.51 to -0.98 to -0.71, it becomes statistically less significant over time, with the t-statistics dwindling from -1.83 to -1.01 to -0.97. These results validate the hypothesis that as the formal institution of China's FDI regulatory framework matures over the years, investors have less of a need to count on informal cultural means, such as linguistic familiarities, personal friends, and kinship ties.

By contrast, the coefficient of market size generally grows across the three periods, from -0.13 to 0.86 to 0.92 for the goods market, and from -0.25 to 0.85 to 0.76 for the assets market. More impressive still, their statistical significance improve dramatically, with the t-statistics moving up from -0.18 to 2.19 to 4.65 for the goods market and from 0.38 to 2.30 to 5.14 for the assets market. These results show that for foreign investors, what matters is market access, which in turn is a function of institutional arrangements. This is especially true in a transitional economy like that of China. As bureaucratic intervention gradually recedes from the market-place over time, it is only natural that we see a growing correlation between FDI and market size. Foreign investors have been gradually allowed more market access. And this is quite consistent with anecdotal sectoral evidence reported elsewhere.

In the goods market, Coca-Cola sales in China, for instance, rocketed 76% in 1994, making China Coke's fastest-growing market by far. By 1997, Coca-Cola had set up 23 plants in China, from Harbin in the northeast, to Wuhan in the center, to Xi'an in the northwest, presenting a total investment of more than US$500 million (Burstein and de Keijzer 1998:236). In the assets market, the foreign presence also grew rapidly. To illustrate, of the four so-called pillar industries designated by the Chinese government, foreign investors have significant participation in two of them. According to Huang (1999:7), in electronics and telecommunications, FIEs accounted for 53% of the assets in 1997. In the auto industry, foreign firms accumulated a significant stake by 1997, at 21%, as compared to 63% held by the government and only 3% held by Chinese private firms. Overall, as of 1996, there were 43,543 industrial FIEs and 240,447 FIEs in the entire economy. Industrial FIEs accounted for 16% of the industrial value-added and 17% of assets.

Regression Diagnostic Tests

As a precaution against the problem of multicollinearity among the independent variables that can potentially be so severe as to distort the signs of the coefficients into the wrong directions, thus perverting our judgment, regression diagnostic tests are in order. For this, I have run regressions of FDI on policy, culture, and markets (both goods and assets market), individually and separately across the three periods.

The test results are reported in Table VI-5. As these results show, even though on average the sizes of the coefficients for each individual variable when tested in isolation across the three periods increase tangibly, they nevertheless do so in a consistent fashion. In other words, there is no change in the direction of the signs. Looked at across the three periods, the effect of the policy advantage variable continues to decrease over time; the effect of culture variable continues to dwindle over time; and the effect of the market size variable continues to grow over time.

Table VI-5: Results of Regression Diagnostic Tests

	Period I (1979-84)		Period II (1985-90)		Period III (1991-96)	
POLICY	12.58***	(5.23)	8.04 ***	(5.15)	3.68 ***	(4.20)
R^2	0.49		0.48		0.40	
Adjusted R^2	0.47		0.46		0.38	
CULTURE	-1.02 ***	(-4.76)	-0.63 ***	(-3.60)	-0.50***	(-3.48)
R^2	0.45		0.40		0.44	
Adjusted R^2	0.43		0.38		0.42	
MARKETgoods	0.03	(0.52)	1.48 ***	(3.81)	1.30 ***	(5.54)
R^2	0.01		0.35		0.53	
Adjusted R^2	-0.02		0.33		0.51	
MARKETassets	0.43	(0.53)	1.50 ***	(3.83)	1.92***	(5.33)
R^2	0.01		0.35		0.51	
Adjusted R^2	-0.02		0.32		0.49	

T-statistics are in parentheses. *** Statistically significant at the 1% level.

Concluding Remarks

In this chapter, we have reviewed some of the theoretical literature on the determinants of FDI. Guided by theoretical insights, we then developed a formal investment model. This model covers both space (29 provinces) and time (1979-96), and it puts us in a better position to test institutional effects on investment behavior, controlling for economic variables, such as market size, labor costs/skills and physical infrastructure.

Empirical results yielded by multiple regression analyses validate the central hypothesis of this study; that is, as the institutional framework of China's FDI regulatory regime gradually liberalized and strengthened over the reform years, along a continuum from a command economy to a rule-based market system, it has had a systematic and positive effect on investment behavior. Specifically, we have observed that over time, the statistical association between the levels of FDI and the economic variables (market size, both the goods and assets; labor costs/skills; and infrastructure) across the different regions in China become *stronger*. This indicates that foreign investors enjoy a *growing* degree of freedom (from bureaucratic barriers or worries about weak institutional protection of investment) to invest in ways that make most sense economically. Not surprisingly, the cultural advantage, while still relevant as a predictor of FDI, becomes less important over time. The policy advantage, while still a plus in attracting FDI, becomes less potent. Domestic markets, while in many ways still restricted, are more accessible to foreign investors throughout China.

Conclusions

With the economic reforms and the open door that began in China in 1978, the economy has undergone radical structural change, and this has been accompanied by dramatic economic results. The country's gross domestic product has enjoyed an average annual growth rate of close to 10% for the past two decades, and its foreign trade has registered an even more impressive record, averaging about 15% per year. Among the various facets of its economic achievements has been a massive influx of foreign direct investment. Starting from a very moderate level, averaging less than US$1 billion per year in the initial years of reforms (1979-85), FDI inflows steadily picked up tempo in the latter part of the 1980s, averaging US$2.8 billion per year (1986-90). They began to skyrocket in the early years of the 1990s, averaging about US$26 billion per year for the 1991-96 period. Even in the wake of the Asian financial crisis, China managed to attract US$45.28 billion and US$45.58 billion in realized FDI for 1997 and 1998 respectively.[1]

The aim of the current study, as stated in the Introduction, is to go beyond standard economic and cultural explanations to arrive at a more nuanced understanding of the underlying forces that shape the variant patterns of FDI inflows to China. In carrying out this study, our intent is theoretical; our method is empirical. Applying the logic of neo-institutionalism, our search began with a simple hypothesis that investments, where current costs are incurred for future benefits, are not shaped by market forces alone. Being inherently intertemporal, investments are vulnerable to opportunistic behavior, and their growth therefore logically requires the presence and improvement of non-market institutions for the protection of property rights and the

---

1. The contractual amounts for 1997 and 1998 were US$51.78 billion and US$52.13 billion. By comparison, it was US$73.27 billion in 1996. The drop largely resulted from the slowing down of FDI flows from Asian countries/regions (e.g., South Korea, Hong Kong, Taiwan), indicating that the Asian financial crisis is also hurting China.

reduction of transaction costs. In particular, we have argued that the gradual yet steady improvements in the formal institution of China's FDI regulatory regime, albeit still imperfect and in many ways not entirely adequate, have had a systematic and positive effect on investment behavior. In this chapter, we summarize the principal findings that, taken together, provide strong empirical support to our central argument.

China's FDI Regulatory Framework: A Retrospect

On the eve of China's economic reform, the Chinese economy was virtually closed to the outside world. Just as China's opening to the world has been a step-by-step endeavor, so too has been the building process of China's FDI regulatory framework. In other words, China's FDI regulatory framework was not erected in one day, one year, or one decade; instead it has been the result of an on-going cumulative process throughout the reform years. Generally speaking, there are two dimensions, policy and legislative, of China's FDI regulatory framework. While the legislative dimension, once put in place, such as the 1979 EJV Law, was meant to be applied evenly nationwide, FDI-related policies, such as preferential tax treatment were often localized initially as experiments, and then expanded gradually over time. Starting literally from scratch in 1979, the evolution of China's FDI regulatory framework has undergone three easily identifiable periods, i.e., 1979-84, 1985-90, and 1991-96, each of which has its own distinct hallmarks.

During the initial period China's FDI regulatory framework was rudimentary. The 1979 EJV Law, China's first foreign investment law, was too brief and general to provide clearly defined operational guidance for foreign investors. Moreover, the law was meant only to govern joint ventures, and it did not apply to wholly foreign-owned enterprises. On the policy front, even though China established four Special Economic Zones in Guangdong and Fujian provinces and the local governments there were authorized to offer special policies and generous fiscal concessions to foreign investors, the rest of the country remained in uncertainty as an investment outlet. For instance, while WFOEs were allowed to operate in the SEZs, they were not allowed elsewhere.

During the second period China's FDI regulatory framework apparently improved. With the promulgation of the WFOE Law in 1986, operations of 100% foreign-owned subsidiaries were legalized. To ameliorate the problems that many foreign investors had in balancing their foreign exchange accounts, institutional innovations, such as the so-called swap centers, were introduced during this period. If the initial legal framework was very prone to arbitrary interpretations because it lacked legal precision and specificity, things were looking up by the second period. For instance, the Detailed Implementation Act of the EJV Law was in place. A separate law was enacted in 1988 to further clarify the legal status of contractual joint ventures. In addition, a flurry of auxiliary rules and regulations also came out, all trying to encourage foreign investment by clarifying operational issues ranging from tax incentives to land-use fees to management autonomy regarding employment of local workers.

On the policy front, 14 major cities and 3 delta regions along China's coastline were authorized by the central government to offer similar (although by no means the same) preferential treatment hitherto available only in the SEZs. And the whole of Hainan island was turned into another SEZ during the second period. What is more, conditions for foreign access to domestic markets were apparently relaxed. Whereas investors had earlier been "encouraged" to market their products internationally, now they could sell "import-substitutes" domestically.[2] All at the same time, greater authority was delegated by the central government to the coastal provinces in terms of their approval powers of FDI projects. As a result, FDI project application procedures were greatly expedited.

The Tiananmen events of 1989 and their immediate aftermath may have caused jitters among foreign investors. But liberalization and improvement of China's FDI regulatory framework still continued during the third period. On the policy front, less than one year after Tiananmen, Shanghai's Pudong New Area was opened up to foreign investment. That move was followed by significant reforms aimed at removing sectoral restrictions on FDI. In addition, following Deng Xiaoping's tour of South China in early 1992, preferential policies to

2. These terms, quoted directly from Chinese documents, reflect changes in policies regarding foreign access to Chinese domestic markets. See the 1979 EJV Law and the "22 Articles."

foreign investment were expanded from the coastal areas to all the principal cities in the interior regions of the country.

Fast-paced policy liberalization was accompanied by progress on the legal front in the post-Tiananmen period. For instance, both the Detailed Implementation Acts of the WFOE Law and the CJV Law were now put in place. Of particular significance was the 1990 amendment to the 1979 EJV Law. The amendment in effect lifted the ban on foreign nationals from holding the position of chairperson of the board of directors of JVs, and allowed the duration of joint ventures to continue without limits. Also during this period China published a unified tax code in 1991, which effectively put an end to the discriminatory tax treatment of WFOEs vis-à-vis JVs. Accompanying all these developments was a continued effort to align the country's investment framework more in line with international standards.

By the early 1990s China had already entered into a rather sophisticated web of international institutional guarantees regarding foreign investment. China was a signatory to both the New York Convention (i.e., the UN Convention on the Recognition and Enforcement of Foreign Arbitral Awards), and the Washington Convention (i.e., the Convention on the Settlement of Investment Disputes between States and the Nationals of Other States). It also joined the Multinational Investment Guarantee Agency, thus committing itself to the principle of subrogation, which greatly increased the costs China would have to pay should it choose to renege on its obligations vis-à-vis foreign private investors. In addition, as of 1996 the list of bilateral investment protection treaties China had signed was lengthened to six dozen countries, covering all major capital-exporting countries.

Indeed, to enhance its creditworthiness China proceeded even to the extent of allowing foreign nationals to sit in on its arbitration courts. More pointedly, China's Supreme Court ruled that where China is a party to an international treaty, unless explicit reservations are made beforehand, treaty provisions override domestic provisions in resolving disputes.[3] In addition, in view of the fact that the Chinese legal system is still evolving and legislation may thus be inadequate,

---

3. Response of the Supreme People's Court to Certain Questions Concerning the Application of the Foreign Economic Contract Law (issued on 19 October 1987).

China's Foreign Economic Contract Law thoughtfully contains provisions which permit reference to "international practice" as a means to fill the gaps, and "grandfathering" is allowed in many cases to provide continuity and stability in an era of changes.

In retrospect, even though the statement – made in October 1989 by Ren Jianxin, the President of China's Supreme Court – that China "is turning from a country which is ruled mainly by government and Party policies to a country chiefly by laws"[4] may be a far cry from reality, it is by no means irrelevant if progress is what we are looking for. Indeed, in comparison with other developing and transitional economies, after about two decades of experimentation, or "crossing the river by groping for stepping stones" as the Chinese say, China has already put in place an FDI regulatory framework that is relatively mature and liberal by international standards. China's recent intensive efforts to enter the WTO further demonstrates its determination to build up a modern economy that is pro-competition, transparent, and based on the rule of law.

Commenting on what changes the reforms have brought to China, William Overholt (1997), an investment banker and keen China observer, said: "If one takes China as a snapshot, poverty and tyranny are most vivid. If one takes China as a moving picture, it is the improvements in the standard of living and freedom that amaze." The same logic applies fittingly to the institutional building process that has a bearing on investments in China in the reform years.

Institutions and Investments: A *Prima Facie* Case

In exploring the relationship between institutions and investments in this study, we have aimed first to build up a *prima facie* case by looking at the variant patterns of FDI in China that are apparently beyond the explanatory power of either cultural or economic accounts.

In order to provide a micro-foundation for our examination of investment behavior under changing institutional circumstances, we began with an organizational analysis of different modes of FDI in China. Drawing upon Oliver Williamson (1985), we proposed that investment risks can be a function of asset specificity. Generally,

---

4. "Top Judge Feels Law Has Made Big Gains," *China Daily*, 3 October 1989, p. 4.

lumpy, fixed, and site-specific investments are more risk-prone than mobile and general investments. The reason is that whereas the value of mobile and general investments can remain more or less the same in alternative uses, fixed and site-specific investments often have a salvage value which is significantly below their original levels at the site. In vernacular terms, in the case of fixed and site-specific investments, you can't afford to take your wares and leave, without suffering great losses.

Thus, of the principal modes of FDI in China, i.e., WFOE, EJV, and CJV, the form of WFOE is most risky in light of its unique organizational imperatives. WFOE by definition does not have local partners, which can be crucial for reducing information and transaction costs in an alien part of the world. As one business executive in China reflected: "Partners are someone to help point you in the right direction; navigation – they help you to save time. Which projects are going to get approved; what can be done, what can't. A good partner is a critical source of good information" (cited in Rosen 1998:42). In addition, WFOE would also have to make all the necessary lumpy investments, such as land and buildings, which might otherwise be provided by local partners as equity contributions.

On the other hand, between the two modes of JVs, i.e., CJVs and EJVs, CJVs are a safer bet than EJVs under institutional uncertainties. Because, according to Chinese investment laws, unlike EJVs where the benefit-sharing schedule has to be made strictly in accordance with equity ratios, CJVs leave the profit-sharing schedule to negotiations between JV partners regardless of equity positions, thus making quick returns possible for foreign investors. As a matter of fact, interview results confirm that Chinese partners in CJVs do often let their foreign partners take a greater portion of their profits than their equity share warrants in early years, and in turn net all the assets when the JV terminates.

On the basis of this micro-organizational analysis, the facts that: (A) CJVs as a share of total FDI inflows in China dwindled consistently over time from an initial dominant position (over 80% to less than 20%); (B) EJVs rose gradually in the 1980s from an initial low position (about 10%) and largely stabilized in the 1990s (about 60%); and (C) WFOEs started to pick up in the latter part of the 1980s and increased significantly in the 1990s (over 30%), suggest strongly that the confidence of foreign investors grew as the formal institution of China's FDI regulatory regime gained strength over the reform years.[5]

Standard economic explanations would be at loss to account for these dramatic changes in different modes of FDI in China over time. And to the extent that we take cultural explanations seriously here, these trends suggest that culture becomes less important, if only because CJVs as a mode of investment were particularly popular among overseas Chinese investors. And WFOEs, by going it alone without local partners, undercut cultural arguments.

Variant patterns of FDI in China in the reform years, of course, have manifested themselves not just in investment modalities. Changes also took place in geographical distribution, source country/region configuration, as well as sectoral composition. While all these dimensions have been extensively documented in this study, a summary of that documentation, with some brief comments, are appropriate in conclusion here.

In terms of sectoral composition, the bulk of FDI (about 60%) in China is concentrated in the manufacturing sector, spread out over many industries such as textile, garments, food, chemicals, metals, electronics, and plastic products. Within the manufacturing sector, a major portion is involved in small-scale and labor-intensive operations like apparel, footwear, leather processing, toy manufacturing, and simple electronics assembling.[6] While an economic account of China's relatively low labor costs certainly goes a long way in explaining the high presence of labor-intensive FDI projects in the country, a closer examination of sectoral composition of FDI flows *over time*, however, indicates that institutional factors also mattered.

Indeed, as our analytical focus moved across time, this study has found that the number of capital-intensive and high-tech investments by big multinational corporations, including long-term infrastructure projects, increased rapidly. The trend was especially clear in the 1990s. Because infrastructure projects normally would involve a great deal of lumpy, fixed, and site-specific investments and therefore are more

5. The changing patterns of FDI inflows in different modes over time are graphed in Figure III-1.

6. According to *Zhongguo tongji nianjian 1997* [China Statistical Yearbook, 1997], the top four industries in China, measured by FIEs equity shares, are electronics and telecommunications (55%); leather products (52%); garments (49%); and good manufacturing (47%).

exposed to risks associated with institutional uncertainties, the rise of FDI in these projects can therefore be generally interpreted as a sign of increased confidence on the part of foreign investors in the institutional guarantees of property rights in the host country.

In terms of geographical distribution, while FDI has penetrated every province of China, an overwhelming share (about 80% in realized amount) is concentrated in the coastal areas. In particular, Guangdong alone has hosted close to 30%. It is followed by Jiangsu (11%), Fujian (10%), Shanghai (9%), and Shandong (6%). In terms of source country/region configurations, Hong Kong (including Macao) leads the way (63% in realized amount). It is followed by the US (8.7%), Japan (8.6%), Taiwan (8.1%), Singapore (3%), Britain (2%), and Germany (1%). A cursory look at these figures apparently bolsters the cultural accounts. But, a closer look, again, calls for answers that go beyond cultural explanations. Evidence suggests that, while culture has doubtless worked as a facilitator of investment especially under institutional uncertainties, its role has gradually been eclipsed as China's FDI regulatory framework improved over time.

For instance, Guangdong's high share (30%), relative to the rest of China, is largely a function of its extremely dominant position (about 80%) in the initial years (1979-84). This is no surprise, since China's FDI regulatory framework was rudimentary at the time. Under institutional uncertainties, it makes sense that investors cluster in areas where they can make better use of their informal institutional means, such as kinship ties in order to hedge against investment risks. But even along this line of reasoning, one should be aware that analysis of the cultural role is complicated by the fact that Guangdong, after all, was authorized early on by the central government to adopt very special policies to attract foreign investment. Recall that Guanghong was home to three SEZs, i.e., Shenzhen, Zhuhai, and Shantou, as the very front-line of China's open door policy.

Note also that while Hong Kong has a large share (60%) of total FDI in China, this impressive figure masks significant changes over time. The fact is that measured by the number of FDI projects, the relative share of FDI by Hong Kong investors showed a dramatic and consistent downward trend, from a very high of about 85% in 1983 to less than 50% in 1995, and it is still shrinking.[7] By contrast, the share

---

7. See Figure IV-4.

of other countries that are not in cultural proximity to China rose over time. Note, as well, that investment from Hong Kong is complicated by the fact that many Western firms often choose to invest in China via Hong Kong, and the precise amount of that investment is unclear. Note, further, that it is conceptually imprecise simply to assume that Hong Kong, or for that matter Taiwan, investors, because they are Chinese, do not benefit from the improvements in China's legal framework.[8]

To build up a *prima facie* case linking institutions and investments, we also engaged in case studies. Specifically, we looked at Taiwan and contrasted it with Hong Kong. The idea is to hold culture "constant" so that we can net out the institutional effects (the formal type) on investment behavior. Interestingly, significant variations in investment behavior existed between Hong Kong and Taiwan investors in comparable stages of investment flows. When Hong Kong investors started to invest in China in the early 1980s, many of them chose the CJV mode, the least risky form of investment in a China under institutional uncertainty. Besides, the duration of their projects also tended to be short, averaging no more than 15 years. By contrast, when Taiwan investors started to invest in earnest in the late 1980s, after the Taiwan authorities lifted the ban on visits to the mainland in 1988, many opted for long-term projects (over 30 years) and mostly in the WFOE mode, the most risky form of investment if institutional guarantees are assumed tenuous.[9]

Note that Taiwan investors resembled early Hong Kong investors in that they were also relocating their labor-intensive operations to the mainland to take advantage of the relatively low labor costs. But given that both Hong Kong and Taiwan investors are on a relatively equal footing culturally, the variations in their investment behavior at comparable stages suggest strongly that it was the institutional variable (the formal type) that mattered. By the late 1980s, China already had had a decade to develop and consolidate its FDI regulatory framework, with the benefits of a growing amount of positive feedback from policy experiments in the SEZs and the coastal open cities.

---

8. Interestingly, when people discuss the economic rise of Hong Kong, few argue that Hong Kong has risen simply because Hong Kong people are Hong Kong people. While they take that as a constant, they look for other variables, among which the rule of law is often cited. For a thoughtful discussion of the rule of law in Hong Kong, see DeLisle and Lane (1997).

9. See Table IV-20 and Table IV-21.

Indeed, our institutional argument would have been all the stronger had we factored in the cold political relations and, at times, animosity, across the Taiwan straits. Even in the wake of the 1996 Taiwan straits crisis in which the mainland lopped missiles over Taiwan to warn the island against sliding toward independence, few Taiwan investors whom I interviewed seriously doubted the safety of their investments in the mainland.

Institutions and Investments: Beyond *Prima Facie* Case

Proceeding on the basis of a *prima facie* case that highlights a linkage between institutions and investments, this study has taken a step further. It has made an effort to increase the rigor of our institutional analysis by developing an investment model which allows us to control for the effects of both economic and cultural factors. Our effort to do so is guided by a recognition that any single-minded focus, be it institutional, economic or cultural, cannot satisfactorily paint the whole picture of the variant patterns of FDI in China. For the fact of the matter is, investors are not only concerned about avoiding investment risks but are also concerned about investing in a way that makes economic sense. Thus, instead of setting institutional, economic, and cultural accounts up against one another, a balanced analytical framework has to give space not only to institutional effects but also to economic and cultural factors.

Within that framework, one may ask better questions, such as: Assuming foreign investors go to China for big markets, relatively cheap labor, and good infrastructure, can they scout the country up and down to put their investments where they want? If they did not have that freedom initially – either because of policy restrictions on the part of the host government or because of a lack of confidence on their own part in the institutional guarantees provided at the local spot – do they have more freedom over time? If, for instance, a province, A, argues that its neighboring province, B, had a higher share of FDI because A did not enjoy the preferential policies that B did (e.g., higher FDI project approval power or lower tax rates to foreign investors), now that A has similar preferential policies, does that make the policy advantage of B less important? Or, indeed one may ask: all else being equal, do special policies make a difference to begin with?

Furthermore, one may also ask: If cultural advantage is understood as linguistic familiarity and kinship ties, are those provinces – such as Guangdong, Fujian, and Shanghai – whose natives dominate Chinese business communities overseas – more able (or less able) to take advantage of the cultural factor in attracting FDI over time, relative to the rest of China, all else being equal? Obviously, an institutional (the formal type) argument would predict "less able." Since to argue that the formal institution of the FDI regulatory regime has improved over time implies that property rights are now better protected, information is now more readily available, and business is now more predictable, there should be less of a need for investors to rely on informal institutional means such as kinship ties for a reduction of information and transaction costs.

In search for answers to these and other questions that are relevant to assessing the validity of our institutional arguments beyond a mere *prima facie* case, in Chapter 6 we developed a formal investment model which allowed us to perform systematic empirical analysis in two ways. One way was to examine spatial variations in investment behavior among 29 Chinese provinces. The other was to examine variations in investment behavior over time in light of the evolutionary dynamics of China's FDI regulatory framework documented in length in Chapter 1 of this study. The empirical results yielded by our investment model support the central contention of this study.

In particular, this study has found that: First, while cultural advantage has had an effect on investment behavior, it was more powerful in the initial period and less so subsequently. This supports our institutional argument. Second, while foreign investors are driven by their desire to seek big markets, use cheap (and yes skilled) labor, and opt for good infrastructure, they were more able to fulfill their wish-list in later rather than in earlier periods. No surprise, because in China's transitional economy from plan to market, foreign access to domestic markets is a function of the gradual and continuous efforts to nudge bureaucrats out of the marketplace. This, too, supports our institutional argument. Finally, while policy advantages in the form of lower tax rates and higher FDI project approval power were a critical factor in a province's ability to attract FDI in the initial period, over time, they became less important. No surprise either, now that preferential policies are no longer offered exclusively in the SEZs and open coastal cities. This, again, supports our institutional argument.

In short, the findings of this study support the conclusion that, for all its remaining problems, the gradual yet steady improvements in China's FDI regulatory framework have had a positive and systematic effect on FDI in China over the reform years. In the broad context of China's reform efforts, the findings of this study indicate that in the past two decades, in spite of its seemingly gradual pace, China has come a long way along a continuum from a command economy to a rule-based market system. Seen in the time-honored intellectual tradition that looks at the relationship of political institutions and economic growth – that of law and economics in particular (Bentham 1789; 1827; 1830; Coase 1960; Posner 1980; Cooter and Ulen 1997), China is no exception. The Chinese story, as told in this study through the prism of FDI in an era of reforms, confirms a basic institutional postulate; that is, economic development and, for that matter, investment growth, are predicated upon an improvement and consolidation of a non-market institution that is pro-competition, transparent, reliable, and predictable.

But to be sure, as Chinese experience shows, institutions take time to build and consolidate, and cannot be wished into reality overnight. To underscore this normative lesson, we only need to contrast it with the Russian experience of *perestroika.* In a haste to replace plan with market, while Russia was effective in destroying the plan, it failed to build a functioning market as a replacement. In the process, everything seems to have gone awry. The point that has been sorely missed is that for a market to function properly, non-market institutions that are pro-competitive, transparent, reliable and predictable are imperative. But alas, such non-market institutions take time to develop and consolidate. This is so if only because recruiting, training, overseeing, and managing the armies of new civil servants required to man such non-market institutions in a large economy will take decades.

As Dani Rodrik has cautioned in his book *Has Globalization Gone Too Far?* (1997:3), the problems associated with developing and transitional economies in times of increasing globalization require more nuanced and imaginative solutions than simple slogans, such as "low-wage competition," or "leveling the playing field," or "race to the bottom." It seems that in designing and developing new institutions, having the skills of governance is just as important as having a bright vision.

A Caveat

Throughout much of this study, we have shown that institutional developments have had a systematic and positive effect on the variant patterns of FDI in China. However, lest too rosy a picture be inadvertently painted out of what in many ways continues to be a problematic investment situation, a caveat against over-interpretation is in order.

There seems little question that the reforms that began in the late 1970s have gradually strengthened a sound regulatory environment in China, and considerable progress has also been made toward establishing economic and legal institutions that were virtually non-existent prior to 1978. This, however, does not mean that the formal institution of China's FDI regulatory regime is now perfect or even entirely adequate. In fact, in China's current marketplace there are areas, many transitional in nature, that remain very problematic.

One such area, for instance, is the disparate treatment between FIEs and domestic firms, the implications of which we explored at considerable length in Chapter 5. There is strong evidence that the different treatment gave rise to a range of questionable investment behavior at the local levels in China, notable among which is the phenomenon of "round-tripping" or "fake" FDI, that is, Chinese capital going offshore first and then returning camouflaged as FDI to take advantage of the policy benefits – such as tax holidays and import rights – offered exclusively to FIEs and not to domestic enterprises. The problem with round-tripping FDI is that while it artificially inflates inward FDI figures, it does not result in actual transfers of capital, technology, or managerial skills to China and yet it costs the government in the form of lost tax revenues and other policy benefits. In short, it reflects continued market distortions in China.

Although this study has suggested that the problem was ameliorated after 1994 when the enterprise income tax rate for domestic firms was finally lowered from the previous 55% to 30% – the general income tax rate for FIEs – round-tripping FDI is nevertheless expected to continue, since in many instances FIEs continue to have an edge over domestic firms in terms of policy-conveyed advantages. FIEs continue to enjoy a varying degree of tax exemptions and reductions that domestic enterprises do not, and they continue to enjoy a wide range of duty-free imports that are off-limits to domestic firms.[10] Indeed, theoretically at least, the phenomenon of "round-tripping" FDI will not disappear altogether until the task of building a veritable level playing field is completed for both FIEs and their domestic counterparts.

Beyond continued, albeit much abated, market distortions, there are many other undesirable aspects in the investment environment in China, prominent of which is corruption. According to a World Bank report (1996:95), corruption commonly occurs in economies in transition, when traditional controls are breaking down and new legal restraints, particularly those affecting conflicts of interest, are not yet firmly established. In this regard, China seems to be the norm rather than exception. As Lieberthal (1995:267) has observed, while there is no easy way to measure the overall level of corruption in China, corruption has apparently increased significantly in the reform era. It thrives on the fact that the current Chinese system is only semi-reformed, subject neither to a disciplined plan nor driven primarily by the market via activities constrained by the rule of law.

Indeed, both foreign investors and Chinese nationals have reported widespread corruption, especially at the local government levels (Business Monitor International 1995:89; Gong 1994; Wank 1995). Rosen notes (1998:218) that the universe of the possibly corrupt ranges from the clearly corrupt (bribes to get customs duties lowered) to the likely corrupt ("rep fees" to facilitate large government procurement contracts) to the murky (gift giving and extravagant entertainment for officials or children of high-level officials). Anecdotally, in some cases, corruption may simply expedite the government approval process and not add significantly to costs. In others, however, it may seriously distort the capacity of FIEs to compete in what has increasingly become a very competitive business environment, and therefore may have depressed inward FDI.[11]

---

10. In the late 1990s China decided to phase out duty-free imports for FIEs. But in the wake of the Asian financial crisis, China made new concessions to FIEs by offering a wide range of duty exemptions for high-tech capital goods. It is conceivable that competitive pressures from neighboring countries that devalued their local currencies motivated China to increase incentives to FIEs so as to keep FDI flowing in, especially as the temptation to devalue the RMB was resisted.

11. For small firms, for instance, sponsoring study tours abroad for officials in China certainly adds tremendously to their costs, and therefore

Even though the precise effects of corruption on FDI volume in China are not totally clear, international evidence suggests that its effects are negative and serious. In a recent cross-country study, Wei (1997:16), after controlling for GDP, population, distance, tax rates, and linguistic ties, finds that an increase in the corruption level from that of Singapore to that of Mexico is equivalent to raising the tax rate by over 24 percentage points. This indicates the depressing effects of corruption on inward FDI are very significant.

How does China compare with other countries in terms of level of corruption? According to a corruption perception index based on a survey of 2,400 firms in 58 countries conducted by the Global Competitiveness Report (1997), China is cleaner than Colombia, India, Indonesia, the Philippines, Russia, Thailand, and is similar to South Korea and Malaysia. But compared to economies where market institutions are mature, such as Britain, Canada, Japan, Hong Kong, Singapore, and the US, China is significantly behind (see Table 3).

Table 3: Corruption Ratings for Selected Countries

Asian countries/regions	1-10 scale	Non-Asian countries	1-10 scale
Singapore	1.77	United Kingdom	1.93
Hong Kong	2.17	Canada	2.37
Japan	2.96	United States	2.41
Taiwan	4.60	Germany	2.61
Malaysia	5.67	France	3.51
China	5.86	Mexico	6.24
South Korea	6.20	Colombia	7.41
India	7.30	Russia	7.61
Thailand	7.93		
Indonesia	7.94		
Philippines	7.94		

Note: In the original index, smaller numbers imply more corruption. The index has been re-scaled on a 1-10 basis so that large numbers imply more corruption. The values in the table = (8 - original values) 10/7.

This suggests that while China has come a long way in reforming its command economy into a rule-based market-oriented system, enormous challenges remain to further strengthen its legal system and

---

negatively affects their ability to compete. But as Wei (1997:6) notes, and my interviews confirm, sponsoring foreign study tours and even providing financial support for family members of high officials to study abroad are popular ways of cultivating relations with Chinese officials.

key economic institutions to provide a sound regulatory framework for a market economy. As James Wolfenson, President of the World Bank, has advised, "we need to deal with the cancer of corruption.... We can give advice, encouragement, and support to governments that wish to fight corruption and it is these governments that, over time, will attract the larger volume of investment."[12]

But beyond its negative effects on FDI inflows, it is important to recognize as well that corruption can have many other detrimental effects. It may reduce the growth rate, possibly as a result of reduced domestic investment (Mauro 1995; Knack and Keefer 1995), and contribute to unfair income or wealth distribution. More crucially, it may thus give rise to popular resentment, resulting in political instability. In 1996 China finally promulgated its Administrative Penalty Law which contains criminal penalties for officials involved in bribery. While this is an intermediate step in the right direction toward building up a rule-based market economy, ultimately China must ponder and find the wisdom to solve the riddle posed by an ancient poet: "Who is to control the controller?" (cited in Huang 1996:329).

---

12. *Transition,* vol. 10, nos. 9-10, Sept./Oct. 1996, p. 9.

References

Books and Articles

Agrawala, Ramgopal. 1992. "China: Reforming Intergovernmental Fiscal Relations," Discussion Paper, no. 178, World Bank.

Akerlof, George. 1970. "The Market for Lemons: Qualitative Uncertainty and the Market Mechanism," *Quarterly Journal of Economics,* vol. 84, pp. 488-500.

Alchian, Armen and Harold Demsetz. 1972. "Production, Information Costs, and Economic Organization," *American Economic Review,* vol. 62, pp. 777-95.

Alesina, Alberto and Dani Rodrik. 1994. "Distributive Politics and Economic Growth," *Quarterly Journal of Economics,* vol. 108, pp. 465-90.

Alford, William. 1995. *To Steal a Book is an Elegant Offense: Intellectual Property Law in Chinese Civilization.* Stanford: Stanford University Press.

Alt, James and Kenneth Shepsle, eds. 1990. *Perspectives on Positive Political Economy.* New York: Cambridge University Press.

Amsden, Alice. 1989. *Asia's Next Giant: South Korea and Late Industrialization.* New York: Oxford University Press.

Aoki, Masahiko. 1984. *The Cooperative Game Theory of the Firm.* New York: Oxford University Press.

Ariff, M. and C.P. Lim. 1987. "Foreign Investment in Malysia," In V. Cable and B. Persaud eds., *Developing with Foreign Investment.* London: Croom Helm.

Arrow, Kenneth. 1970. "The Organization of Economic Activity: Issues Pertinent to the Choice of Markets versus Non-market Allocation." In R. Haveman and J. Margolis, eds., *Public Expenditures and Policy Analysis,* Chicago: Markham.

———. 1974. *The Limits of Organization.* New York: W.W. Norton.

Art, Robert and Minkang Gu. 1995. "China Incorporated: The First Corporation Law of the People's Republic of China," *Yale Journal of International law,* vol. 20.

Ash, R. F. and Y. Y. Kueh. 1993. "Economic Integration within Greater China: Trade and Investment Flows between China, Hong Kong and Taiwan," *China Quarterly,* no. 136, pp. 711-46.

Axelrod, Robert. 1984. *The Evolution of Cooperation.* New York: Basic Books.

Bahl, Richard and Christine Wallich. 1992. "Intergovernmental Fiscal Relations in China," WPS 863, World Bank.

Barro, Robert. 1991. "Economic Growth in a Cross Section of Countries," *Quarterly Journal of Economics,* vol. 106, pp. 407-44.

———. 1994. "Democracy and Growth," NBER Working Paper, no. 4909.

Barzel, Yoram. 1982. "Measurement Costs and the Organization of Markets," *Journal of Law and Economics,* vol. 25, pp. 27-48.

———. 1989. *Economic Analysis of Property Rights.* New York: Cambridge University Press.

Bates, Robert. 1988. "Contra Contractarianism: Some Reflections on the New Institutionalism," *Politics and Society,* vol. 16, pp. 387-401.

———. 1997a. "Institutions as Investments." In Zubair Iqbal and Ravi Kanbur, eds., *External Finance for Low-Income Countries.* Washington, DC: International Monetary Fund, pp. 177-78.

———. 1997b. *Open-Economy Politics: The Political Economy of the World Coffee Trade.* Princeton: Princeton University Press.

Baum, Richard. 1994. "The Road to Tiananmen: Chinese Politics in the 1980s." In Roderick MacFarquhar, ed., *The Politics of China: The Eras of Mao and Deng.* Cambridge: Cambridge University Press.

Becker, Gary. 1964. *Human Capital: A Theoretical and Empirical Analysis, with Special Reference to Education.* New York: Columbia University Press.

Bennett, Amanda and Roger Thurow. 1984. "VW and China Complete Auto Production Pact," *Wall Street Journal,* 7 October. p. 37.

Benoit, Philippe. 1996. "Project Finance at the World Bank: An Overview of Policies and Instruments," Technical Paper, no. 312, World Bank.

Bentham, J. 1789. "An Introduction to the Principles of Morals and Legislation." In *The Utilitarians*, 1973 ed. New York: Anchor Books, pp. 5-398.

———. 1827. *Rationale of Judicial Evidence*, vol. 5. London: Hunt and Clarke.

———. 1830. *The Theory of Legislation*, 1931 ed. by C.K. Ogden, trans. by R. Hildreth. London: Kegan Paul and Co.

Berger, Peter L. 1994. "Our Economic Culture." In William Boxx and Gary Quinlivan, eds., *The Cultural Context of Economics and Politics.* Lanham, MD: University Press of America.

Berman, Harold. 1983. *Law and Revolution: The Foundation of the Western Legal Tradition.* Cambridge, MA: Harvard University Press.

Bersani, Mathew D. 1992. "Enforcement of Arbitration Awards in China," *China Business Review,* vol. 19, no. 3.

Blau, Peter, Danching Ruan and Monika Ardelt. 1991. "Interpersonal Choice and Networks in China," *Social Forces,* vol. 69, no. 4.

Bohrnstedt, George and David Knoke, David. 1994. *Statistics for Social Data Analysis*, Itasca, IL: F.E. Peacock Publishers, Inc.

Borensztein, Eduardo, Jose De Gregorio and Jong-Wha Lee. 1995. "How Does Foreign Direct Investment Affect Economic Growth?" NBER Working Paper no. W5057, March.

Borrus, Amy and Richard Brandt. 1994. "Will China Scuttle Its Pirates?" *Business Week*, 15 August.

Brahm, Laurence. 1989. "Arbitration Disputes on the Rise," *China Trade Report*, vo. 27, no. 4.

Breslin, Shaun, 1996. *China in the 1980s: Centre-Province Relations in a Reforming Socialist State.* London: Macmillan.

Broadman, Harry G. 1996. "Policy Options for Reform of Chinese State-owned Enterprises," Discussion Paper, no. 335, World Bank.

Brownlees, Kit. 1997. "A Private Market Comes of Age." *Reinsurance,* June, pp. 30-1.

Buckley, Peter and Mark Casson. 1976. *The Future of the Multinational Enterprise*. London: MacMillan.

———. 1988. "Theory of Cooperation in International Business." In F. Contractor and P. Lorange, eds., *Cooperative Strategies in International Business*. Lexington, MA: Lexington Books. pp. 31-53.

Burawoy, Michael. 1996. "The State and Economic Involution: Russia Through a China Lens," *World Development*, vol. 24, no. 6, pp. 1105-17.

Burstein, Daniel and Arne de Keijzer. 1998. *Big Dragon -- China's Future: What It Means for Business, the Economy, and the Global Order.* New York: Simon and Schuster.

Business Monitor International. 1995. *China 1995-97: Annual Report on Government, Economy, the Business Environment and Industry.* London: Business Monitor International.

Cable, V. and B. Persaud. 1987. "New Trends and Policy Problems in Foreign Investment: The Experience of Commonwealth Developing Countries." In V. Cable and B. Persaud, eds., *Developing with Foreign Investment.* London: Croon Helm, pp. 1-27.

Cardose, Eliana A. and Rudiger Dornbusch. 1989. "Foreign Private Capital Flows. In Hollis Chenery and T. N. Srinivasan, eds., *Handbook of Development Economics,* vol. 2. London: Elsevier Science.

Caves, Richard E. 1996. *Multinational Enterprise and Economic Analysis.* New York: Cambridge University Press.

CCP. 1992. "Political Report to the 14th Party Congress," translation in FBIS-CHI, 13 October. pp. 23-43.

CERD Consultants Ltd. 1991. *Shanghai-Pudong baogao* [Shanghai-Pudong report]. Hong Kong, September.

Chan, Hing Lin.1995. "Chinese Investment in Hong Kong," *Asian Survey*, vol. 39, no. 10, pp. 941-54.

Chandler, Alfred. 1962. *Strategy and Structure: Chapters in the History of the American Industrial Enterprise.* Cambridge, MA: MIT Press.

———. 1977. *The Visible Hand: The Managerial Revolution in American Business.* Cambridge, MA: Belknap Press.

Chen, Jinghan. 1993. "The Environment for Foreign Direct Investment and the Characteristics of Joint Ventures in China," *Development Policy Review*, vol. 11, no. 2.

Chen, Jinghua, ed. 1996. *1996 nian Zhongguo guomin jingji he shehui fazhan baogao* [Report on China's National Economy and Social Development, 1996]. Beijing: Zhongguo jihua chubanshe.

Chen, Wenjin, ed. 1996. *Yatai diqu maoyi he touzi ziyouhua de xin langchao* [New Waves of Trade and Investment in the Asian-Pacific Region]. Beijing: Zhongguo tuiwai jingji maoyi chubanshe.

Chen, Yun. 1986. *Chen Yun wenxuan, 1956*-1985 [Selected Works of Chen Yun, 1956-1985]. Beijing: Renmin chubanshe.

Cheng, Chu-yuan. 1964. *Economic Relations between Peking and Moscow, 1949-63*. New York: Praeger.

Cheng, Dejun, et al., eds. 1995. *International Arbitration in the People's Republic of China.* Hong Kong: Butterworths Asia.

Cheung, Stephen. 1969. "Transaction Costs, Risk Aversion, and the Choice of Contractual Arrangements," *Journal of Law and Economics,* vol. 12, pp. 23-42.

———. 1983. "The Contractual Nature of the Firm," *Journal of Law and Economics,* vol. 17, pp. 53-71.

Chi, Francis. 1981. "China's Newborn SEZs and their Strategic Significance," *Economic Reporter*, August.

China Investment Guide 1984/1985. 1984. Hong Kong: Longman Group Limited.

———*. 1986. 1985*. Hong Kong: Longman Group Limited.

China Staff. 1997. *China Staff*, vol. 3, no. 8, July-August.

Chitrakar, Ramesh. 1994. *Foreign Investment and Technology Transfer in Developing Countries*. Hong Kong: Avebury.

Chodosh, H. 1991. "Swap Centers in the People's Republic of China: A Step towards Partial Convertibility of a Local Currency," *International Lawyer*, no. 25. pp. 415-29.

Chu, Baotai. 1987. "The Effectiveness of China's Absorption of Foreign Investment." In Richard Robinson, ed., *Foreign Capital and Technology in China*. New York: Praeger.

Clague, Christopher, Philip Keefer, Stephen Knack and Mancur Olson. 1996. "Property and Contract Rights under Democracy and Dictatorship," *Journal of Economic Growth*, June, pp. 243-76.

Clark, Aubert J. 1960. *The Movement for International Copyright in Nineteenth Century America*. Washington, DC: Catholic University of America Press.

Clark, Donald, Nicholas Howson and Ganliang Qian. 1997. "China's New Partnership Law," *China Business Review,* vol. 24, no. 4 July-August.

Clark, William and Sylvia Maxfield. 1996. "Credible Commitments, International Investment Flows and Central Bank Independence in

Developing Countries: A Signaling Model." Paper presented at the Annual Meeting of the American Political Science Association, San Francisco, August.

Coase, Ronald. 1937. "The Nature of the Firm," *Economica,* no. 4. pp. 386-405.

———. 1960. "The Problem of Social Cost," *Journal of Law and Economics*, vol. 3, pp. 1-44.

Cohen, Jerome. 1982. "Equity Joint Ventures: 20 Potential Pitfalls that Every Company Should Know About," *China Business Review*, vol. 9, no. 6, pp. 23-30.

Commons, John. 1931. "Institutional Economics," *American Economic Review,* vol. 21, pp. 648-57.

Conner, Alison. 1991. "To Get Rich is Precarious: Regulation of Private Enterprise in the People's Republic of China," *Journal of Chinese Law*, vol. 5, no. 1, pp. 18-31.

Cooter, Robert and Thomas Ulen. 1997. *Law and Economics,* 2nd ed. Reading, MA: Addison-Wesley.

Coughlin, C.C., J. Terza and V. Arromdee. 1991. "State Characteristics and the Location of Foreign Direct Investment within the United States," *Review of Economics and Statistics,* vol. 73, no. 4, pp. 675-82.

Council of State Governments. 1989. *Economic Development in the States: State Business Incentives and Economic Growth: Are they Effective? A Review of the Literature.* Washington, DC: Council of State Governments.

Crane, George, T. P. 1990. *The Political Economy of China's Special Economic Zones.* Armonk, NY: M. E. Sharpe.

Cukierman, Alex, Steven Webb and Bilin Neyapti. 1992. "Measuring the Independence of Central Banks and Its Effect on Policy Outcomes," *World Bank Economic Review,* vol. 6 no. 1, pp. 353-98.

Davidson, W. H. 1980. "The Location of Foreign Direct Investment Activity: Country Characteristics and Experience Effects," *Journal of International Business Studies*, vol.11, Fall, pp. 9-22.

Davis, Virginia and Carlos Yi. 1992. "Balancing Foreign Exchange," *China Business Review*, vol. 19, no. 2, pp. 14-16.

Dean, Genevieve. 1988. "Investment Incentives throughout Asia," *China Business Review,* vol. 15, no. 2, pp. 49-51.

Deane, R. S. 1970. *Foreign Investment in New Zealand Manufacturing.* Wellington, NZ: Sweet and Maxwell.

DeLisle, Jacques and Kevin Lane. 1997. "Cooking the Rice without Cooking the Goose: The Rule of Law, the Battle over Business, and the Quest for Prosperity in Hong Kong after 1997." In Warren I. Cohen and Zhao Li eds., *Hong Kong Under Chinese Rule: The Economic and Political Implications of Reversion.* New York: Cambridge University Press.

Demsetz, Harold. 1983. "The Structure of Ownership and the Theory of the Firm," *Journal of Law and Economics*, vol. 26, June, pp. 375-90.

Deng Xiaoping, 1983. *Deng Xiaoping wenxuan, 1975-82* [Selected Works of Deng Xiaoping, 1975-82], Beijing: Renmin chubanshe.

———. 1993. *Deng Xiaoping wenxuan, 1982-1992* [Selected Works of Deng Xiaoping, 1982-1992], Beijing: Renmin chubanshe.

Department of International Liaison of the Ministry of Foreign Economic Relations and Trade of China, ed. 1992. *GATT: A Handbook.* Beijing: Jingji guanli chubanshe.

Dicken, P. and P. Lloyd. 1990. *Location in Space: Theoretical Perspectives in Economic Geography.* New York: Harper and Row.

Donnithorne, Audrey. 1967. *China's Economic System,* London: George Allen and Unwin.

Du, Xianzhong, ed. 1994. *Zhongguo waishang touzi qiye guanli* [The Management of Foreign-invested Enterprises in China], Wuhan: Wuhan daxue chubanshe.

Dunning, John H. 1979. "Explaining Changing Patterns of International Production," *Oxford Bulletin of Economies and Statistics*, vol. 41, pp. 269-96.

———. 1980. "Towards an Eclectic Theory of International Production: Some Empirical Tests," *Journal of International Business Studies*, vol. 11, no. 1, pp. 9-31.

———. 1988. "The Eclectic Paradigm of International Production: A Restatement and Some Possible Extensions," *Journal of International Business Studies*, vol. 19, no. 1, pp.1-31.

———. 1993. *Multinational Enterprises and Global Economy.* New York: Addison Wesley.

———. 1995. "Re-appraising the Eclectic Paradigm in an Age of Alliance Capitalism," *Journal of International Business Studies*, vol. 26, no. 3, pp. 461-91.

EAAU (East Asia Analytical Unit, Australian Department of Foreign Affairs and Trade). 1995. *Overseas Chinese Business Networks in Asia.* Canberra: Department ofForeign Affairs and Trade.

———. 1997. *China Embraces the Market: Achievements, Constraints and Opportunities.* Canberra: Department of Foreign Affairs and Trade.

Eggertsson, Thrainn. 1990. *Economic Behavior and Institutions.* New York: Cambridge University Press.

EIU (Economist Intelligence Unit). 1997. *Multinational Companies in China: Winners and Losers.* Research Report. Hong Kong: EIU.

Elster, Jon. 1979. *Ulysses and the Sirens: Studies in Rationality and Irrationality.* Cambridge: Cambridge University Press.

Emmott, Bill. 1993. "A Survey of Multinationals," *Economist*, 17 March.

Fairbank, John King. 1983. *The United States and China.* Cambridge, MA: Harvard University Press.

Fan, Gang and Chunying Xin. 1998. "The Role of Law and Legal Institutions in Asian Economic Development: The Case of China," HIID, Harvard, Development Discussion Papers, no. 664, November.

Fang, Frank. 1997. "A Balanced Equation," *Independent Power,* October, pp. 29-31.

Fang, James and David Tang. 1988. "The Wholly Foreign-Owned Enterprise Law: Defining the Legislative History and Interpreting the Statute," *Journal of Chinese Law*, vol. 2.

Fang, Weizhong, ed. 1984. *Zhonghua renmin gongheguo jingji dashiji, 1949-1980* [A Record of the Major Economic Events of the PRC, 1949-1980]. Beijing: Zhongguo shehui kexue chubanshe.

Fei, Zhongji and Chengyuan Tang, eds., 1992. *Zhongguo sifa xiezhu de lilun yu shijian* [Theory and practice of Judicial Assistance in China]. Beijing: Renmin fayuan chubanshe.

Feng, Peter. 1997. *Intellectual Property in China.* Hong Kong: Sweet and Maxwell Asia.

Feng, Yushu. 1997. "China and the Multilateral Investment Guarantee Agency," World Bank Group, MIGA, Policy Research Working Paper, no. 1763, May.

Fenwick, Ann. 1984. "Evaluating China's Special Economic Zones," *International Tax and Business Lawyer*, no. 2, p. 376.

Foreign Investment Administration, MOFTEC. 1994. *Summary of China's Foreign Investment Policy*. Beijing: MOFTEC.

Frieden, Jeffry. 1989. *Banking on the World: The Politics of International Finance*. New York: Basil Blackwell.

Frisbie, John. 1992. "Surveying the Foreign Exchange Climate," *China Business Review*, vol. 19, no. 2, p. 15.

Frobel, Heinrichs and O. Kreye. 1980. *The New International Division of Labor: Structural Unemployment in Industrialized Countries and Industrialization in Developing Countries.* Cambridge: Cambridge University Press.

Fudenberg, D. and E. Maskin. 1986. "A Folk-theorem in Repeated Games with Discounting and with Incomplete Information," *Econometrica,* vol. 54, pp. 533-554.

Fukasaku, K. and D. Wall. 1994. *China's Long March to an Open Economy*, Paris: OECD.

Gao, Chang. 1995. Dalu jinggai yu liang'an maoyi guanxi [Mainland Economic Reforms and Trade Relations across the Taiwan Straits]. Taiwan: Wunan tushu chubanshe.

Gelatt, Timothy A. 1983. "New Constitution Improves, Clarifies Legal Position of Foreign Investors," *East Asian Executive Reports*, 5 February, p. 23.

———. 1986. "The Foreign Exchange Quandary," *China Business Review*, vol. 13, no. 3, pp. 28-31.

Gillis, Malcom, Dwight Perkins, Michael Roemer and Donald Snodgrass. 1996. *Economics of Development,* 4th ed. New York: W.W. Norton.

Goldstein, Carl. 1992. "Numbers Games," *Far Eastern Economic Review*, 24 December.

———. 1994. "Pirates' Lair," *Far Eastern Economic Review,* 19 May.

Goldstein, Morris. 1998. *The Asian Financial Crisis: Causes, Cures, and Systemic Implications.* Washington DC: Institute for International Economics.

Gomez, Berta. 1997. "Industry's Losses Estimated at $11,200 Million," United States Information Agency, 5 May.

Gong, Ting. 1994. *The Politics of Corruption in Contemporary China: An Analysis of Policy Outcomes.* London: Praeger.

Graham, Edward M. and Paul R. Krugman. 1991. *Foreign Direct Investment in the United States.* Washington DC: Institute for International Economics.

Green, Milford and Rod McNaughton. 1995. *The Location of Foreign Direct Investment: Geographic and Business Approaches.* Aldershot: Avebury.

Greif, Avner. 1989. "Reputation and Coalitions in Medieval Trade: Evidence on the Maghribi Traders," *Journal of Economic History,* vol. 49, pp. 857-82.

Grieo, Joseph M. 1986. "Foreign Investment and Development: Theories and Evidence." In Theodore H. Moran, ed., *Investing in Development: New Roles for Private Capital?* New Brunswick, NJ: Transaction Books.

Grossman, Gene. ed. 1994. *Imperfect Competition and International Trade.* Cambridge, MA: MIT Press.

Grossman, Sanford. 1981. "The Informational Role of Warranties and Private Disclosure About Product Quality," *Journal of Law and Economics,* vol. 24, pp. 461-83.

Grub, Phillip and Jianhai Lin. 1991. *Foreign Direct Investment in China.* New York: Quorum Books.

Guisinger, Stephen. 1985. "A Comparative Study of Country Policies." In Stephen Guisinger and Associates, eds., *Investment Incentives and Performance Requirements.* New York: Praeger.

———. 1986. "Host-country Policies to Attract and Control Foreign Investment." In Theodore Moran, ed., *Investing in Development: New Roles for Private Capital?* New Brunswick, NJ: Transaction Books, pp. 157-172.

———. 1989. "Total Protection: A New Measure of the Impact of Government Interventions on Investments Profitability," *Journal of International Business Studies,* vol. 20, no. 2, pp. 280-95.

Guojia guoyou zichan guanliju [Bureau of Management of State-owned Assets], ed. 1995a. *Zhongguo haiwai qiye guoyou zichan guanli tansuo* [On Management of Chinese State-owned Assets Abroad]. Beijing: Jingji kexue chubanshe.

———. ed. 1995b. *Zichan pinggu gongzuo fagui zhidu huibian* [A Collection of Rules and Regulations Regarding the Work of State Assets Appraisals]. Beijing: Jingji kexue chubanshe.

———. ed. 1995c. Guoyou zichan chanquan guanli shouce, [A Reference Book on the Management of State Assets]. Beijing: Jingji kexue chubanshe.

Guthrie, Doug. 1998. "The Declining Significance of Guanxi in China's Economic Transition," *China Quarterly*, no. 154, pp. 254-82.

Haddad, Mona, and Ann Harrison. 1993. "Are There Positive Spillovers from Direct Foreign Investment? Evidence from Panel Data for Morocco," *Journal ofDevelopment Economics,* vol. 42, no.1, pp. 51-74.

Hamilton, Gary G., ed. 1991. *Business Networks and Economic Development in East and Southeast Asia.* Hong Kong: Center for Asian Studies, University of Hong Kong.

———, 1992. "Overseas Chinese Capitalism," Program in East Asian Business and Development, Working Papers, no. 42. UC Davis.

———, and Tony Waters. 1995. "Chinese Capitalism in Thailand: Embedded Networks and Industrial Structure." In Edward K.Y. Chen and Peter Drysdale, eds., *Corporate Links and Foreign Direct Investment*. New York: Harper Collins.

Hansen, Wendy. 1990. "The International Trade Commission and the Politics of Protectionism," *American Political Science Review,* vol. 84, no.1, pp. 21-46.

Harrison, Ann. 1996. "Determinants and Effects of Direct Foreign Investment in Cote de'Ivoire, Morocco and Venezuela." In Mark Roberts and James Tybout ed., *Industrial Evolution in Developing Countries: Micro Patterns of Turnover, Productivity, and Market Structure*. New York: Oxford University Press.

Harrison, Selig S. 1977. *China, Oil, and Asia.* New York: Columbia University Press.

Harrold, Peter and Rajiv Lall. 1993. "China: Reform and Development in 1992-1993,"World Bank Discussion Paper, no. 215, World Bank.

Harding, Harry. 1987. China's Second Revolution: Reform after Mao. Washington, DC: Brookings Institution.

Hart, Oliver and Bengt Holmstrom. 1987. "The Theory of Contracts." In T. Bewley, ed., *Advances in Economic Theory: Fifth World Congress*. Cambridge: Cambridge University Press.

Harvard Business School. 1993. *Adam Opel AG.* Case 9-392-100, 101, 127. Cambridge, MA: Harvard Business School.

Hayek, Friedrick A. 1945. "The Use of Knowledge in Society," *American Economic Review,* vol. 35, pp. 519-30.

———. 1974. "The Price System as a Mechanism for Using Knowledge." In Morris Bornstein, ed., *Comparative Economic Systems*. Homewood, IL.: Richard Irwin.

Head, Keith and John Ries. 1996. "Inter-City Competition for Foreign Investment: Static and Dynamic Effects of China's Incentive Areas," *Journal of Urban Economics,* vol. 40, pp. 38-60.

Hennart, Jean-Francois. 1991. "The Transaction Cost Theory of the Multinational Enterprise." In Christos Pitelis and Roger Sugden, eds., *The Nature of the Transnational Firm.* London: Routledge.

Hicks, John. 1969. *A Theory of Economic History.* Oxford: Oxford University Press.

Hill, Hal. 1988. *Foreign Investment and Industrialization in Indonesia.* New York: Oxford University Press.

Hines, James. 1993. "On the Sensitivity of R&D to Delicate Tax Changes: The Behavior of U.S. Multinationals in 1980s." In A. Giovannini, R. Hubbard and J. Slemrod eds., *Studies in International Taxation*. Chicago: University of Chicago Press, pp. 149-87.

———. 1996. "Tax Policy and the Activities of Multinational Corporations," NBER Working Paper, no. 5589.

Hinman, George. 1980. "China, Modernization, and Sino-United States Trade: Will China Submit to Arbitration?" *California WILJ*, no. 10. pp. 53-91.

Ho, Samuel. 1984. *China's Open Door Policy.* Vancouver: University of British Columbia Press.

Hodder, Rupert. 1996. *Merchant Princes of the East: Cultural Delusions, Economic Success, and Overseas Chinese in Southeast Asia.* Chichester: J. Wiley.

Hodgson, Geoffrey. 1998. "The Approach of Institutional Economics," *Journal of Economic Literature*, vol. 36, pp. 166-92.

Holden, Jeanne. 1997. "Backgounder on 'Special 301' Trade Law Review," United States Information Agency, 25 February.

Holmstrom, Bengt and Jean Tirole. 1989. "The Theory of the Firm." In in R. Schmalensee and R. Willig, eds., *Handbook of Industrial Organization.* New York: North-Holland.

Horsley, Jamie P. 1985. "Chinese Labor," *China Business Review,* vol. 11, no. 3.

Howe, Christopher and Y.Y. Kueh. 1984. "China's International Trade: Policy and Organizational Change and Their Place in the 'Economic Readjustment,'" *China Quarterly,* no. 100, pp. 836-66.

Hsieh, Chiao-min and Jean Kan Hsieh. 1995. *China: A Provincial Atlas.* New York: Simon and Schuster.

Hu, Peizhao, et al. 1991. "Xiamen de touzi baogao" [Report on Investment in Xiamen]. *Zhongguo jingji wenti* [Chinese Economic Issues]. no. 1. Xiamen: Xiamen Daxue.

Huang, Cen. 1998. "The Organization and Management of Chinese Transnational Enterprises in South China," *Issues & Studies,* vol. 34, no. 3, pp. 51-70.

Huang, Yasheng. 1998. *FDI in China: An Asian Perspective*. Hong Kong: The Chinese University Press.

———. 1990. "Web of Interests and Patterns of Behavior of Chinese Local Economic Bureaucracies and Enterprises during Reforms," *China Quarterly*, no. 123, pp. 431-58.

———. 1996. *Inflation and Investment Controls in China: The Political Economy of Central-local Relations during the Reform Era*. New York: Cambridge University Press.

———. 1999. "Why is there so Much Demand for Foreign Equity Capital in China? An Institutional and Policy Perspective." WCFIC Working Paper, 99-04, Harvard University.

Huo, Shitao. 1994. "Regional Inequality Variations and Central Government Policy." In Jia Hao and Lin Zhimin, eds., *Changing Central-Local Relations in China.* Boulder: Westview Press, pp. 181-206.

Hymer, Stephen H. 1976. *The International Operations of National Firms.* Cambridge, MA: MIT Press.

"ICC Arbitration in the Asia/Pacific Region," 1991. *ICC International Court of Arbitration Bulletin Special Supplement*, no. 2, 5 June.

IMF. 1977. *IMF Balance of Payments Manual* (4th ed.).

Jackson, John H. 1991. *The World Trading System: Law and Policy of International Economic Relations.* Cambridge, MA: The MIT Press.

Jacobson, Harold K. and Michel Oksenberg. 1990. *China's Participation in the IMF, the World Bank and GATT.* Ann Arbor: University of Michigan Press.

Jansson, Hans. 1994. *Transnational Corporations in Southeast Asia: An Institutional Approach to Industrial Organization.* Aldershot, England: Edward Elgar.

Jen, Hui-wen. 1997. "Zhu Rongji Presides Over Work of Screening State-owned Assets Erosion," *Hong Kong hsin pao* [Hong Kong Economic Journal], 10 January, p. 22.

Jensen, Michael and William Meckling. 1976. "Theory of the Firm: Managerial Behavior, Agency Costs and Ownership Structure," *Journal of Financial Economics*, vol. 3, no. 4, pp. 305-60.

Johansson, S. Ryan. 1988. "The Computer Paradigm and the Role of Cultural Information in Social Systems," *Historical Methods*, vol. 21, pp. 172-88.

Johnson, Todd M. 1999. "Foreign Involvement in China's Energy Sector." In Elizabeth Economy and Michel Oksenberg eds., *China Joins the World: Progress and Prospects.* New York: Council on Foreign Relations.

Kamath, S. J. 1990. "Foreign Direct Investment in a Centrally Planned Developing Economy: The Chinese Case," *Economic Development and Cultural Change,* vol. 39, no. 1, pp. 107-30.

Kao, John. 1993. "The Worldwide Web of Chinese Business," *Harvard Business Review,* March-April.

Katzenstein, Peter. 1977. *Between Power and Plenty.* Madison: University of Wisconsin Press.

Keefer, Philip and Stephen Knack. 1997. "Why Don't Poor Countries Catch Up? A Cross National Test of an Institutional Explanation." *Economic Inquiry*, vol. 35, no. 3, pp. 590-602.

Kennedy, Scott. 1997. "The Stone Group: State Client or Market Pathbreaker?" *China Quarterly,* no. 152.

Khan, Azizur Rahman and Carl Riskin. 1998. "Income and Inequality in China," *China Quarterly,* no. 154, pp. 221-53.

Kindleberger, Charles P. 1969. *American Business Abroad: Six Lectures on Direct Investment.* New Haven: Yale University Press.

Klein, Benjamin, Robert Crawford and Armen Alchian. 1978. "Vertical Integration, Appropriable Rents, and the Competitive Contracting Process," *Journal of Law and Economics,* no. 21, pp. 297-326.

Knack, Stephen and Philip Keefer. 1995. "Institutions and Economic Performance: Cross Country Test Using Alternative Institutional Measures," *Economics and Politics,* vol. 7, no. 3, pp. 207-27.

Knight, Frank. 1921. *Uncertainty and Profit.* London: London School of Economics.

Kobler, Arthur L. 1999 "Trade, Investment, and the Information Age: A Level Playing Field in China Would Help American Businesses While Promoting China's Own Interests," *Harvard China Review*, vol. 1, no. 2, pp. 63-65.

Kornai, Janos. 1980. *The Economics of Shortage*. Amsterdam: North-Holland.

Kraar, Louis. 1994. "The New Power in Asia," *Fortune,* vol. 130, 31 October, pp. 80-82.

Krasner, Stephen D. 1978. *Defending the National Interest.* Princeton: Princeton University Press.

———. ed. 1981. *International Regimes*. Ithaca: Cornell University Press.

Kreps, D., P. Milgrom, J. Roberts and R. Wilson. 1982. "Rational Cooperation in the Finitely Repeated Prisoners' Dilemma." *Journal of Economic Theory,* vol. 27, pp. 245-52.

Kreps, D. and R. Wilson. 1982. "Reputation and Imperfect Information," *Journal of Economic Theory,* vol. 27, pp. 253-79.

Krugman, Paul R. 1994. *Rethinking International Trade.* Cambridge, MA: MIT Press.

La Croix, Sumner, ed. 1997. *Emerging Patterns of East Asian Investment in China.* New York: M.E. Sharpe.

Lampton, David, ed. 1987a. *Policy Implementation in Post-Mao China.* Berkeley: University of California Press.

———. 1987b. "Chinese Politics: The Bargaining Treadmill," *Issues and Studies*, vol. 23, no. 3, pp. 12-15;

Lardy, Nicholas. 1987. *China's Entry into the World Economy.* Lanham. MD: University Press of America.

———. 1992a. *Foreign Trade and Economic Reform in China, 1978-1990.* Cambridge: Cambridge University Press.

———. 1992b. "Chinese Foreign Trade," *China Quarterly*, no. 131. pp. 691-720.

———. 1994. *China in the World Economy.* Washington DC: Institute for International Economics 1994.

———. 1995. "The Role of Foreign Trade and Investment in China's Economic Transformation," *China Quarterly*, no. 144..

———. 1998. *China's Unfinished Economic Revolution.* Washington DC: Brookings Institution.

Lawrence, Robert Z. 1993. "Japan's Low Levels of Inward Investment: The Role of Inhibitions on Acquisitions." In Kenneth A. Froot ed., *Foreign Direct Investment.* Chicago: University of Chicago Press, pp. 85-112.

Leblang, David. 1997. "Political Democracy and Economic Growth: Pooled Cross Sectional and Times-Series Evidence," *British Journal of Political Science,* vol. 27, pp. 453-66.

Lee, Sue-Jean and Andrew Ness. 1986. "Investment Approval: A Step-by-step Guide to Finalizing a Contract in China," *China Business Review*, vol. 13, no. 3, pp. 14-18.

Li, Anita. 1981. "Foreign Investors Are Encouraged Despite the Labor Problems," *China Business Review*, vol. 8, no. 5.

Li, Guang'an and Liqun Wei. 1982. "Nengyuan shi jingqi fazhan de zhanlue zhongdian" [Energy Is the Key Point in Economic Development Strategy], *Jingji Yanjiu* [Economic Research], no. 11.

Li, Haopei. 1986. "A Comparative Study of the Internal Application of Treaties." Symposium on Chinese and European Concepts of Law. Hong Kong Arts Center, March 20-25.

Li, Lanqing, ed. 1995. *Zhongguo liyong waizi jichu zhishi* [Essential Information on China's Utilization of Foreign Investment]. Beijing: Jingji guangli chubanshe.

Li, Linda Chelan. 1998. *Centre and Provinces: China 1978-1993.* Oxford: Clarendon Press.

Li, Nianhua. 1991. "Shuilianjiao haishi lianjiaoshui" [Reluctance to Pay taxes or Difficulty in Collecting Taxes], *Liaowang* [Outlook], no. 27.

Li, Tieying. 1995. "15 Years of Reform of State-Owned Enterprises," *Beijing Review*, 9-15 January, p. 15.

Li, Yong. 1997. "Waiguo gongsi zai Tianjin kaifaqu de touzi," [Foreign Investment in the Development Zone in Tianjin]. In Wang, Zhile, ed., *Zhuming kuaguo gongsi zai zhongguo de touzi* [Investment of Transnational Corporations in China], Beijing: Zhongguo jingji chubanshe.

Li, Xin. 1997. "US$13 Billion in China's Stock Market from Overseas," *China Economic News,* 10 November, p. 3.

Li, Zhanwu and Qiang Wu. 1995. "Woguo yinjin waizi gongzuo mianlin de xintiao zhan" [New Challenges Facing China in Attracting Foreign Investment], *Jingji yanjiu cankao* [Reference Materials for Economic Research], 8 April, pp. 2-8.

Liang, Huaping. 1989. "Jiaqiang yusuanwai zijin guanli banhao zonghe caili pingheng" [Strengthen Control over Extra-budgetary Funds and Strive for a Comprehensive Fiscal Balance], *Jianghuai Luntan* [Jianghuai Forum], no. 4.

Liang, Shibin, ed. 1993. *Zhongwai hezi qiye guanli*, [Management of Chinese-foreign Joint Ventures]. Beijing: Zhongguo duiwai jingji maoyi chubanshe.

Lieberthal, Kenneth. 1995. *Governing China: From Revolution through Reform.* New York: W.W. Norton.

Lieberthal, Kenneth and Michel Oksenberg. 1988. *Policy Making in China: Leaders, Structures, and Processes.* Princeton: Princeton University Press.

Lim, David. 1983. "Fiscal Incentives and Direct Foreign Investment In Less developed Countries," *Journal of Development Studies*, vol. 19, pp. 207-12.

Lin, Teh-chang. 1998. "An Analysis of Taiwan's Investment in Guangdong," *Issues & Studies*, vol. 34, no. 3, pp. 71-87.

Lipson, Charles. 1985. *Standing Guard: Protecting Foreign Capital in the Nineteenth and Twentieth Centuries.* Berkeley: University of California Press.

Lizondo, J. Saul. 1991. *Determinants and Systemic Consequences of International Capital Flows.* Washington DC: International Monetary Fund.

Liu, Changgen. 1996. *Qiye kuaguo jingying lun* [About Business Operations Overseas]. Beijing: Zhongguo jingji chubanshe.

Liu, Guoping. 1993. "Waizi zhengche huanjing de bijiao" [A Comparison of Investment Environments], *Jingji yanjiu cankao* [Reference Materials for Economic Research], 25 May.

Liu, Xiangdong, ed. 1993. *Zhonggou duiwai jingji maoyi zhengce zhinan* [A Guide to China's Policies regarding Foreign Economic and Trade Relations]. Beijing: Jingji guanli chubanshe.

Liu, Yiming. 1989. "1988 nian waiguo zai Zhongguo de touzi xianzhu zengjia" [Foreign Investment in China Increased Significantly in 1988]. *Zhongguo duiwai jingji maoyi nianjian* 1989 [Almanac of China's Foreign Economy and Trade, 1989]. Beijing: Zhongguo jingji chubanshe.

Liu, Yuesheng. 1999. *Gouji zhijie touzi yu zhongguo liyong waizi* [FDI and China's Use of Foreign Capital]. Beijing: Zhongguo fazhan chubanshe.

Low, Alfred. 1976. *The Sino-Soviet Dispute*, Rutherford, NJ: Fairleigh Dickinson University Press.

Lubman, S. and G. Wajnowski. 1991. "Arbitration Fair, But Frustrating," *China Trade Report,* vol. 29, (April).

Luo, Gengmo, ed. 1994. *Shige zhuanti jiancha yanjiu*, [A Study of Ten Special Subjects]. Dalian: Dongbei caijing daxue chubanshe.

Ma, Hong and Mengkuai Wang. 1999. *Zhongguo jingji xingshi yu zhanwang* [Economic Situation and Prospect of China]. Beijing: Zhongguo fazhan chubanshe.

MacCormac, Susan. 1993. "Eyeing the GATT," *China Business Review*, vol. 20, no. 2.

MacFarquhar, Roderick, ed. 1997. *The Politics of China: The Eras of Mao and Deng*. Cambridge: Cambridge University Press.

Mann, Jim. 1989. *Beijing Jeep: The Short Unhappy Romance of American Business in China*. New York: Simon and Schuster.

Mauro, Paulo. 1995. "Corruption and Growth," *Quarterly Journal of Economics,* vol. 110, pp. 681-712.

Marx, Karl. 1976. *Capital: A Critique of Political Economy,* trans. by Ben Fowkes. Harmondsworth, UK: Penguin Books.

Maxfield, Sylvia. 1997. *Gatekeepers of Growth.* Princeton: Princeton University Press.

McKenzie, Paul. 1990. "Foreign Exchange and Joint Ventures with China: Short-term Strategies and Long-term Prospects," *Canadian Business Law Journal*, vol. 17, pp. 114-30.

McKern, Bruce. 1993. *Transnational Corporations and the Exploitation of Natural Resources.* London: Routledge.

Michalet, C. A. and M. Delapierre. 1976. *The Multinationalization of French Firms*. Chicago: Academy of International Business.

Milgrom, Paul and John Roberts. 1990. "Bargaining Costs, Influence Costs, and the Organization of Economic Activity. " In James Alt and Kenneth Shepsle, eds. *Perspectives on Positive Political Economy*. Cambridge: Cambridge University Press.

Minford, Patrick. 1993. "The Magic of Capitalism," *Quarterly Economic Bulletin,* (Liverpool Macroeconomic Research Group), vol. 14, no. 3.

Ministry of Finance. 1983. "Ministry of Finance Notice (1983)." In *Cai Shui Wai Zi*, no. 271, 9 September.

MOFTEC. 1993. *Liyong waizi wenjie huibian* vol. 3 [Documents regarding the Utilization of Foreign Capital]. Beijing: Zhongguo jihua chubanshe.

Moran, Theodore. ed. 1986. *Investing in Development: New Roles for Private Capital?* Washington DC: Overseas Development Council.

———. 1998. *Foreign Direct Investment and Development: The New Policy Agenda for Developing Countries and Economies in Transition.* Washington DC: Institute for International Economics.

Mufson, Steve. 1995. "Chinese Congress Vote Shows Surprising Dissension," *Washington Post,* 18 March.

Mulvenon, James. 1998. *Soldiers of Fortune: The Rise of the Military-Business Complex in the Chinese People's Liberation Army, 1978-1998.* Los Angeles: UCLA dissertation.

Nash, J. 1950. "The Bargaining Problem," *Econometrica*, vol. 18, pp. 155-62.

———. 1953. "Two-Person Cooperative Games." *Econometrica,* no. 21: pp. 128-40.

National Council for US-China Trade. 1987. *US Joint Ventures in China: A Progress Report*. Washington DC: National Council for US-China Trade.

Naughton, Barry. 1995. *Growing Out of the Plan: Chinese Economic Reform, 1978-1993.* New York: Cambridge University Press.

———. 1996. "China's Dual Trading Regimes: Implications for Growth and Reform. Adelaide, Australia: Center for International Economic Studies, Seminar Paper 96-20, University of Adelaide.

Nimmer, Melville B. 1978. *Nimmer on Copyright: A Treatise on the Law of Literary, Music and Artistic Property, and the Protection of Ideas*. New York: M. Bender.

Nolan, Peter. 1995. *China's Rise, Russia's Fall.* London: Macmillan.

Nordhaus, William. 1975. "The Political Business Cycle," *Review of Economic Studies,* vol. 42, pp. 169-90.

North, Douglass C. and Robert Thomas. 1973. *The Rise of the Western World: A New Economic History.* Cambridge: Cambridge University Press.

———. 1981. *Structure and Change in Economic History.* New York: W. W. Norton.

———. 1984. "Government and the Cost of Exchange," *Journal of Economic History,* no. 44, pp. 255-64.

———. 1995. *Institutions, Institutional Change and Economic Performance.* Cambridge: Cambridge University Press;

———. 1990. "A Transaction Cost Theory of Politics," *Journal of Theoretical Politics,* vol. 2, no. 4, pp. 355-67.

North, Douglass and Barry Weingast. 1989. "Constitutions and Credible Commitments: The Evolution of the Institutions of Public Choice in 7th Century England," *Journal of Economic History,* vol. 59, no. 4, pp. 803-32.

Oborne, Michael, 1986. *China's Economic Zones.* Paris: Development Center for OECD.

OECD. 1982. *Controls and Impediments Affecting Inward Direct Investment in OECD Countries.* Paris: OECD.

———. 1983. *Investment Incentives and Disincentives, and the International Investment Process*. Paris: OECD.

———. 1992. *Industrial Support Policies in OECD Countries: 1986-89.* Paris: OECD.

———. 1996. *Public Support to Industry: Report by the Industry Committee to the Council at Ministerial Level.* Paris: OECD.

Oi, Jean. 1992. "Fiscal Reform and the Economic Foundations of Local State Corporatism in China," *World Politics*, vol. 45, no. 1.

———. 1995. "The Role of the Local State in China's Transitional Economy," *China Quarterly*, no. 144, pp. 1132-49.

Oksenberg, Michael and James Tong. 1991. "The Evolution of Central-Provincial Fiscal Relations in China, 1971-1984: The Formal System," *China Quarterly*, no. 125, pp. 1-32.

Olson, Mancur. 1993. "Dictatorship, Democracy and Development." *American Political Science Review,* vol. 87, no. 3, pp. 567-76.

Ong, Aihwa and Donald M. Nonini, eds. 1997. *Ungrounded Empires: The Cultural Politics of Modern Chinese Transnationalism.* New York: Routledge.

Onida, F. and G. Viesti. 1988. *The Italian Multinationals*. London: Croom Helm.

O'Sullivan, P. 1985. "Determinants and Impact of Private Foreign Direct Investment in Host Countries," *Management International Review*, vol. 25, pp. 28-35.

Overholt, William. 1997. "One Man's Legacy for One Billion," *Asian Wall Street Journal,* 26 February.

Oxfeld, Ellen. 1993. *Blood, Sweat, and Mahjong: Family and Enterprise in an Overseas Chinese Community*. Ithaca, NY: Cornell University Press.

Ozawa, T. 1979. "International Investment and Industrial Structure: New Theoretical Implications from the Japanese Experience," *Oxford Economic Papers*, vol. 31, pp. 72-92.

Pastor, Manuel and Jae Ho Sung. 1995. "Private Investment and Democracy in the Developing World," *Journal of Economic Issues,* vol. 29, pp. 223-43.

Pauly, Mark. 1968. "The Economics of Moral Hazard," *American Economic Review,* vol. 58, pp. 31-58.

Pearson, Margaret. 1991. *Joint Ventures in the People's Republic of China.* Princeton: Princeton University Press.

———. 1997. *China's New Business Elite: The Political Consequences of Reform.* Berkeley: University of California Press.

People's China Press, ed. 1993. *Zhongguo gedi touzi youhui zhengce* [Preferential Policies Up and Down China]. 2 vols. Beijing: Renmin Zhongguo chubanshe.

Perkins, Dwight. 1994. "Completing China's Move to the Market," *Journal of Economic Perspectives,* vol. 8, no. 2, pp. 21-46.

Persson, Torsten. 1988. "Credibility of Macro-economic Policy: An Introduction and a Broad Survey," *European Economic Review,* vol. 32, pp. 519-32.

Pomfret, Richard. 1991. *Investing in China.* New York: Harvester Wheatsheaf.

———. 1992. "Financial Breakthrough," *China Trade Report*, March.

Posner, Richard. 1980. "A Theory of Primitive Society, With Special Reference to Law," *Journal of Law and Economics,* vol. 7.

Potter, Barbara. 1993. "China's Equity Joint Venture Law: A Standing Invitation to the West for Foreign Investment?" *University of Pennsylvania Journal of International Business*, vol. 14, pp. 4-6.

Przeworski, Adam. 1991. *Democracy and the Market.* New York: Cambridge University Press.

Przeworski, Adam and Fernando Limongi. 1993. "Political Regimes and Economic Growth," *Journal of Economic Perspectives,* vol. 7, no. 3.

Qi, Yuan. 1998. *Zhongguo duiwai kaifang 20 nian* [20 Years of China's Reforms and Open Door]. Henan: Zhongzhou guji chubanshe.

Qian, Yingyi and Barry R. Weingast. 1995. "China's Transition to Markets: Market Preserving Federalism, Chinese Style," Hoover Institution, Stanford University.

Qian, Yingyi and Chenggang Xu. 1993. "Why China's Economic Reforms Differ: The M-Form Hierarchy and Entry/Expansion of the Non-State Sector," *The Economics of Transition,* vol. 1, no. 2, pp. 135-70.

Radelet, Steven and Jeffrey Sachs. 1999. "What Have We Learned, So Far, From the Asian Financial Crisis," Harvard Institute of International Development. <www.hiid.harvard.edu/pub/other/aea/zz.pdf>.

Rama, M. 1993. "Rent-seeking and Economic Growth: A Theoretical Model and Some Empirical Evidence," *Journal of Development Economics,* vol. 42, pp. 35-50.

Ranis, G. and C. Schive. 1985. "Direct Foreign Investment in Taiwan's Development." In W. Galenson, ed., *Foreign Trade and Investment: Economic Development in the Newly Industrializing Asian Countries*. Madison: University of Wisconsin Press.

Redfern, Alan and Martin Hunter. 1991. *Law and Practice of International Commercial Arbitration.* London: Sweet & Maxwell.

Reuber, Grant L. 1973. *Private Foreign Investment in Development.* Oxford: Clarendon Press.

Rieu, E.M. 1986. "The Application of the General Agreement on Tariffs and Trade to the Countertrade Practices of Less-Developed and Developing Countries," *California Western International Law Journal*, vol. 16.

Robinson, Richard. ed. 1987. *Foreign Capital and Technology in China*. New York: Praeger.

Rodman, Kenneth A. 1988. *Sanctity vs. Sovereignty: The United States and the Nationalism of Natural Resource Investments.* New York: Columbia University Press.

Rodrik, Dani. 1989. "Promises, Promises: Credible Policy Reform via Signaling," *The Economic Journal,* vol. 99, pp. 52-62.

———. 1997. *Has Globalization Gone Too Far?* Washington DC: Institute for International Economics.

Rogowski, Ronald. 1987. "Trade and the Variety of Domestic Institutions," *International Organization*, vol. 41, no. 2, pp. 203-23.

———. 1989. *Commerce and Coalitions.* Princeton, NJ: Princeton University Press.

Rong, Yiren. 1979. "Rong Yiren Expounds Problems Concerning Joint Ventures Using Chinese and Foreign Investment," *Ta Kung Pao*, 3 October, p.77.

Root, Hilton. 1989. "Tying the King's Hands: Credible Commitments and Royal Fiscal Policy During the Old Regime," *Rationality and Society,* vol. 1, no. 2, pp. 240-58.

Rosen, Daniel. 1998. *Behind the Open Door: Foreign Enterprises in the Chinese Marketplace.* Washington DC: Institute for International Economics.

Rosen, Daniel, Ligang Liu and Lawrence Dwight. 1988. "Financial Fallout," *China Business Review*, vol. 25, no., 2, pp. 44-47.

Rosenberg, Nathan and L.E. Birdzell, Jr. 1986. *How the West Grew Rich: The Economic Transformation of the Industrial World.* New York: Basic Books.

Rosenberg, Peter D. 1983. *Patent Law Fundamentals.* New York: Clark Boardman Co.

Rosenn, Keith.1991. *Foreign Investment in Brazil.* Oxford: Westview Press.

Ross, Steven. 1973. "The Economic Theory of Agency: The Principal's Problem," *American Economic Review,* vol. 63, pp. 134-39.

Rostow, W.W., ed. 1963. *The Economics of Take-off into Sustained Growth.* New York: St. Martin's Press.

Rugman, Alan M. 1985. "Internalization Is Still a General Theory of Foreign Direct Investment," *Weltwirtschaftliches Archive,* vol. 121, no. 3, pp. 564-69.

———. 1986. "New Theories of Multinational Enterprises: An Assessment of Internalization Theory," *Bulletin of Economic Research*, vol. 38, no. 2, pp. 101-18;

———. D. J. Lecraw and L. D. Booth. 1985. *International Business: Firm and Environment.* New York: McGraw-Hill.

Rutherford, Malcolm C. 1994. *Institutions in Economics: The Old and the New Institutionalism.* New York: Cambridge University Press.

Santiago, Carlos. 1987. "The Impact of Foreign Direct Investment on Export Structure and Employment Generation," *World Development*, vol. 15, no. 3, pp. 317-28.

Scaperlanda, Anthony. 1969. "The Determinants on US Direct Foreign Investment in the EEC," *American Economic Review*, vol. 59.

Schelling, Thomas. 1966. *Arms and Influence.* New Haven, CT: Yale University Press.

Schlesinger, Michael N. 1995. "A Sleeping Giant Awakens: The Development of Intellectual Property Law in China," *Journal of Chinese Law*, vol. 9, pp. 93-140.

Schneider, F. and B. S. Frey.1985. "Economic and Political Determinants of Foreign Direct Investment," *World Development*, vol. 13, no, 2.

Schulberg, M. 1989. "China's Accession to the New York Convention: An Analysis ofthe New Regime of Recognition and Enforcement of Foreign Arbitral Awards," *Journal of Chinese Law,* vol. 1.

Schweke, William, Carl Risk and Brian Dabson. 1994. *Bidding for Business: Are Cities and States Selling Themselves Short?* Washington, DC: Corporation for Enterprise Development.

Scully, Gerald W. 1988. "The Institutional Framework and Economic Development,"*Journal of Political Economy*, vol. 96, pp. 52-62.

Sender, Henry. 1991. "Inside the Overseas Chinese Network," *Institutional Investor*, September.

Shen, Gong. 1995. "Progress in Intellectual Property Protection," *China Information*, February.

Shepsle, Kenneth A. 1991. "Discretion, Institutions, and the Problem of Government Commitment." In Pierre Bourdieu and James S. Coleman, eds., *Social Theory for a Changing Society*. Boulder: Westview Press.

Shirk, Susan L. 1993. *The Political Logic of Economic Reform in China.* Berkeley: University of California Press.

———. 1994. *How China Opened Its Door: The Political Successes of the PRC's Foreign Trade and Investment Reforms.* Washington, DC: The Brookings Institute.

Sicular, Terry. 1992. "Public Finance and China's Economic Reform," Harvard Institute of Economic Research Discussion Paper. no.1618, November.

Simmons, Beth A. 1994. *Who Adjusts?* Princeton: Princeton University Press.

Simon, Herbert. 1957. *Models of Man.* New York: John Wiley & Sons.

———. 1982. *Models of Bounded Rationality,* Cambridge, MA: MIT Press.

Simone, J. T. Jr. 1992. "Improving Protection of Intellectual Property," *Chinese Business Review*, vol. 19, no. 2.

Sladkovskii, M. I. 1966. *History of Economic Relations between Russia and China*. Jerusalem: Israel Program for Scientific Translations.

Smith, Adam. 1976. *An Inquiry into the Nature and Causes of the Wealth of Nations,* ed. By W. B. Todd. Oxford: Clarendon Press.

Sobel, Andrew. 1994. *Domestic Choices, International Markets: Dismantling National Barriers and Liberalizing Securities Markets.* Ann Arbor: University of Michigan Press.

———. 1999. *State Institutions, Private Incentives, Global Capital.* Ann Arbor: University of Michigan Press.

Solnick, Steven L. 1996. "The Breakdown of Hierarchies in the Soviet Union and China: A Neo-institutional Perspective," *World Politics*, vol. 48, no. 2, pp. 209-39.

Song, Jingyuan, et al., eds. 1998. *Zhengfeng yu guoyou qiye de caizheng guanxi* [Fiscal Relations between the State and State-owned Enterprises]. Henan: Huanghe shuili chubanshe.

Spence, Jonathan D. 1990. *The Search for Modern China.* New York: W. W. Norton.

Spence, Michael and Richard Zeckhauser. 1971. "Insurance, Information and Individual Action," *American Economic Review,* vol. 61, pp. 380-87.

Spinanger, Dean. 1983. "Economic Activity Zones: Objectives and Impact: Some Evidence from Asia," Working Paper, Kiel Institute of World Economics, November.

State Planning Commission. 1994. "Woguo liyong waiguo zhijie touzi wenti de yanjiu baogao," [A report on China's Utilization of Foreign Direct Investment], *Jingji Yanjiu Cankao* [Reference Materials for Economic Research], vol. 12, October, pp. 2-59.

State Statistical Bureau. 1996. *Gaige kaifang shiqinian Zhongguo jingji* [China Regional Economy: A Profile of 17 Years of Reform and Opening Up]. Beijing: Zhongguo tongji chubanshe.

Stein, Laura. 1987. "Wholly Foreign-owned Ventures in China: A Comparison of 3M China, Ltd., Grace China, Ltd., and the New Foreign Enterprise Law," *China Law Reporter*, vol. 4, no. 1.

Stepanek, Jim. 1982. "China's SEZs, Terms in the Special Economic Zones Compare Well with Those in Other Parts of the World," *China Business Review,* March-April, p. 39.

Steven, Rob. 1990. *Japan's New Imperialism.* New York: M.E. Sharpe.

Stiglitz, Joseph E. 1994. *Whither Socialism?* Cambridge, MA: MIT Press.

Strange, Susan. 1988. *States and Markets: An Introduction to International Political Economy.* New York: Basil Blackwell.

Sun, Haishun. 1998. *Foreign Investment and Economic Development in China: 1979-96.* Singapore: Ashgate.

Sun, Shangqing and Xingzhou Ren eds. 1997. *A Grand Market in China: Retrospect and Prospect*. Beijing: New World Press.

Sun, Shujun and Hongxi Shi, "Policy on the Development of China's Offshore Oil." In Richard Robinson, ed., *Foreign Capital and Technology in China*. New York: Praeger.

Suryadinata, Leo. 1995. "China's Economic Modernization and the Ethnic Chinese in ASEAN: A Preliminary Study." In Leo Suryadinata, ed., *Southeast Asian Chinese and China: The Political-Economic Dimension.* Singapore: Times Academic Press.

Svensson, Jacob. 1998. "Investment, Property Rights and Political Instability: Theory and Evidence," *European Economic Review,* vol. 42, pp. 1317-41.

Swedenborg, B. 1979. *The Multinational Operations of Swedish Firms: An Analysis of Determinants and Effects*. Stockholm: Industrial Institute for Economic and Social Research.

Sylvester, Kirsten. 1995. "China's Key Foreign Investment Laws and Regulations," *China Business Review,* vol. 22, no. 3, p. 12.

Szeto, Wanda. 1994. "Raid Nets One Million Pirate CDs," *South China Morning Post*, 4 October, p. 6.

Tanzer, Andrew. 1994. "The Bamboo Network," *Forbes,* 18 July, p. 140.

Taylor, Michael. 1976. *Anarchy and Cooperation.* London: Wiley.

Tian, Gang. 1996. *Shanghai's Role in the Economic Development of China*. Westport, CT: Praeger.

Tirole, Jean. 1988. *The Theory of Industrial Organization.* Cambridge, MA: MIT Press.

Tong, James. 1988. "Fiscal Reform, Elite Turnover and Central-Provincial Relations in Post-Mao China," *Australian Journal of Chinese Affairs,* no. 22, pp. 1-28.

Torbert, Preston. 1986. "Wholly Foreign-Owned Enterprises Come of Age: New Law Protests Nascent Form of Investment." *China Business Review*, July-August, pp. 50-53.

Torstensson, Johan. 1994. "Property Rights and Economic Growth: An Empirical Study," *Kyklos,* vol. 47, no. 2, pp. 231-47.

Tsurumi, Y. 1976. *The Japanese Are Coming: A Multinational Interaction of Firms and Politics*. Cambridge, MA: Ballinger.

UNCTAD. 1997. *World Investment Report 1997: Transnational Corporations, Market Structure and Competition Policy.* New York: United Nations.

——. 1998. *World Investment Report 1998: Trends and Determinants. New York: United Nations.*

——. 1999. *World Investment Report 1999: Foreign Direct Investment and the Challenge of Development.* New York: United Nations.

UNCTC. 1985. *Transnational Corporations in World Development.* New York.

——. 1991. "Government Policies and Foreign Direct Investment," no. 17, series A.

United Nations. 1991. *The Challenge of Free Economic Zones in Central and Eastern Europe.* New York: United Nations.

US Department of Energy. 1995. *China: Country Energy Profile.* Washington, DC: Energy Information Administration, February.

US-China Business Council. 1996. *Labor Developments in China.* Washington, DC: US-China Business Council.

Van Read, Kees, ed. 1990. *Model Income Tax Treaties*, 2nd ed. Boston: Kluwer.

Vernon, Raymond. 1971. *Sovereignty at Bay.* New York: Basic Books.

Veugelers, R. 1991. "Locational Determinants and Ranking of Host Countries: An Empirical Assessment," *Kyklos*, no. 3, pp. 363-82.

Verdier, Daniel. 1994. *Democracy and International Trade.* Princeton: Princeton University Press.

Vogel, Ezra. 1989. *One Step Ahead of China, Guangdong under Reform.* Cambridge, MA: Harvard University Press.

Wall, David, Boke Jing and Xiangshuo Yin. 1996. "China's Opening Door," *Royal Institute of International Affairs.*

Wall Street Journal. 1994. "China Limits Sale of Assets Held by State Companies," 17 May, p. A15.

Wang, Bingqian. 1988. "1987 nian guojia yusuan zhixing qingkuang" [The Situation of Government Budgetary Funds in 1987]. In Chinese Financial Society, ed., *Zhongguo jinrong nianjian, 1988* [1988 Yearbook of Chinese Finance]. Beijing: Zhongguo jinrong chubanshe.

Wang, Chunping, et al., eds. 1996. *Zhongwai shuizhi gaige yu jianjie* [The Reform of Tax Systems, Chinese and Foreign, Compared], Beijing: Zhonghua gongshang lianhe chubanshe.

Wang, Hongying. forthcoming. *Weak State, Strong Networks: The Institutional Dynamics of Foreign Investment in China.* Oxford University Press.

Wang, Gungwu. 1990. "The Culture of Chinese Merchants," University of Toronto-York University Joint Center for Asia Pacific Studies, Working Papers, no. 57.

Wang, Luolin. ed. 1997. *Zhongguo waishang touzi baogao* [Report on Foreign Investment in China]. Beijing: Jingji guanli chubanshe.

Wang, N. T. 1984. *China's Modernization and Transnational Corporations*. Lexington, MA: Lexington Books.

Wang, Shaoguang. 1994. "Central-local Fiscal Politics in China." In Jia Hao and Lin Zhimin, ed., *Changing Central-Local Relations in China.* Boulder: Westview Press.

Wang, Shaoguang and Hu Angang, 1993. *Zhongguo guojia nengli baogao* [A Report on State Capacity in China]. Shengyang: Liaoning renmin chubanshe.

Wang, Wentong and Houxiong Xiao. 1992. "Guanyu 100 hu qiye shuifei fudan qingkuang de diaocha baogao" [Report on the Tax and Non-tax Burdens of 100 Enterprises], *Hubei caizheng yanjiu* [Hubei Financial Studies], no. 1.

Wang, Zhile, ed. 1996. *Zhuming kuaguo gongsi zai Zhongguo de touzi* [Investment of Transnational Corporations in China]. Beijing: Zhongguo jingji chubanshe.

Wank, David L. 1995. "Private Business, Bureaucracy, and Political Alliance in a Chinese City," *Australian Journal of International Affairs,* no. 33, pp. 55-71.

Weber, Max. 1978. *Economy and Society,* ed. By Guenther Roth and Charles Witt. Berkeley: University of California Press.

Wedeman, Andrew Hall. 1995. *Bamboo Walls and Brick Ramparts: Rent Seeking, Inter-regional Economic Conflict, and Local Protectionism in China 1984-1991.* Ph.D. dissertation. University of California, Los Angeles.

Wei, Shang-Jin. 1997. "How Taxing Is Corruption on International Investors?" NBER Working Papers, no. 6030.

Weidenbaum, Murray and Samuel Hughes. 1996. *The Bamboo Network: How Expatriate Chinese Entrepreneurs Are Creating a New Economic Superpower in Asia.* New York: Martin Kessler Books.

Weinstein, David E. 1996. "Foreign Direct Investment and Keiretsu: Rethinking U.S. and Japanese Policy." NBER Working Papers, no. W5612, June.

Wells, Louis T. Jr. 1986. "Investment Incentives: An Unnecessary Debate," *CTC Reporter,* 22 (Autumn), pp. 51-62.

Wilkins, Mira. 1989. *The History of Foreign Investment in the United States.* Cambridge, MA: Harvard University Press.

Williamson, Oliver. 1975. *Markets and Hierarchies: Analysis and Antitrust Implications.* New York: Free Press.

———. 1979. "Transaction Cost Economics: The Governance of Contractual Relations," *Journal of Law and Economics*. vol. 22, pp. 233-61

———. 1985. *The Economic Institutions of Capitalism.* New York: Free Press.

———. 1989. "Transaction Cost Economics." In R. Schmalensee and R. Willig, eds., *Handbook of Industrial Organization.* New York: North-Holland.

Wong, Christine, ed. 1997, *Financing Local Government in the People's Republic of China*. Hong Kong: Oxford University Press.

Woo, Wing Thye. 1994. "The Art of Reforming Centrally Planned Economies: Comparing China, Poland and Russia," *Journal of Comparative Economics,* vol. 18, pp. 274-308.

Woodard, Kim. 1980. *The International Energy Relations of China.* Stanford: Stanford University Press.

Woodward, D. P. 1992. "Locational Determinants of Japanese Manufacturing Startups in the United States," *Southern Economic Journal*, vol. 58, no. 3, pp. 690-708;

——— and R. J. Rolfe. 1993. "The Location of Export-Oriented Foreign Direct Investment in the Caribbean Basin," *International Journal of Business Studies*, vol. 24 (First Quarter), pp. 121-44.

World Bank. 1988. *China: External Trade and Capital.* Washington, DC: World Bank.

———. 1994a. *World Debt Tables: External Finance for Developing Countries, 1994-95*, vol. 1. Washington, DC: World Bank.

———. 1994b. *China: Reform of State-Owned Enterprises.* Washington, DC: World Bank.

———. 1995. *Infrastructure Development in East Asia and the Pacific: Towards a New Public-Private Partnership.* Washington, DC: World Bank.

———. 1997a. *China's Management of Enterprise Assets: The State as Shareholder*. Washington, DC: World Bank.

———. 1997b. *Clear Water, Blue Skies: China's Environment in the New Century Century*. Washington, DC: World Bank.

———. 1997c. *China Engaged: Integration with the Global Economy*. Washington, DC: World Bank.

———. 1998, *Global Development Finance*. World Bank Debtor Reporting System. Washington, DC: World Bank.

———. 1999. *World Development Indicators*. Washington, DC: World Bank.

Wu, Chao, ed. 1991. *Waishang duihua zhijie touzi diaoyan baogao* [Report on Foreign Direct Investment in China]. Beijing: Zhongguo caizheng jingji chubanshe.

Wu, Deming. 1987. *Guojia yusuan guanli tizhi gailun* [An Outline of the State Budget Management System]. Beijing: Zhongguo caizheng jingji chubanshe.

Wu, Jianghu. 1994. "An Analysis of Cross-Strait Economic and Trade Relations," *Taiwan jingji* [Taiwan Economy], no. 211, July.

Wu, Qiang. 1996. "Gaige kaifang yilai woguo liyong waizi de zhongti huigu," [A Review of China Utilization of Foreign Capital since Reform and Open Door], *Jingji gongzuozhe xuexi ziliao*, [Study Material for Economic Workers], nos. 46-47.

Wu, Nengquan. 1995. *Guangdong sanzi qiyie jixiao fengxi* [An Analysis of FDI Firms in Guangdong]. Guangzhou: Zhongshan Daxue chubanshe.

Wu, Yi, et al., eds. 1995. *Maoyi touzi zhinan: yuenan* [Trade and Investment Guide: Vietnam]. Beijing: Jingji guangli chubanshe.

———. *Maoyi touzi zhinan: yindu* [Trade and Investment Guide: India]. Beijing: Jingji guangli chubanshe.

———. *Maoyi touzi zhinan: lamei* [Trade and Investment Guide: Latin America]. Beijing: Jingji guangli chubanshe.

Xiao, Yanming. 1999. *The State and Economic Development in Early Republican China*. Ph.D. dissertation, Harvard University.

Xie Zhao Hua Lushi Shiwusuo [Xie Zhao Hua Law Firm]. 1995. *Zhongguo shangshi falu yaolan* [An Outline of China's Commercial Laws]. Beijing: Falu chubanshe.

Xin, Ming. 1995. "Liyong waizi xuyao zhuajin yanjiu zhiding he luoshi de ruogan zhongda zhengce" [Several Important Policy Issues that Need to be Addressed in the Utilization of Foreign Capital], *Jingji yanjiu cankao* [Reference Materials for Economic Research], 8 April, pp. 8-26.

Xu, Jinhe. 1995. *Zhongguo liyong waizi falu shiwu daquan* [A Comprehensive Collection of Chinese Laws regarding the Utilization of Foreign Capital]. Beijing: Zhongguo Renmin Daxue chubanshe.

Yang, John, et al. 1999. "The Evolution of Chinese Consumers: What Will They Want Next?" *Harvard China Review*, Summer, vol. 1, no. 2, pp. 67-72.

Yao, Ximin and Xin Zhong. 1986. "Foreign Exchange Redistribution Center Set Up to Encourage Foreign Investment," *Guoji Shangbao* [International Business], 13 November.

Yarbrough, Beth and Robert Yarbrough. 1988. "International Institutions and the New Economics of Organizations," *International Organization,* vol. 44, no. 2, pp. 235-60.

Yi, Gang. 1994. *Money, Banking, and Financial Markets in China.* Boulder: Westview.

Yin, Xin. 1993. "Government to Tighten Restrictions on Zones," *China Daily Business Weekly*, 7 February, p. 1.

Yoshihara, K. 1978. *Japanese Investment in Southeast Asia*. Honolulu: University of Hawaii Press.

Yoshino, M. Y. 1976. *Japan's Multinational Enterprises*. Cambridge MA: Harvard University Press.

Yu, Jian. 1996. "The Predicament and Solution for State-owned Enterprises," *Jinrong shibao* [Financial News], 29 January, p. 3.

Yuan, Jiashi and Liping Yang, eds. 1995. *Duiwai jingji maoyi xin guifan* [New Policies regarding Foreign Economy and Trade]. Shanghai: Fudan Daxue chubanshe.

Yuill, Douglas and Kevin Allen. 1981. *European Regional Incentives 1981.* Glasgow, Scotland: University of Strathclyde.

Zeichner, L. 1987. "Chinese Solutions to Legal Problems: Repatriating Business Profits from the People's Republic of China," *Law and Policy in International Business*, vol. 19.

Zhang, Guilong and Liu Shuqiang, ed. 1994. *Taiwan tongbao touzi baohufa,* [Investment Protection Law regarding Taiwanese Compatriots]. Beijing: Zhongguo zhengfa daxue chubanshe.

Zhang, Ren, 1993. *Meiguo zaihua de zhijie touzi 1980-1991* [US Direct Investment in China 1980-1991]. Shanghai: Fudan daxue chubanshe.

Zhang, Shangtang and Youfu Xia, et al. eds. 1997. *Zhongguo xishou waishang zhijie touzi redian wenti tantao* [China Attracts FDI: Hot-button Topics]. Beijing: Zhongguo duiwai jingji moyi chubanshe.

Zhao,Yujiang. 1986. "Yusuanwai zijin fenbu he difang zhengfu de guanli xingwei" [The Distribution of Extra-budgetary Funds and the Management Behavior of Local Governments]. In Chinese Institute for Economic System Reform, ed., *Gaige: Women mianlin de wenti yu silu* [Reform: Problems and Resolutions]. Beijing: Zhongguo jingji guanli chubanshe.

Zhen, Daoxian, et al. 1992. "Beijingshi waishang touzi gongye qiye zai xianjieduan zuoyong he diwei wenti de tantao" [Present Status and Problems of Foreign Invested Industrial Enterprises in Beijing]. Beijing: Beijing jingji weiyuan hui, April.

Zheng, Jianhui. 1984. "The Birth of an Important Decision - A New Step in Opening the Country to the World," *Liaowang* [Outlook], no. 24, 11 June.

Zheng, Yan'er. 1985. "Domestic Sales of Joint Ventures Production," *Intertrade*, May-June, pp. 57-59.

Zhou, Taihe, ed. 1984. *Dangdai zhongguo de jingji tizhi gaige* [Economic System Reforms in Contemporary China]. Beijing: Zhongguo shehui kexue chubanshe.

Almanacs and Statistical Sources

Almanac of China's Foreign Economic Relations and Trade (various years). Hong Kong: China Resource Advertising Co. Ltd.

Huaren jingji nianjian [Yearbook of Overseas Chinese Economy] (various years). Beijing: Shehui kexue wenxian chubanshe.

Gaige kaifang shiqinian de zhongguo diqu jingji [China Regional Economy: A Profile of 17 Years of Reform and Opening Up]. 1996. Beijing: Zhongguo tongji chubanshe.

Guangdong tongji nianjian [Statistical Yearbook of Guangdong] (various years). Beijing: Zhongguo tongji chubanshe.

Zhongguo chengshi tongji nianjian [Yearbook of Chinese Urban Cities] (various years). Beijing: Zhongguo tongji chubanshe.

Zhongguo duiwai jingji maoyi nianjian [Almanac of China's Foreign Trade and Economic Relations] (various years). Beijing: Zhongguo jingji chubanshe, and Hong Kong : Jingji dao bao she.

Zhongguo duiwai jingji tongji nianjian [China Foreign Economic Statistical Yearbook] (various years). Beijing: Zhongguo tongji chubanshe.

Zhongguo duiwai jingji tongji daquan, 1979-1991 [China Foreign Economic Statistics]. Beijing: Zhongguo tongji xinxi zixun fuwu zhongxin chuban, 1992.

Zhongguo falu nianjian [Almanac of Chinese Law] (various years). Zhongguo falu nianjian chubanshe.

Zhongguo jingji nianjian [Almanac of China's Economy] (various years). Beijing: Jingji guanli chubanshe.

Zhongguo jingji tequ kaifaqu nianjian [China Special Economic Zones and Development Zones Yearbook]. Beijing: Gaige chubanshe 1995.

Zhongguo guoyou zichan nianjian [China Yearbook of State Assets] (various years). Beijing: Jingji kexue chubanshe.

Zhongguo nianjian [People's Republic of China Yearbook] (various years). Beijing: PRC Yearbook Ltd., and Hong Kong: Economic Information and Agency.

Zhongguo tongji nianjian [China Statistical Yearbook] (various years). Beijing: Zhongguo tongji chubanshe.

Zhongguo tongji zhaiyao [A Statistical Survey of China] (various years). Beijing: Zhongguo tongji chubanshe.

Laws, Rules and Regulations

- Law of the PRC concerning Sino-Foreign Joint Ventures (1979)
- Guangdong Province Special Economic Zone Act of the PRC (1980)
- Taxation Law of the PRC concerning Sino-Foreign Joint Ventures (1980)
- Taxation Law of the PRC concerning Wholly Foreign-owned Enterprises (1981)
- Amended Constitution of the PRC (1982)
- Regulations of the PRC concerning the Exploitation of Offshore Petroleum Resources in Cooperation with Foreign Enterprises (1982)
- Trade-mark Law of the PRC (1982)

- Detailed Implementation Act of the Law of the PRC concerning Sino-Foreign Joint Ventures (1983)
- Patent Law of the PRC (1984)
- The Procedures for Implementing the Regulations on Labor Management in Sino-Foreign Joint Ventures (1984)
- Provisional Regulations on the Reduction and Exemption of Enterprise Income Tax in the Special Economic Zones and 14 Coastal Cities (1984)
- Foreign Economic Contract Law of the PRC (1985)
- Foreigners' Entry and Exit Law of the PRC (1985)
- Enterprise Bankruptcy Law of the PRC (1986)
- General Principles of the Civil Law of the PRC (1986)
- Law of the PRC concerning Wholly Foreign-owned Enterprises (1986)
- Land Administration Law of the PRC (1986)
- Provisions for the Encouragement of Foreign Investment [the "22 Articles"] (1986)
- Provisions concerning Autonomous Rights of Personnel Employment, and Salary, Insurance and Welfare Expenses in Foreign-Invested Enterprises (1986.
- Provisions on the Question of Balancing Foreign Exchange Receipts and Expenditures of Sino-Foreign Joint Ventures (1986)
- Certain Provisional Regulations Governing the Operation of Foreign Banks in the Special Economic Zones (1987)
- Measures for the Substitution of Importation with Products of Sino-Foreign Joint Ventures (1987)
- Procedures concerning Purchasing Domestic Products by Foreign-Invested Enterprises to Resolve Problems of Foreign Exchange Balance (1987)
- Response of the Supreme People's Court to Certain Questions Concerning the Application of the Foreign Economic Contract Law (1987)
- Rules of the Ministry of Finance for the Implementation of Recent Articles concerning Preferential Tax Terms Stipulated in the Provisions for the Encouragement of Foreign Investment (1987)
- Amended Version of the Land Administration Law of the PRC (1988)
- Foreign Economic Contract Law of the PRC (1988)

- Law of the PRC concerning Sino-Foreign Cooperative Joint Ventures (1988)
- Regulations on Encouraging the Investment of Taiwan Compatriots (1988)
- Opinion on Further Insuring the Autonomy of Personnel Management in Foreign-Invested Enterprises (1988)
- Amended Version of the Law of the PRC concerning Sino-Foreign Joint Ventures (1990)
- Copyright Law of the PRC (1990)
- Detailed Implementation Act of the Law of the PRC concerning Wholly Foreign-owned Enterprises (1990)
- Interim Administrative Measures concerning Investment in and Development and Management of Land by Foreign Businesses (1990)
- Procedural Law of the PRC for Concluding Treaties (1990)
- Regulations concerning Contracting for the Operation of Sino-Foreign Equity Joint Ventures (1990)
- Returned Overseas Chinese and Relatives of Overseas Chinese Protection Law of the PRC (1990)
- Shanghai Regulatory Measures concerning Foreign Financial Institutions and Joint Sino-Foreign Financial Institutions (1990)
- Civil Procedure Law of the PRC (1991)
- Computer Software Protection Regulations (1991)
- PRC Tax Law concerning Enterprises with Foreign Investment and Wholly Foreign-owned Enterprises (1991)
- Corporation Law of the PRC (1993)
- Regulations of the PRC concerning Sino-Foreign Cooperation in the Development of Continental Petroleum Resources (1993)
- Law of the PRC against Unfair Competition (1993)
- Law Regarding the Protection of the Investment by Taiwan Compatriots (1994)
- Regulatory Provisions of the PRC concerning Foreign Financial Institutions (1994)
- Detailed Implementation Act of Law of the PRC concerning Sino-Foreign Cooperative Joint Ventures (1995)
- Administrative Penalty Law of the PRC (1996)
- Partnership Law of the PRC (1997)

Index

T indicates tables and figures